T0330131

Sin Padres, Ni Papeles

Sin Padres, Ni Papeles

UNACCOMPANIED MIGRANT YOUTH
COMING OF AGE IN THE UNITED STATES

Stephanie L. Canizales

 UNIVERSITY OF CALIFORNIA PRESS

University of California Press
Oakland, California

Library of Congress Cataloging-in-Publication Data

Names: Canizales, Stephanie L, author.
Title: Sin Padres, Ni Papeles : unaccompanied migrant youth coming of age
    in the United States / Stephanie L. Canizales.
Description: Oakland, California : University of California Press, [2024] |
    Includes bibliographical references and index.
Identifiers: LCCN 2024003734 (print) | LCCN 2024003735 (ebook) |
    ISBN 9780520396180 (cloth) | ISBN 9780520396197 (paperback) |
    ISBN 9780520396203 (epub)
Subjects: LCSH: Unaccompanied immigrant children—California—
    Los Angeles—Social conditions. | Unaccompanied refugee children—
    California—Los Angeles—Social conditions. | Immigrant youth—
    California—Los Angeles—Social conditions.
Classification: LCC JV6344 .C36 2024 (print) | LCC JV6344 (ebook) |
    DDC 305.23086/910979494—dc23/eng/20240222
LC record available at https://lccn.loc.gov/2024003734
LC ebook record available at https://lccn.loc.gov/2024003735

33 32 31 30 29 28 27 26 25 24
10 9 8 7 6 5 4 3 2 1

MAMÁ PATY, I am because you are.

Contents

Illustrations

FIGURE

TABLES

Acknowledgments

This research began when I met the *jóvenes* of Voces de Esperanza in 2012. I am indebted to them for opening their worlds up to me and generously sharing their time, ideas, and experiences. I am especially indebted to one participant, Caleb. The first person to accept an interview invitation in the group, Caleb's trust in me and kind words about our conversation afterward led to a cascade of interviews within the group, invitations to other spaces where youth congregated, and introductions to other unaccompanied Central American and Mexican youth. I am also grateful to the group coordinators, Wilfredo and Jorge, who kept me abreast of group meeting days and times and informal group gatherings and affirmed my trustworthiness in every new space they introduced me to. *Gracias a todos por su confianza, apoyo, y cariño.*

I owe immense gratitude to Pierrette Hondagneu-Sotelo and Jody Agius Vallejo, my coadvisors, mentors, and fierce defenders throughout my PhD program and today. Pierrette was my North Star well before I arrived at USC. Her scholarly rigor, sharp ethnographic eye, evocative writing style, and dedication to scholar advocacy are only matched by her commitment to mentoring others interested in developing those skills. Jody has been an unwavering source of support since our meeting. On the day we met, I remember thinking,

"This is who I want to be when I grow up," a conviction I maintain. They would never agree, but I firmly believe this book would not exist without them. Pierrette and Jody, with all my heart, thank you.

I am also thankful to Manuel Pastor Jr. and George Sanchez, members of my dissertation committee, whose influence on my thinking and writing is laced throughout the chapters of this book. I thank especially Manuel for inspiring the title of this book. I had proudly landed on the title *Without Parents nor Papers* as I was preparing my proposal for UC Press. When I shared the title with Manuel, he said, "Okay, now say that in Spanish." I did. He smiled, winked, and walked away. When I shared the title of the book with a group of the *jóvenes* in late 2023, they loved it. Caleb said, "*Ah, si, porque así se vive acá, sin padres, ni papeles*" (Ah, yes, because that's how we live here, without parents, nor papers). I am so proud of the title's resonance.

A special thanks goes to Naomi Schneider and the UC Press editorial board for their confidence in this project. Thanks also to LeKeisha Hughes and Aline Dolinh for their editorial assistance. I am indebted to the reviewers assigned to this manuscript for their critical comments and insightful recommendations. Pierrette Hondagneu-Sotelo and Carola Suárez-Orozco were the first to read this book in its entirety in 2022. I am deeply grateful for their enthusiasm about this project, attention to detail, and all the holes they poked and left me to patch up. Our conversation was a turning point for me and this work. Thank you. Finally, I am thankful to my UC Merced mentors, Tanya Golash-Boza, Zulema Valdez, Marjorie Zatz, and Laura Hamilton, and Sociology Department colleagues for their support of my career during my years there.

I received generous support from numerous funders throughout this work. The National Science Foundation, Stanford University's Center on Poverty and Inequality, University of California at Davis's Center for Poverty and Inequality Research, USC Center for the Study of Immigrant Integration (now Equity Research Institute), USC Latin American and Latino Studies, USC Tomas Rivera Policy Institute, and the USC Sociology Department funded data collection. The Russell Sage Foundation, Ford Foundation, John Randolph and Dora Haynes Foundation, the American Sociological Association's Minority Fellowship Program, Sociologists for Women in Society, and the University of Wisconsin-Madison's Institute for Research on Poverty funded data analysis. The University of California at Merced's Chancellor's Postdoctoral Fellowship Program funded the completion of this book manuscript. Finally, the UC Merced Center for the Humanities and UC Press FirstGen Program funded editorial support and indexing.

I have also been privileged to publish peer-reviewed articles and other public works related to this research. These include *Ethnic and Racial Studies* (2015), the *Journal of Ethnic and Migration Studies* (2019, 2023), *Sociology of Education* (2021), *Sociology Compass* (2022), *Social Forces* (2023), and the *Journal of Health and Social Behavior* (2023). I am thankful to the editors and reviewers at each journal for their thoughtfulness when reading my work and providing suggestions as I sharpened my arguments, clarified my writing, and strengthened my voice.

I began writing *Sin Padres, Ni Papeles* in January 2021 with a blank Word document that could have paralyzed me. Weekly writing meetings with Abigail Andrews sustained me as I wrote the first draft of this book. Subsequent writing groups with Camila Alvarez, Dalia Magaña, Meredith Van Natta, and Yiran Xu kept me energized during revisions. Thank you all for showing up each week, encouraging me, and celebrating milestones with me. I am incredibly grateful to Laura E. Enriquez, who has been a relentless mentor and inspiration since we met during our overlapping years at UCLA, but especially as I completed the final revision of this book.

To my very best friends—Layna Austin Parra, Rachel Burris, Tissyana Camacho, Dayna Garwacki, Gabriela Gonzalez, Steph Gomez,

Lauren Kenson, Ruby Moran, Koryn Olage, Diana Rivera, Mariah Syrett, Natalia Sztyk—thank you. Your loyalty and kindness ground me; your love is my lighthouse. To Enn Burke and Michela Musto: I don't even know where to start, and I'm sure neither of you wants me to, so I'll just say thank you for being my f-words and HUMANS. To Meredith Van Natta and Whitney Pirtle: you were my home away from home. Thanks, Mer and Whitney, for The Vault, too. I love you all beyond measure and could not have done the last ten years without you.

Antonio Diaz: We entered each other's lives when we least expected, and then again when we were ready. You've held me and my work lightly since. No one knows better than you what finishing this project required of me, and what I hope it will do. Thank you for believing I could, and that it will. I love you endlessly.

Mamá Chita y Papá Peter: Es un orgullo presentarles la cosecha de sus sacrificios por nuestra familia. Gracias por su apoyo y por su amor incondicional. No importa el tiempo, ni la distancia, siempre los tengo en mi corazón. I love you *un chingo.*

Equipo Canizales: You have heard me talk about "my book" for over a decade, and I am honored to finally present it to you. Jessica, Kendrick, and Brianna, you really know how to make a girl feel average, and for that, I am grateful. It's never mattered how we show up, just that we do, and that truth is my landing place. Jessi, thank you for Levi and Ezra. Before becoming Dr. Steph, I was Tía Stephanie. There is no greater joy in this world than hearing those words from the sweetest humans I've known. Dad, I can't remember a time in my life when you weren't steadfastly holding up the guardrails, reminding me that there was more to be done, and I had it in me to do it. You are my place of *desahogo.* Thank you, dad.

Mamá Paty: Of all the moms in the world, what are the odds that I'd get you? I could spend a lifetime telling you how much I love and appreciate you, but it would be insufficient. I could dedicate every meaningful thing I do in this world to you, but it would still fall short. You are my greatest gift in this life, and I live in humble gratitude for you and your love for me. Thank you, *mamita mía*, for every big and small thing. *Mereces el mundo entero. Empiezo con esto*: my first book.

Introduction

This book tells the coming-of-age stories of Central American and Mexican immigrant youth who migrated to the United States and arrived in Los Angeles, California, clandestinely, *sin padres, ni papeles* (without parents nor papers). That is, outside of the purview of adult caregivers and the state. I began my research with unaccompanied and undocumented migrant youth in 2012 just as immigrant communities across the US were settling into the Obama administration's passage of the Deferred Action for Childhood Arrivals. Colloquially known as DACA, this executive order granted a stay on deportation and work authorization renewable in two-year increments to a select group of undocumented immigrant young people who arrived as children and grew up as students.[1] While DACA had a significant positive impact on eligible groups' political, economic, and social mobility, some criticized its limited scope, including that it left out 62 percent of the undocumented youth and young adults who did not meet the policy's educational requirements.[2] Among those excluded were the youth I was meeting in Los Angeles, who because of their unaccompanied status were not growing up as students in schools but as low-wage workers. "They're working because they don't have parents here to look after them, and they have no other means to survive," I'd explain to those who asked why my study participants did not enroll in school to qualify for DACA. Some were garment manufacturers sewing clothes for Americans' favorite brands, others were dishwashers at notable Los Angeles restaurants, and others lived as domestic workers for Los Angeles's elite.

Telling these youth's stories would get more complicated come 2014 when the near doubling of unaccompanied children and youth apprehensions at the US-Mexico border incited "an urgent humanitarian situation" that would eventually launch a decade-long migration crisis. Suddenly it was not just images of undocumented high school and college graduates donning caps and gowns that were spread across printed and digital media, but those of Central American and Mexican children as young as three or four years old at the border, in detention centers, and in courtrooms.

How did we get here?

What would we do now?

US policymakers took to describing children as fleeing violence and poverty and in search of parents already living in the country. Charged with the admission and care of children from noncontiguous border countries under the Trafficking Victims Protection Reauthorization Act of 2008, the federal government's simplified story goes that the US Customs and Border Protection takes eligible children into Department of Homeland Security (DHS) custody. DHS then transfers children to the Department of Health and Human Services' Office of Refugee Resettlement (ORR), where the Flores Settlement Agreement of 1997 determines that they should be detained in the "least restrictive setting appropriate to a minor's age" until released to a sponsor.[3] Adult sponsors are responsible for children's integration into family, school, and community life; because DHS immediately places released children in removal proceedings upon apprehension, sponsors are also responsible for children's legal lives. Children who prove persecution, neglect, or abandonment can qualify for asylum or Special Immigrant Juvenile

(SIJ) status, setting them toward eventual citizenship.[4] All others must await their fates.

Even with the growing discourse around unaccompanied child migration, it remained difficult to square the undocumented immigrant youth workers I was researching in Los Angeles with the children we saw on the news. The unaccompanied youth workers I knew had crossed the US-Mexico border as EWIs, what the federal government designates as Entry Without Inspection. Accessing legal relief would require admission of one's unauthorized entry. Being brought into the legal system would also require teens to adopt adolescence—that is, dependence—which they often could not afford. Without work, they could not financially support themselves and their left-behind families. Their financial precarity constrained their ability to seek legal counsel.

Moreover, many study participants did not maintain documents proving their arrival dates. They explained that no one told them that proof of date and age of arrival or the length of their residency in the US would one day be important to demonstrate. And by the time of this research, many had aged out of eligibility protections designed for unaccompanied children. What becomes evident is that policies like DACA, SIJ, and others geared toward supporting immigrant (and nonimmigrant) youth in the US carry the underlying assumption that parents or other adult figures are present in a child's life, and that these adults will take on the caregiver role and responsibilities that enable immigrant children's incorporation into society and normative transition to adulthood within parent-led households and K–12 schools.

The migration and coming of age of migrant youth *sin padres, ni papeles* do not neatly fit into the existing frames of undocumented students or unaccompanied children and urge us to question our assumptions about who immigrant youth are, how they live in the US, and what it means to grow up as both unaccompanied and undocumented young people. Scholars and policymakers alike have grappled with these questions over the last decade. Indeed, as I wrapped up interviews for this project in the fall of 2016, federal, state, and local governments looked for solutions to the unaccompanied child migrant crisis (and still do). Around that time, a coalition of Los Angeles County officials, advocates, and service providers tapped me for ideas for a regional response. I did what I had learned to do from organizing alongside undocumented students years before: I turned to immigrant youth's perspectives. I was in the habit of doing this in my seventy-five one-on-one interviews, in which I probed young people on their views of the crisis around unaccompanied children and what, based on their experiences, could be done to support the well-being of the affected in Los Angeles. To round out my suggestions to Los Angeles County advocates, I asked a key study participant if he would help me gather a group of Central American and Mexican young people who had grown up in Los Angeles *sin padres, ni papeles* to share some thoughts on these questions. He obliged.

In October 2016 I sat in a wood-paneled room of a Koreatown, Los Angeles, teahouse with sixteen undocumented young adults who had come of age as unaccompanied youth and low-wage workers across the city. Some were the first in their families to migrate; others had arrived in Los Angeles following siblings, cousins, aunts, or uncles. Many remained tied to left-behind families, but a few described themselves as *solitos* (alone). I asked the group several questions: What comes to mind when you hear the news of unaccompanied child migration? Do you relate to these children, and how? What should we do to help kids arriving in Los Angeles today?

The room turned quiet and the youth pensive. I waded through the silence for a few awkward moments until Cristhian, a Guatemalan Maya man in his early twenties, responded. "I am going to talk from my experience," he said. "I'll tell you how I've lived and how I see things," asserting that he did relate to the children arriving in the US at the time. I smiled and nodded as others turned their gazes toward him. "I think, well, the first thing is to understand how people lived in their home country when they were little. Some of us live in a lot of poverty," he began, "Over there, when you're little, you grow up poor and without resources, and you can't get ahead. And the same goes for our parents; they don't have an education. It's not their fault, but that is how we lived in Guatemala. There was no education, no way to get ahead."

For Cristhian, the news of unaccompanied child migration prompted him to think of children's original displacement(s). He understood migrant children's lives in the United States as shaped by what they left behind: intergenerational structural violence, including poverty, that cut futures short. Cristhian described himself and other adolescent migrants as being aware of the unattainability of their imagined futures even when "they were little" because "no one asks you, 'what do you want to do?' And even if you know what you want to do, over there, when you're little, you work. So, you think, 'Oh, this is my life, and people live like this in other places too.'" Supporting children, he proposed, necessitated the understanding that youth possess imagined futures and a curiosity about what they entail. Beyond knowing youth's goals, government and community bodies would need to leverage power and resources to see them through: "I think, the kids that are coming now, I don't know how old they are, but I think we need to ask them what they want to do and maybe have organizations that will give them funding to do that because maybe they [don't want to work, but] want to study."

Turning back to his experience, Cristhian reflected, "Like, I would have liked to study, but there was no one here to support me. There still isn't. So, you get here, and you must work. You come here to work. If you don't work, you end up on the street." Regardless of what future youth imagined they would have at the point of departure, their arrival context—that there "was no one" and "still is no one"—shaped how they would grow up in Los Angeles. Without support, Cristhian became a worker, not a student as he desired. He had no other choice. If he did not work, he would go unhoused. Cristhian ended his reflection by saying, "If someone had helped me financially, if someone had funded my education and my housing, I would at least have a college degree by now. But it wasn't like that. There aren't resources there or here. So, you move very slowly, little by little, because you cannot do everything at once."

"Everything is a process," someone said from across the table.

"Yes, it's a long process," another young person affirmed.

Since the start of my research, I have wrestled with what it means for scholarship and policy that there is a segment of the immigrant youth population that exists outside of the social and institutional bounds of childhood that are often leveraged as evidence of youth's contributions to society to make claims about their rights for legal protection and social inclusion. I have also wrestled with what it means for some of the most marginalized immigrant youth in US society to tell agentic migration stories laced with aspirations for mobility and well-being in the present and future, the disillusionments they face as they come of age across societies, and the hope that success is attainable, however slowly.

By all accounts, the unaccompanied youth transitioning to adulthood at the center of my research would be destined for what social scientists have defined as a downward incorporation into poverty and social exclusion, especially as they navigate the uncertain life stage of adolescence and the transition to adulthood. Social scientists, who define incorporation as patterns of participation and membership in the destination country's economic, social, and political mainstream, characterize successful incorporation in socioeconomic terms, as educational completion, occupational mobility, wealth accumulation, and the adoption of the society's dominant cultural practices.[5] Foundational studies of Latin American–origin youth, whether immigrants themselves or children of immigrants, consistently find that adolescents' absence from, or underachievement in, school during early developmental years can lead to stagnation or downward incorporation in adulthood.[6] The safeguard? Parents. With the help of adult figures in schools and coethnic communities, parents can buffer children from a grim fate by guiding them toward success. These conclusions agree with much research on child development and status attainment over the life course.[7]

Without parental supervision and outside of schools, immigration policymakers might write off youth like Cristhian as deviant, unproductive, and undeserving of legal and social protection and inclusion. Although some research participants experienced extreme poverty and mental and emotional distress that prompted them to adopt risky adolescent behaviors, many achieved material stability as they transitioned to adulthood. Having done so independently, they also achieved emotional growth and stability. And as Cristhian and others suggested, they did so "slowly, little by little," as a process.

Based on the experiences of migrant teens coming of age *sin padres, ni papeles,* I argue that incorporation is not a singular socioeconomic endpoint, as suggested by previous research, but an ongoing process that crosses social, institutional, and national boundaries over the life course. Attending to the simultaneous processes by which these young people adjust to their lives in the United States and transition to adulthood, I move beyond material measures like educational and occupational attainment to include the social and emotional aspects of belonging and investigate how immigrant youth negotiate their material and emotional lives independent of parents. I introduce the concepts of (dis)orientation, adaptation, and perdition—terms used by study participants in the Spanish language (*[des]orientación, adaptación,* and *perdición*)—as phases of the incorporation process, and I elucidate the mechanisms that move young people through each phase.

Throughout this book, my analysis pays close attention to how contexts—from the macro level of the nation-state to the micro level of interpersonal ties, social roles, and intersectional identities— shape immigrant youth's incorporation processes at different stages of migration and coming of age. As processes, the measures of successful incorporation and coming of age are not static endpoints but are subjectively defined. I consider how unaccompanied migrant teens redefine success for themselves as they adjust to roles and responsibilities, make sense of the structure of opportunities before them, and form identities in local and transnational communities as immigrants in a new society while transitioning to adulthood. In centering young people's perspectives of success and well-being, and as rates of unaccompanied youth's migration show few signs of decline, I hope to offer ideas about a way forward that accounts for the diversity of undocumented youth in the US today.

Existing Immigrant Incorporation Theories

In the past several decades, immigration research has focused on whether and how immigrants achieve political, social, and economic incorporation into the mainstream through interaction with and embeddedness in US society. Immigrants' diverging incorporation patterns within groups and across generations are primarily understood as produced by their receiving context.[8] Originally conceptualized as a societal-level phenomenon tied to government policies, labor market conditions, and cultural receptivity or hostility toward newcomers, the reception framework was revised to reflect individuals' and groups' positioning within nested structural and institutional contexts across state and local levels that help or hinder incorporation prospects.[9] Some social scientists debate whether multilevel societal barriers such as exclusionary immigration policies, labor exploitation, and ethnoracial discrimination slow eventual upward mobility or entirely lock multiply disadvantaged groups into downward mobility. However, others assert that the United States fails to offer today's immigrants and their descendants equitable access to opportunities for mobility based on national origin, ethnorace, class, and legal status, positing that marginalized groups' incorporation is that of "differential inclusion" as "distinct and subordinate subjects, rather than as identical peers."[10]

Immigrant Youth Incorporation

Theorizing based on the experiences of immigrant children and children of immigrants—the 1.5 and second generation—within normative family dynamics, studies portray youth as socialized by adults in families and schools. In contrast, adults negotiate workplaces and community life to secure children's futures.[11] Immigrant youth incorporation theorists center parental human capital and family structure as starting points for incorporation during the transition to adulthood. In this way, parents' positions in relation to the receiving government's policies, labor market, and community receptivity determine children's outcomes. Parents' roles enjoy prominence in the segmented assimilation theory—a foundational framework that outlines positive incorporation as achieved by youth members of racialized groups when parents maintain their authority—buffer exposure to discrimination from the cultural mainstream and provide "moral and material" resources that aid their children's social, political, and economic mobility.[12]

Researchers further argue that access to a "really significant other" or a nonparental figure who takes a "keen interest in a child" is decisive in immigrant children's incorporation and complementing strong familial ties.[13] Through a school-centric lens, researchers have identified the trusting relationships students develop with teachers, counselors, and peers as a critical variable in determining immigrant youth's mobility, especially among undocumented teens transitioning to adulthood and "illegality."[14] Attention to unaccompanied children moving through the formal federal government custody and release channels reveals that they are uniquely thrust into a "bureaucratic maze" in which they undergo legal socialization guided by family and immigration lawyers who impart to youth knowledge and resources to navigate their social position as legal subjects in US society while communicating messages of mobility and belonging.[15] In all, parents, coethnic communities, and significant others work together to buffer children from societal exclusion while providing material and emotional resources that guide them toward success.

Yet today's Latin American–origin immigrants and children of immigrants are coming of age in increasingly diverse household dynamics, with precarious class and legal statuses and complex educational and employment trajectories.[16] And despite the typical portrayal of adults as workers and children as students, history reveals that Latin American–origin youth have migrated—in some cases, without parents—in pursuit of work for several decades. My work with unaccompanied teens and young adults, along with that of other scholars, shows that unaccompanied minors do not automatically enter schools in the destination country but are often relegated to low-wage work as a matter of individual and familial survival.[17] Thus, understanding unaccompanied, undocumented immigrant youth incorporation, including that of low-wage workers, requires engaging theories built on the experiences not just of other children but of their adult counterparts.

Undocumented Immigrant Workers' Incorporation

Research on undocumented Latin American immigrant workers in the United States primarily builds from the case of Mexican migrants.

This work demonstrates that migration is strategically deployed to recoup economic opportunities lost during political and economic instability.[18] More recent research with Central American adults tells the stories of adults and families fleeing war, political repression, and labor market inefficiencies.[19] Typically, adult parents navigate migration and labor institutions and endure life in the destination country on behalf of left-behind families. Many Central American and Mexican children are joining the ranks of undocumented adult immigrant workers in the secondary labor market—the dual US labor market segment associated with low wages, job instability, and poor work conditions.

Debates about the effects of secondary labor market entry on immigrant incorporation are ongoing.[20] Relying on a comparative frame, some scholars argue that low-wage labor in the United States offers opportunities for those with low English-language proficiency and limited knowledge about the United States to find work.[21] Others show that the characteristics that enable employability in the secondary labor market, such as undocumented status, limited knowledge about work opportunities, exploitative work conditions, and lack of English-language fluency, can represent significant occupational mobility barriers.[22] As employers' monopolistic power over immigrant employees reduces their bargaining power, undocumented workers endure lower or lost wages, worse conditions, and fewer benefits than those with work authorization.[23] With few occupational prospects and limited earnings mobility, undocumented immigrants might work multiple low-wage jobs for longer hours to make ends meet, breeding social isolation or ethnic-community fragmentation as impoverishment contributes to coethnic opportunism and exploitation.[24] Women and Indigenous migrants may also experience intersectional gendered and ethnoracial disadvantages within society at large and in their coethnic community that worsen job prospects and work conditions and reduce earnings.[25]

Social scientists recognize that immigrant workers in the secondary labor market face near-insurmountable challenges to achieving incorporation as it is traditionally defined under these labor market conditions. These scholars have thus conceptualized immigrant incorporation not as an endpoint but as an active process wherein claims to social membership are subjectively made, and success is subjectively defined.[26] The incorporation process is experienced as an ongoing and dynamic struggle between groups aiming to claim their place within an unequal society.[27] Developed through a study of low-wage Latina/o adult immigrants in the workplace, this theory has explained the incorporation processes of adult immigrants within a single social domain. Here, I expand the incorporation process framework to account for the interdependence of social domains across societies and apply it to the case of unaccompanied and undocumented immigrant youth workers as they come of age in the US.

Reconceptualizing Immigrant Incorporation

Unaccompanied teenage migrants' institutional displacements set the stage for a ground-up reconceptualization of immigrant incorporation. Based on their experiences and perspectives, I bridge the theorization of incorporation as a process occurring within institutions with life-course scholars' socioecological framing of individual development as a series of interactions between structure and agency within distinct institutions like family, school, and work. Socioecological theory argues that interpersonal and institutional interactions are nested within social systems of community, neighborhood, and larger society that are shaped by context and culture over time.[28] This suggests that incorporation processes are also nested and that an individual's navigation of opportunity structures and participation patterns in one social domain shapes their ability to navigate the structures of opportunity and participate in another by granting or denying social status, opportunities, and resources. In this way, attaining stability in one social domain can promote status attainment and resource accumulation in another. The inverse is also true.[29]

In this book, this dynamic and multiscalar process is captured through the interconnected concepts of (dis)orientation, adaptation, and perdition. *Disorientation* refers to immigrants' material and emotional state immediately following arrival, when they are largely unfamiliar with the organization of the destination society and their place within it and are unsure of how they should navigate its structures and institutions, norms, and values. Unaccompanied immigrant youth are uniquely disoriented about how and by whom they will be received, as well as what social roles and responsibilities they will take on upon arrival. *Orientation* is the process by which immigrants learn about the unfamiliar new society. Immigrants who find a welcoming household context might be ushered into their new roles and social position by a long-settled relative, who also teaches them their new social world's norms and values. Those without a welcoming household arrival must do this learning on their own and without support. Some instances of orientation occur by virtue of time and the quotidian interactions born of the need for survival; these are typically material orientations to employment, housing, and neighborhood spaces. Orientation to the need for companionship through coethnic community and social life, especially in adolescence, can orient immigrants to meaningful social ties that offer emotional support. Immigrants who remain disconnected from meaningful social ties might experience material orientation but remain emotionally disoriented. For unaccompanied teens undergoing simultaneous migration and adolescent transitions, access to material and emotional support is critical for their orientation.

Adaptation—how immigrants become materially and emotionally adjusted within and across social domains in the destination society—follows orientation. In adaptation, immigrants activate knowledge and skills learned and resources obtained in orientation to make inroads into material and emotional well-being within the structure of opportunities before them. Over the life course, adaptation is ongoing as orientation to and adaptation in one social domain of interaction (work, school, family, community) shapes subsequent orientation to and adaptation in another. When immigrant families are transnational, immigrants' adaptations are also transnational. But even if materially adapted as a matter of survival, immigrant teens can remain emotionally maladapted. This typically occurs when the grief of migration and indefinite family separation can be too great, leading immigrants toward *perdition*. Participants described perdition as a state of loss, unrelenting emotional disorientation characterized by overwhelming loneliness and angst. In social isolation, immigrants can unwittingly adopt coping strategies, like substance abuse, that destabilize their material lives and worsen their emotional distress. Just as material and emotional orientation and adaptation work together to promote positive incorporation, prolonged material and emotional disorientation creates a feedback loop of perdition. Still, perdition is not an endpoint but a process that can be reoriented toward adaptation through stabilizing material and emotional support.

This conceptual framework corroborates assertions of the existing immigrant incorporation theory, such as its socioeconomic and interrelational features, while foregrounding the importance of socioemotions and interactions across institutions and societies. Moreover, this framework allows for exploring an array of institutional and interpersonal starting points, including the possibility of immigrant youth's coming of age outside parent-led households and schools. It traces the patterns that distinct starting points produce.

Portraits of Unaccompanied Migrant Youth in the United States

The portraits of unaccompanied migrant youth shared throughout this book have remained largely unseen by the state and understudied by academics. In the United States, the term *unaccompanied alien child* was codified into law with the passage of the 2002 Homeland Security Act. It refers to minors (aged eighteen and under) with neither lawful US immigration status nor a parent or legal caregiver in the United States; this includes children separated from their family units.[30] Almost 66 percent of the nearly 11.2 million undocumented immigrants currently living in the United States are from Mexico, El Salvador, Guatemala, and Honduras,[31] with 93 percent of unaccompanied minors also originating from these four countries.[32]

Unaccompanied child migration rates in the United States are measured by the number of apprehensions, which remained relatively stable before 2010. However, between 2011 and 2014 the number of unaccompanied Central American children apprehended annually nearly doubled, culminating in almost 70,000 Central American and Mexican unaccompanied child apprehensions by the end of fiscal year (FY) 2014.[33] There are reports of another 152,000 unaccompanied children being apprehended during 2022.[34] Unaccompanied children apprehended at the US-Mexico border are taken into US federal custody and, if eligible, move through formal custody transferral channels, as outlined earlier in this chapter. The participants of this research were not apprehended at the border; therefore, they were not formally classified as unaccompanied children but grew up experiencing the full reality of childhood without parents or adult caregivers.

While we cannot accurately account for the number of children who enter without inspection, estimates of undocumented Latin

American–origin adult migration show that for every undocumented migrant apprehended at the border, three others are not.[35] Observable trends of unaccompanied children's release from ORR custody suggest that children arrive in states with dense Latin American-origin populations.[36] California—and Los Angeles County in particular—has long been a primary destination for Central American and Mexican immigrants. Since 2014, California has been among the top receiving localities for unaccompanied children and youth released from ORR custody.[37] Participants in this study discussed having set their sights on Los Angeles because they knew of others who had migrated there before them who, they imagined, could facilitate their transition to a new society.[38] Upon arrival, and invisible to the state, unaccompanied teens' social worlds are circumscribed by structure and circumstance. While some oversight and expectations of supervision and care exist for children placed with sponsors through apprehension and custody transferral, migrant children who enter clandestinely rely entirely on informal arrangements to secure support and their futures. Unbeknownst to many study participants when they arrived in Los Angeles, their undocumented, long-settled kin were navigating precarious everyday lives themselves.

California is relatively welcoming toward immigrants. The state hosts over two million undocumented immigrants, constituting about one-quarter of the nation's total unauthorized population, more than 6 percent of the state's total population, and 10 percent of the state's workforce.[39] Although California declared itself a sanctuary state for undocumented immigrants in 2017, Los Angeles recognized itself as a sanctuary city within the state during the rise of Central American migration in the 1980s; in June 2023, the Los Angeles City Council voted to formalize the city's status as such.[40] Codified as legislation, sanctuary status promises to offset the harm imposed on immigrant families by federal law, which

I detail in chapter 2. These places' being named sanctuaries does not shield undocumented immigrants from the force of the legal and social construction of illegality that all but assures adult migrants' exploitation within the secondary labor market occupations that employ them, with consequences for family organization, dynamics, and the distribution of resources.

Despite undocumented immigrants' enormous contributions to California's economic vitality, those who work in industries with high rates of noncompliance with labor laws, like manufacturing, hospitality, and construction, make up one of the most vulnerable segments of the workforce.[41] Undocumented workers endure conditions of underpayment and wage theft, verbal and physical abuse, and illness and injury due to performance demands and lack of safety training or protective materials while at work. Undocumented workers who resist their work conditions may be silenced by employers, who threaten to reduce hours or wages, terminate employment, or call immigration authorities.[42] Legal scholar Kathleen Kim writes that, for undocumented workers to protect themselves, their families, and their futures, "their illegality renders them consensual to that exploitation."[43] Thus, the exploitation of undocumented workers creates intergenerationally resource-impoverished households and communities.

When households and communities are materially insecure, they are constrained in their capacity to receive teenage newcomers and provide them with material and emotional resources to support normative adolescent incorporation. Teens then enter exploitative low-wage labor industries to survive and to secure basic needs like housing, food, clothing, and in some cases, medical attention. This contradicts existing literature's portrayal of adolescents and teens working under adult supervision to supplement parents' earnings or get spending money.[44] Unaccompanied young people must also work to repay migration debt, which ranged from $3,000 to $11,000 among study participants. In most cases, debt accrued interest with each day it went unpaid.[45] In this study, 93 percent of participants grew up in Los Angeles, California, as full-time workers in the secondary labor market and saw their wages, ranging from $60 to $400 per week for study participants, spread thin in Los Angeles. The city of Los Angeles is ranked as the second most expensive place to live in the United States.[46] The cost of living in Los Angeles is 6 percent higher than the state average and 50 percent higher than the national average.[47] Housing and utilities in Los Angeles are 140 percent and 12 percent more expensive than the national average, respectively.[48] It is costly to be a low-wage worker in Los Angeles.

Teenaged migrant workers endure these conditions as they make ends meet for themselves and, for those with transnational ties, remit money to their left-behind families (between $100 and $300 monthly) for daily expenses, medical needs, home-building projects, education of younger siblings, or family business start-ups. Many of these young people arrive in the United States with prior work experience after working alone or alongside their parents or adult caretakers in their home countries. Thus, they anticipate entering full-time employment in manufacturing and service occupations.

Undocumented low-wage workers' financial pressures create a unique condition of incorporation that I refer to as *work primacy*.[49] This concept describes the centrality of work in immigrants' everyday lives when they attempt to fulfill financial obligations to themselves and their left-behind families with the limited financial and social resources accrued through their work in exploitative low-wage jobs in the US. The unexpected unevenness of immigrants' income and expenses prompts them to work more jobs and longer hours to make ends meet. Hence, work and the workplace become the central organizing activities and domains of immigrants' everyday lives and identities, respectively. Constraints on immigrants' finances, time, and bodies—due to illness and injuries caused by work—spill over to their participation in nonwork institutions.

As I show in chapter 4, work primacy is experienced unevenly; immigrants' locations within social hierarchies matter. Latin American-origin immigrants, especially undocumented immigrants, are stigmatized as "unskilled." [50] They are consequently often relegated to so-called immigrant jobs characterized by low wages, dangerous working conditions, and occupational instability.[51] Furthermore, Indigenous groups have historically been characterized "as dangerous, lazy, childlike, or mulish."[52] Once Indigenous immigrants are in the United States, this illicit and stigmatizing generalization affects everyday social interactions within the Latin American immigrant community as well as with law enforcement bodies, in employment and mobility prospects, and in treatment at work.[53] Meanwhile, gender hierarchies circumscribe women to subordinate social positions with fewer mobility opportunities. Immigrant teens learn to patchwork resources to make ends meet despite the compounded disadvantages of limited material resources and constraints on their time. Work primacy invariably contours experiences of (dis)orientation, adaptation, and perdition and informs how immigrant youth make meaning of success in their transition to adulthood.

Coming of Age *sin Padres, ni Papeles*

Adding complexity to teens' unaccompanied and undocumented experiences is their negotiation of the interconnected phases of incorporation during the critical life-course transition between adolescence and adulthood. This is a period of role adoption and goal setting, changes in young people's bodies and identities, experimentation, and development of autonomy.[54] Hence, compounding youth's disorientation at being a newcomer migrant in an unfamiliar society is the disorientation they might feel about who they are and where they belong more generally. This research takes seriously the assertion of critical youth studies scholars that young people embody their objectives, competencies, and perspectives as they cross national borders and settle into local communities and experience, reconfigure, and make meaning of their local and transnational social worlds, including in the transition to adulthood. I introduce the *emergent frame of reference* as a concept that explains how immigrant youth created comparisons between their past and present living conditions and between themselves and other youth in Los Angeles to understand their social position. In some cases, the emergent frame produced a sense of deprivation as young people worked to understand why they lived—and suffered—as they did relative to immigrant and nonimmigrant youth with parents in the US. In other cases, the emergent frame enabled youth to make claims of material mobility and emotional maturation in the transition to adulthood as they compared their present and past selves.[55] As we will learn in chapter 6, these emergent frames inform the subjective meanings youth make of their success in young adulthood.

While I revise the notion that successful incorporation is an outcome, I also attend to the definitions of the successful transitions to adulthood. Scholars have identified five transitions: school completion, independence from the origin family home, entry into full-time work, and family formation through first marriage and then parenthood.[56] Pathways to these markers vary greatly by economic condition and social position, such as race, class, and gender.[57] Studies of Black and White poor, working-class, and middle-class youth transitioning to young adulthood in the US, for example, show that increasingly unequal access to class resources—like education, job training, professional social ties, and a safety net in times of uncertainty—can delay adulthood role attainment.[58] As traditional adulthood markers fall farther out of reach for native-born, poor, and working-class individuals, the subjective classification of successful adulthood has increased in salience.[59]

For immigrant youth, the experience of migration and individuals' social position, including a teen's legal status, shape adulthood transitions by causing them to experience the roles and responsibilities of adulthood early in their lives.[60] Unaccompanied immigrant youth are often thrust into typical adult roles beginning in their origin countries and certainly through migration. Two studies have importantly informed our understanding of unaccompanied youth's transitions to adulthood and the meanings they make of them. A prominent study of independent Mexican youth workers in New York City found that most youth relied on role attainment markers like financial independence and social responsibility to signal adulthood. Others who struggled with self-esteem and feelings of immaturity did not claim to be adults.[61] In another study of Mexican and Central American unaccompanied migrant young people in Chicago, the subjective markers of financial responsibility, overcoming trauma, and social autonomy were more salient than role fulfillment in immigrants' claims of adult status.[62] It is clear from this research that for unaccompanied adolescent arrivals, material and emotional markers set between traditional and subjective measures define successful adulthood. We know less about how the meanings of successful adulthood are made alongside those of successful migration and incorporation.

Attuning to the interplay between social structure and agency, I analyze how the unaccompanied youth who grew up as undocumented low-wage workers made meaning of their dual transitions to incorporation and adulthood. Findings show that once in young adulthood, youth workers made claims of material mobility and emotional inclusion by crafting congruent cultural narratives about "good" immigrants and "competent" adults across institutions and societies.[63] This advances a line of work investigating how marginalized populations claim dignity and respect while occupying devalued and often stigmatized societal positions. There is evidence of "good" immigrant claims making in studies of populations, including but not limited to undocumented adult workers who politically organize across borders, children of immigrants who work alongside street-vending parents, and undocumented students.[64] This claims making points to work ethic, fiscal responsibility, and collectivism to validate immigrants' marginalized and often stigmatized identities.[65] US-born poor and working-class young adults claim competent adulthood through narratives of overcoming childhood pain, achieving parenthood, and building social-community embeddedness.[66] Scholars agree that even if the dominant society does not recognize claims making, it promotes a positive sense of self and confidence in one's social status, decisions, and behaviors.[67] Unaccompanied youth with transnational ties claim status and inclusion across societies. Throughout the book, I explore the nature of these claims and how the incorporation process phases of (dis)orientation, adaptation, and perdition influence them.

Research with Los Angeles's Unaccompanied Migrant Youth

Sin Padres, Ni Papeles brings together research collected across six years (2012–2018) in the Latin American immigrant ethnic-enclave neighborhoods of Pico-Union and Westlake/MacArthur Park, approximately two miles west of downtown Los Angeles. The concentration of coethnic Latin American–origin residents, availability of low-cost shared housing, and proximity to low-wage work in nearby neighborhoods make Pico-Union and Westlake/MacArthur Park primary first destinations for unaccompanied, undocumented youth workers in the United States. My fieldwork began at Voces de Esperanza, a support group for unaccompanied, undocumented Guatemalan young workers employed primarily in the garment industry in downtown Los Angeles. In its nascent stages of development in 2012, this group represented a true grassroots effort to provide culturally responsive support for unaccompanied Maya teens and young adults.

I gained access to this predominantly male group after meeting coordinators Wilfredo, a Salvadoran first-generation immigrant in his early fifties, and Jorge, a Mexican 1.5-generation immigrant in his early twenties. The Voces group initially met at a Pico-Union neighborhood Starbucks patio and later moved about a mile down the street to a cooperative housing complex. The group operated informally, with conversation guided each week by participants' responses to the simple question, "How was your week?" Discussions could focus on work schedules and money management at one meeting, fears of dating and speaking in public at the next, and recent natural disasters or illness and injury among left-behind family members at another.

I attended the group for seven months (between July 2012 and January 2013) before anyone besides the group coordinators interacted with me. Perhaps demonstrating the young people's distrust of strangers, they did not speak to me directly and hardly interacted with me during my first months in attendance. Although participants rarely engaged with my comments when I spoke up in the group, I continued to attend the group meetings at the invitation of their coordinators, who promised that the ice would eventually break. Finally, as we approached 2013, one participant, Caleb, greeted me when I arrived. It was as if a switch was flipped that evening that signaled to others that I was trustworthy and had a place in the group. At that point, my fieldwork turned from distant observation into participant observation, as I was engaged directly by group participants before, during, and after the group meetings. I shared my research interests in one-on-one conversations rather than having my research be described to the young people by Wilfredo or Jorge. To my delight, Caleb was the first to accept an invitation to be interviewed, in January 2013. Others quickly followed his lead. I honor the space Caleb created for me, the rapport he facilitated within this group, and the others who followed by profiling the complexity of his migration, incorporation, and coming of age throughout the book.

Within one year of observing the group, I was invited to accompany members to local church gatherings, community garden cleanups, book clubs, holiday dinners, recreational activities, fundraisers, baptisms, and funerals. In the fall of 2014 and winter of 2015, a handful of youth I had come to know learned of the Labor Commissioner's Office in downtown Los Angeles and its emphasis on providing legal protection to garment workers. Two of them filed claims, later inspiring others to do the same. Several requested that I attend their meetings at the office to act as an interpreter, and I readily agreed.

Following this, in spring 2015, at the request of a group of teens, I prepared an English-language class, which met biweekly in the classroom of a shared community space in Westlake/MacArthur Park. I shadowed participants across informal spaces such as coffee shops, teahouses, and fast-food restaurants. Still, most of my formal observations took place in the support group and church youth-group meetings. In all, I conducted six years of participant observation with unaccompanied, undocumented young adults throughout Los Angeles between 2012 and 2018, which included intensive weekly site visits between 2012 and 2016 that decreased as I turned to focus on writing my dissertation during the 2017–2018 academic year. Still, I continued to engage in episodic fieldwork until the end of 2018 and sporadic follow-up conversations in 2019. As this book goes into press, I have continued to stay in touch with a handful of participants.

Alongside fieldwork, I conducted seventy-five Spanish-language, semistructured interviews. I organized interviews as life histories that drew on participants' expertise in pre- and postmigration work, school, family, and community life through storytelling, which facilitated trust and comfort as the interviews progressed. On several occasions, participants thanked me for speaking with them, asking questions no one had previously asked them, and showing an interest in their lives. Participants clarified that my interest in their stories made them feel important and valued and that their presence in Los Angeles would somehow be documented and made real. This spoke to the youth's need to unburden (chapter 3) and be witnessed (chapters 4 and 5), to counter feelings of loneliness and angst. While I provide the participant demographic table and my methodological reflections in appendixes A and B, I summarize information about the interviewees below.

As noted earlier, all interviewees arrived in Los Angeles from Guatemala, El Salvador, Honduras, and Mexico. Five received full financial support from a long-settled nonparent relative upon arrival and were therefore not full-time workers. The other seventy grew up as full-time workers. Most worked in garment manufacturing, service, janitorial, and domestic work. Others worked in hairdressing, construction, car washing, mechanics, and day labor. Two men were unemployed at the time of our meeting but had grown up as garment workers. Undocumented youth workers, unlike newcomer English-language learners or Dreamer and DACA youth, do not enroll in the US K–12 educational system, although some interviewees eventually enrolled in adult schools centered on learning English as a second language for a few hours each day, Monday through Thursday. Some falsified their age and entered these after-work classes as minors; others entered as young adults. Twenty-two of the seventy full-time workers in my study sample had enrolled in adult English-language schools at some time since their arrival.

Reflecting recent statistics, Guatemalans are overrepresented in my sample because of my entry into the field and the preliminary study questions, which specifically focused on the experiences of Guatemalan unaccompanied minors. Of the Guatemalan participants, nearly three-quarters originated from rural highland communities. Land privatization has created widespread poverty and underdeveloped educational infrastructure, leading to youth's incomplete education and early entry into the workforce. Identifying as Indigenous, these young people grew up speaking K'iche', Q'anjob'al, Mam, and Akateko, four of the twenty-one Indigenous Maya languages spoken in Guatemala. Unlike non-Indigenous youth—young people living in city centers and those middle- or upper-class youth who might have been educated in Spanish in their origin countries and eventually in English—Indigenous youth learn Spanish as a second language in their home communities or the United States.

The interview sample was made up predominantly of men, reflecting the historical predominance of males in unaccompanied youth's migration. The interviewees' median age was twenty-three, and the median age at migration was sixteen, with the youngest participant migrating at eleven and the oldest at seventeen; participants had spent an average of 8.6 years in the United States. Participants arrived in the United States as adolescents and teens and transitioned to young adulthood before or during this research. Our retrospective conversations illuminated how migration and coming-of-age trajectories intermingle in the incorporation process. This is the focus of the remainder of the book.

Overview of the Book

Sin Padres, Ni Papeles illuminates how immigrant incorporation works as a process over time that shapes subjective meanings of success in the transition to adulthood. Each chapter takes a step in the migration and coming-of-age journey. Chapter 1 examines unaccompanied teens' departure contexts to explain the macro-historical forces that displace children from culturally specific childhoods and imagined futures. Unable to imagine futures in their origin countries, fraught with intergenerational violence and poverty, young people contemplate migration *metas* and plan for departure in ways that reflect their complex relationships and responsibilities. In cases where youth were navigating poverty and violence alongside family, migration decisions may be framed as a mechanism for collective mobility and well-being. For other youth, their family had experienced fragmentation before migration, and they made decisions individually. In each case, migration *metas* included hopes for economic mobility and social belonging in the short and long term.

Chapter 2 turns to arrival contexts and introduces households into the nested context of reception theory to illuminate the critical role of long-settled relatives' welcome in unaccompanied migrant youth's coming of age in the US. Constrained by their precarious political, economic, and social positions as undocumented immigrants, many long-settled relatives could not offer full material and emotional support. As a result, they relied on gendered cultural logics and social expectations to make decisions about the degree (e.g., supportive or unsupportive) and type (e.g., material and emotional) of support they would provide young people. Here, again, we see how macro- and micro-structural forces coalesce to determine young people's fate, in this case by determining newly-arrived teens' material and emotional incorporation starting points.

Chapter 3 explores how, given the household arrival context, unaccompanied youth experience (dis)orientation and learn whether and to what extent their migration *metas* are attainable in Los Angeles. Participants confronted varying degrees of disorientation. Most actively learned to navigate unfamiliar social, cultural, and institutional realms of everyday life without a clear source of guidance. While most young people were oriented to their roles as workers, discovered the falsehood of the "American Dream," and developed emergent understandings of their marginalized social positions as undocumented and unaccompanied immigrant adolescents, they were also oriented to the possibilities of enacting agency in navigating their new lives in the United States. Critical in the youth's orientation and determining their pathways to adaptation or perdition were their relationships with significant adult figures and peers who provided *desahogo* (unburdening) spaces from the emotional distress of loneliness and angst looming over them in their transitions to adulthood.

Chapter 4 analyzes the youth's experiences of material and emotional adaptation. I draw attention to how participants actively patchworked the knowledge, skills, and resources acquired through orientation to increase their material and emotional well-being and pursue social belonging. Institutional context patterns adaptation by determining the material and emotional drains and resources that youth negotiate as they come of age. With a focus on work primacy, I analyze how, through ongoing processes of orientation and adaptation, youth effectively navigate their structure of opportunities and set new *metas*, make decisions, and adopt behaviors that allow them to achieve their goals. Chapter 5 provides an alternate portrait: youth in *perdición* (perdition). Emotional disorientation can destabilize their lives even when immigrants are materially oriented and adapted. In perdition, teens often adopt harmful coping strategies influenced by gendered social expectations of emotional expression; hence, their social worlds do not expand as they do in adaptation but get trapped in a loop of harm. Here, I explore the three practices of substance (ab)use, romantic relationship formation, and self-harm.

The first five chapters show that unaccompanied, undocumented teens are locked out of normative migration and coming-of-age trajectories. Consequently, they are also excluded from the socioeconomic markers that scholars, policymakers, and the public rely on to judge successful incorporation and transition to adulthood. Chapter 6 sets out to untangle how participants made meaning of their coming-of-age experiences and to elucidate the importance of giving back as an embodiment of achieved material stability, emotional maturation, and an attainable but evolving measure of success. For youth who remain tied to left-behind families, giving back transnationally fulfilled their original migration *meta* of providing care for their loved ones. In this way, undocumented young adults understood incorporation as an ongoing experience that is contextually defined and expansive over time.

I revisit the book's empirical and theoretical advancements in the concluding chapter. Moreover, I offer several suggestions for how US federal, state, and regional policymakers and advocates can respond to the suffering and promote the well-being of unaccompanied and undocumented migrant teens, young adults, and families like those profiled in this book.

1 *Departures*

Caleb's mother confessed her concern for his future in Guatemala when he was fourteen. "There is no money here," he remembered her saying. "There is no way for you to get ahead to become a better person and build your house." He grew up one of nine children—the second-oldest sibling but the oldest son. He had several half siblings, including older brothers, but because they grew up separately, Caleb's immediate family relied heavily on him. After completing the first four years of primary education, Caleb dedicated himself to paid and unpaid work to make ends meet, sometimes with his father in the fields and sometimes with his mother at home. Caleb's family was considering what could become of his future in Guatemala, not only as a matter of survival but with concern for his potential to belong in the future, anchored in home and community life. After several long talks with his parents, Caleb felt confident that migration held some promise in achieving his *metas*, his goals to become a better person, earn money, and build a house. These were meant to increase his participation in his local community and society in his transition to adulthood.

When the prospects of fulfilling expected social roles and achieving imagined futures in the origin country narrow, young people set their sights on migration. Migrant youth (and their families) rely on local and transnational social ties to create new possibilities. Caleb explained that his parents contacted his uncle in Los Angeles and "asked him if he could do us the favor of helping us with some money for my passage [through Mexico]." His uncle agreed. "What was that time like for you?" I asked Caleb in 2013 as we sat at a Pico-Union Starbucks. Securing his migration passage was bittersweet. "I started to feel sad the week before I left," he confessed. "I would tell my brothers and sister, 'When I get over there, I will send things. I'll call you.' I'd say that to them, and they'd get excited." Caleb's parents did not have migration experience, nor had they ever visited Los Angeles, but the night before Caleb was set to leave, his parents warned him of the *vicios* (vices) he would encounter in the US—drug and alcohol use primarily, but gangs and community violence, and excessive spending, too. The following day, his parents walked him to the house of the two men who would take him from his family home in the Guatemalan highlands to Los Angeles.

Unaccompanied youth's decision to migrate is made not only in the origin country but continuously in transit as young people balance the material and emotional realities of the present alongside the *metas* they have for themselves and their families in the future. Caleb made his way across the Guatemala-Mexico border and through Mexico by riding buses with twenty-two other migrants led by two immigrant smugglers, known by the slang term *coyotes*. While the group was crossing through the Mexican desert, Caleb noticed that some of his companions were younger than he—twelve- and thirteen-year-old boys—and that "there were girls, too, maybe fourteen, fifteen, sixteen years old." He remembered that as a fourteen-year-old, "there were moments for me that were like, a game. But then there are moments of sadness, there are moments of fear." He observed that other unaccompanied youth migrants shared similar emotional journeys alongside their physical ones. "We couldn't handle it anymore. I couldn't walk anymore. It was then that I started to see sadness there. You see people crying. The *jóvenes* [youth] start to talk about their parents: 'What could they be doing now?' That's what we'd talk about every time [the coyotes] would let us rest." Despite the grim circumstances Caleb was leaving behind and his role in the decision to migrate, going alone was challenging for him.

As high rates of unaccompanied children's migration persist, understanding decisions to migrate from young people's perspectives is vital. Doing so, as this chapter does, reveals that age and life stage critically determine the conditions of their displacement, their migration *metas*, and the meanings they make of their departures. While growing up in their origin countries, youth are acutely aware of the intergenerational violence and poverty—the legacies of colonialism and US imperialism—that threaten their physical, economic, and social lives in the present but also diminish their possibilities for a full and productive future. In adolescence, youth develop their identities and understandings of their roles and positions in society. As they imagine their futures, they contemplate the decisions they will need to make to move them toward their goals. Migration decisions reflect this duality—youth migrate in response to the urgency of their circumstances as adolescents in the present. But they also make migration decisions in the shadow of an imagined future, considering whether and to what extent they can fulfill their roles and responsibilities in adulthood tomorrow.

This framing advances scholarship that conceptualizes youth migration as motivated by either individual aims or collective responsibility. Considering individuals, the literature explains youth migration as the pursuit of their rite of passage into their desired social identity or role. For some, this passage might be to adulthood, as it marks the end of adolescence through independence from family, especially emancipation from parents.[1] For young men, migration can be a rite of passage to masculinity, as it allows them to engage in economic activities that demonstrate their capacity to be husbands and fathers.[2] Young women might pursue migration as a rite of passage to economic independence and less constrained gender roles.[3] Once migration flows are initiated, the quantity and quality of social ties across which information and resources are shared increase, thereby facilitating future acts of migration.[4] The normalization of migration in response to structural disadvantages can create a culture of migration in which it is accepted and expected. Among youth, this manifests as a "youth culture of migration."[5]

A growing body of research on unaccompanied child migration centers youth as knowing and collectively minded agents within oppressive origin countries. It explains their migration not merely as a pursuit of life's milestones but as the pursuit of life itself. Many young people resort to migration—and unintentionally enter the child labor market—to cope with natural and political crises and economic insecurity and to manage urgent familial safety and labor market risks.[6] Youth, like their adult counterparts, engage in multiple migrations—seasonal, regional, and internal—as a means of survival and an act of care before making the transnational migration journey.[7] In each case, they have been found to leverage their skills, knowledge, and resources to escape violence and poverty and, for those with families in the destination country, to pursue reunification.[8] The ability to meet family care goals, even at the cost of separation, adds a sense of purpose and belonging within families and communities.[9] Through this lens, youth migration is regarded as having "overlapping dimensions of compulsion and choice" as "young people enlist their paid labor, unpaid care work, and mobility to ensure the survival of their multigenerational household amid marginality and precarity."[10]

Bringing these threads together, this chapter argues that Central American and Mexican youth's unaccompanied migrations are motivated by individual and collective socioeconomic and socioemotional urgencies of the present and *metas* for the future. At the micro-societal level, migration decisions are made relationally, considering youth's social roles and responsibilities to themselves and their families. In some cases, youth made migration decisions collectively, alongside their families, such as in Caleb's case. For these young people, migration was the family and community splinter point. For others, family and community splintering occurred before migration, and decisions were framed as being made individually with the plan to escape. Relying on existing transnational migrant networks and knowledge, young people gathered the necessary financial, social, and emotional resources to embark on their migration journeys. Youth's displacement and migration journeys were laced with complex material and emotional decisions in each case.

The futurity of youth's individual and collective decisions to migrate is couched within macro-historical systems and structures that displace them from the social roles and opportunities they need to reach their imagined futures. To disentangle the micro- and macro-level forces at play, I begin with an account of contemporary Central American and Mexican displacements and migration histories to bring forward the origin-country dynamics that exclude young people across Central America and Mexico from institutions like schools and experiences like learning, exploration, and play that are associated with "getting ahead" and "becoming a better person," as Caleb's mother put it, during the transition to adulthood.[11] Youth's departure contexts have a bearing on their experiences of arrival and eventual incorporation into the destination society. Moreover, departure contexts and the *metas* they establish within them are essential in how migrant teens measure success in young adulthood.

Departure Contexts

In the contemporary period of enduring global human mobility of adults and children, unaccompanied youth migration is an extension of centuries-long migration from Latin America to the United States; this is not a new phenomenon.[12] Scholars agree that today's trends of Latin American migration are at their very foundations a product of Spanish colonialism, later reincarnated as US imperialism, which reconfigured land, labor, rights, population, and, ultimately, power in Mexico, Central America, and the Caribbean.[13] The history of Mexican migration is long and winding.[14] I refrain from recounting it fully here but note that Mexican immigrants—including unaccompanied children and youth—have made the journey to the United States in response to failing markets and corrupt governments for several decades.

As early as the beginning of the nineteenth century, Mexican children filled jobs in the construction of railroads and other industrial developments.[15] Later, migrant children, typically boys, were among the Mexican males displaced from the Mexican labor market and recruited and smuggled into the United States during the Bracero Program (1942–1964; also known as the Mexican Farm Labor Program). This was a federal initiative meant to redress labor shortages in the agricultural and railroad industries during World War II and address workers' displacement in a changing Mexican society.[16] These young children would claim to be older to evade immigration laws that prohibited their enrollment in the program as minors. Eventually, some would return to Mexico to formally enroll in the program upon meeting the age requirement.[17] Historian Ivón Padilla-Rodríguez summarizes the experiences of unaccompanied Mexican youth as having "had their labor exploited on commercial farms; [they] were denied educational opportunity and subjected to the United States deportation regime as unaccompanied workers and members of 'wet farm families'" throughout the twentieth century.[18]

Although the Bracero Program ended in 1964, labor migration patterns were sustained by migrant networks.[19] Fifty years after the establishment of the Bracero Program, the United States and

Mexico entered into a bilateral trade agreement, the North American Free Trade Agreement (NAFTA) of 1994. NAFTA introduced several economic reforms directed by the World Bank and the International Monetary Fund that were intended to lift Mexicans out of poverty and into prosperity. However, in practice NAFTA heightened economic instability and increased the displacement of workers through the deregulation of the agricultural labor market and the elimination of tariffs and subsidies. Subsistence farmers lost their income-earning potential and means of survival as industrialization devalued working-class people's skills.[20] Opportunities for survival and social mobility dwindled in Mexico under NAFTA, and Mexico witnessed a mass out-migration of adults and teenage workers to the United States—a history well documented in migration scholarship.[21] Indeed, the abovementioned theories of the culture of migration and the broader social process of cumulative causation of migration from which the culture is born were developed in response to the persistence of Mexican labor migration since the nineteenth century. The 2014 humanitarian crisis, in which Central American unaccompanied children apprehended at the border outnumbered those from Mexico, shocked many. Still, this crisis has deep historical roots, some of which mirror Mexico's past.

The contemporary migration history within and from El Salvador, Guatemala, and Honduras is marked by repression and resistance to imperialist agendas. In El Salvador and Guatemala, where governments began privatizing land, commercializing goods and resources, and consolidating power and wealth to benefit political and economic elites in the 1920s, violent and heavily militarized governments historically repressed social movements led by young people, dispossessed farmers and peasants, and Indigenous peoples.[22] Other oppressed people resisted through migration. Central America was soon caught in the crosshairs of the Cold War, a forty-five-year standoff between the United States and the Soviet

Union from 1947 to 1991 that distinctly shaped adult and youth migration patterns starting in the 1970s. The proxy wars ushered in a new era of crippling state violence and political repression, land dispossession and poverty, and fear and mistrust of government. The United States, haunted by the specter of communism and the fear of communist governments being installed in Central America, supported right-wing governments in El Salvador, Guatemala, and Nicaragua and used Honduras as a strategic military site. These interventions increased the Central American population in the United States from 350,000 to more than 2 million between 1980 and 2000.[23]

In El Salvador, the civil war from 1979 to 1992 resulted in the murder of seventy thousand civilians and the displacement of millions more. In Guatemala, an estimated two hundred thousand civilians were killed, forty-five thousand disappeared, and one million were displaced during the thirty-six-year-long civil war between 1960 and 1996. Indigenous communities endured the most brutal violence through targeted persecution, rising to the level of genocide, as they made up approximately 83 percent of those murdered in Guatemala during the war.[24] The current high rates of Guatemalan youth migration and the fact that 95 percent of children under age seventeen who are apprehended and returned to Guatemala are Indigenous serve as evidence of the enduring structural and institutional violence against Indigenous communities.[25] This invariably contributes to high rates of Indigenous community poverty and malnutrition, low education and investment in infrastructure, and the highest rates of child labor across the region.[26] Today, Indigenous communities in Guatemala consider the continued privatization of natural resources by foreign corporations, which forces human displacement and land degradation, a "fourth invasion," following Spanish colonization, the rise of the plantation economy between the 1870s and 1930s, and the civil war.[27]

Although Honduras did not endure a civil war, the nation's fate was sealed when the United States determined that the country, which shares borders with El Salvador, Nicaragua, and Guatemala, presented a strategic site for its covert military operations. Before the civil war period, American corporations controlled much of Honduran economic and political life.[28] When the civil wars broke out in Nicaragua and El Salvador in the 1980s, the United States quickly poured military spending into Honduras to advance its geopolitical and economic agendas. During the years of regional political conflict, funding was used to establish covert training groups, called Contras, as a counterforce against the communist Sandinista government in Nicaragua. The same disappearance tactics used in El Salvador and Guatemala were deployed against Honduran civilians who resisted the militarization of Honduras and the rising violence along the Honduras-Nicaragua border. The country's militarization persisted despite the wars' ending and the peace agreements reached by the 1990s.

Honduras's status as a critical geopolitical player was maintained during the US war on crime and drugs in the 2000s. Honduras was the first country to receive Central American Regional Security Initiative (CARSI) funding—totaling $176 million—to develop military strategies to halt drug and weapons trafficking. But the money did little to end the drug trade and did nothing to address US demand.[29] As occurred in South America decades prior and through Mexico's Mérida Initiative signed in 2008, US intervention pushed criminal organizations to devise more clandestine and violent ways of staying in business, including recruiting women and children as drug mules, spurring their migration.

For generations, Central Americans have fled their origin countries and sought refuge in cities like Los Angeles, forming communities in neighborhoods like Pico-Union and MacArthur Park, where the majority of research for this book took place. In the 1980s, during a period of mass exodus, young people faced discrimination from and conflict with established cliques of Mexican young people to their east and Korean young people to their west. In response, Central American youth formed their own protective cliques—currently the notorious MS-13 and 18th Street gangs—that became more violently organized through incarceration and transnational deportation policies that took exclusion across borders.[30] Once Los Angeles gang members were deported, they returned to their communities, only to face social ostracism and structural conditions of poverty, high unemployment, food insecurity, and educational disinvestment.[31] Some gang members began extorting families and neighbors to survive and to claim some power. Others attempted migration back to the United States, creating what Rodrigo Avila, El Salvador's vice minister of security at the time, referred to as an "unending chain" and "merry-go-round" of gang members moving between the United States and Central America.[32] The deportation regime, initiated by then president Bill Clinton, was strengthened by the George W. Bush and Barack Obama administrations, and persists today.

The United States has denied culpability in these events across Central America. Instead, it has framed itself as a charitable neighbor responding to the political, economic, and social havoc it covertly wreaked in the region with promises of development and stability through neoliberal economic modernization and securitization policies.[33] The 2004 Central American Free Trade Agreement (CAFTA), modeled after the failed NAFTA, is a case in point. CAFTA promised "transparency" and "regional integration" by eliminating trade tariffs, opening markets, and reducing service barriers to strengthen the region's economies. But CAFTA brought with it educational disinvestment, privatization of industries and goods, and increased displacement—including that of teens. Despite their promises to create alternatives to migration, the Mérida initiative and CARSI, implemented in the 2000s, as well as the 2014 Southern Border Program and the 2015 Alliance for Prosperity Plan, have served only to exacerbate regional destabilization and increase child migration.[34]

Compounding political, economic, and human catastrophes have weakened Central American countries' institutional and social infrastructure and built environments so that when natural disasters and global crises hit, they cannot endure them. For example, when Hurricane Mitch struck Honduras, Guatemala, and Nicaragua in 1998, 7,000 people were killed, and 1.5 million people (20 percent of the total population) were displaced in Honduras alone. In 2001 El Salvador suffered two earthquakes that worsened fragile social, political, and economic postwar stabilization efforts. In 2005 Guatemala endured the extensive flooding of Hurricane Stan, which resulted in the deaths of 800 Guatemalans and the destruction of entire towns. These natural crises have continued into the present. In 2020, Hurricanes Eta and Iota and the COVID-19 pandemic killed and displaced thousands of people and spurred the migration of many more.

Altogether, these events and interventions have produced deeply embedded "mundane and dramatic forms" of violence that devastate youth's present and cut short their futures.[35] Latin America has been considered one of the most violent regions in the world, and its economies are among the most stratified.[36] Across Central America and Mexico, violence ranges from the structural violence of entrenched poverty and ethnoracial and gender discrimination, to the direct violence of gang and cartel targeting and extortion, to domestic abuse and abandonment, all of which deny children and their families the right to live well.[37] Vulnerable groups adopt various survival strategies as they navigate the intertwining forms of structural and interpersonal violence to which they are subjected. Some people might engage in migration as a collectivist survival strategy, as the new economics of labor migration theory proposed.[38] Scholars describe the prioritization of collectivism in Latin American origin countries, especially among rural and Indigenous communities that have leveraged collective strategies to combat government neglect, persecution, and genocide; to construct local-level governance and economic systems; and to uphold sacred rituals and cultural practices.[39] Others might succumb to their experiences of extreme violence and poverty and reproduce it more locally, weakening the bonds within families and communities.[40] Given the critical role of the home and family in youth's sense of self and hope for the future, home and family life disruptions can prompt youth's feelings of displacement and nonbelonging and, ultimately, their migration.

Youth's displacement and migration stories will show that their decisions to depart are undeniably informed by their origin countries' long histories of exploiting, persecuting, and excluding the most vulnerable groups, including women, children and youth, and Indigenous communities. From within societies that threaten childhood and protected transitions to adulthood but from which youth have learned cultural expectations and values, youth contemplate and make decisions about their futures.[41] These country conditions force children to become knowing political and economic actors within their families and communities early in life. In this context, youth grow up thinking about their own and their loved ones' fates. Their migrations are imbued with moral obligations to their personal and familial well-being. They are thus caught at the intersection of compulsion and choice as they make collective and independent decisions to mitigate immediate hardship while contemplating an imagined future.

Migration and *Metas* for the Collective Future

Poverty is violence that is normalized in everyday life. In Latin America, 201 million people living in the region (32 percent of the total population) experience poverty; 82 million live in extreme poverty.[42] The majority of those living in poverty are children. In this study, young people who grew up experiencing extreme poverty and who observed their parents struggling to make ends meet in their origin countries believed that migration to the United States was a mechanism by which they could alleviate familial suffering and achieve a more stable future. Among study participants, these tended to be Guatemalan youth, particularly Guatemalan Maya youth, who were shut out of educational opportunities and thrust into paid and unpaid work at an early age.[43]

All study participants who described their migration to escape poverty shared their early exposure to and involvement in their family's economy and the precarity of their collective survival. Andrés, for example, remembered being around ten years old when he started working with his father. His older brother, Jayson, had migrated to Los Angeles some years earlier, but the family did not receive remittances from him as promised, so Andrés, the second eldest son, left school during the fifth grade and joined his father at work. He explained that he started working with his father because *"ahí no se puede ganar el pan de cada día"* (you cannot earn a day's bread [meaning that one's work does not produce a living wage]). They sewed shirts, he told me, and *unas chumpas*. Knowing that I am not Guatemalan and might not have been familiar with the term *chumpas*—the Guatemalan term for jackets—Andrés added, *"¿Se llaman chamarras aquí, verdad?"* (They're called jackets here, right?). I nodded along as Andrés detailed his memories of sewing Adidas logos onto tracksuit jackets with his father. Sewing labels onto jackets by hand was tedious, and despite their long hours at the task, the pair's combined earnings were insufficient to keep the family's heads above water.

Andrés's father decided to find new work in agriculture. He instructed Andrés to find a different job because of agricultural work's arduous and exploitative nature, especially the mistreatment of Indigenous people. At thirteen, Andrés was more aware of the family's economic circumstances and had confidence in resisting his father's instructions. He insisted that he be allowed to work in the fields as well. "I just didn't feel good, you know? Because I felt this [economic] insecurity because I knew we wouldn't have anything to eat." Andrés's father relented.

Andrés's intense insecurity pushed him to "work really hard" harvesting corn so that he could "feel good." But there were two looming discontents. First, the cornfields Andrés worked in were not his own but *de otras personas* (belonging to other people), which meant the profits of his labor were not his either. Second, as Andrés explained, "Sometimes, there are moments that you, as a kid, want to play, right? And I never had that." Instead, his father insisted Andrés and his siblings had to work to support the family. "You have to help," his father would say. Andrés agreed, saying, "He had good reason." There were seven other mouths to feed, after all. Andrés eventually decided to leave agricultural work and found independent employment in the garment industry. He was still only thirteen, but he had prior work experience in this, so he was able to find work quickly making men's button-down shirts at home. "I started to earn about three hundred *quetzales* per day" (the current equivalent of $38). That was hard-earned money. Andrés said in an exasperated tone:

It was so much work because it's not like you have a machine like over here. No, over there, it's all by hand and with only one needle. You sew them one by one and all through the night, so you aren't getting any sleep so that you can finish the work. First, you cut the fabric, then make the collar, then do a ton of work to put it all together. So, you suffer a lot.

"Is this when you decided to migrate?" I asked him, thinking that his individual suffering may have propelled his departure. Andrés explained that his experiences at school and work, up to his decision to migrate, convinced him that he would be unable to attend school or find stable work. Depressingly, he could not even guarantee food for his family. Meanwhile, he was learning of his brother's tales of success in Los Angeles, which piqued his curiosity. "The idea came to me because I started to think about my brother. He migrated first, and he had started to make a house over there [Guatemala]. That's what motivated me." The two realities merged, and he tethered his imagined mobility to alleviating his family's pains. Andrés desired to relieve his father, whom he had witnessed toiling at difficult labor for years. "I thought if I could work here [Los Angeles], I would be able to help my dad so that he wouldn't suffer anymore. I didn't want my family to suffer in this life anymore. That's where the idea came from. 'Okay, I'm going to the United States.'" Andrés would soon learn that his imagined future would not be easy to attain.

Young women described similar experiences of poverty, learning of their family's social and economic position from working within the home. Camelia grew up in Guatemala; her family had deployed the youth migration strategy several times before she finally departed. Since Camelia was the third-oldest sibling and second-oldest daughter, her departure was never a part of the family's plan. It was not part of Camelia's plan until she had exhausted all other options. "I saw the need. I saw how we were living," she recalled. "I saw how my parents were living, too, so I decided to come [to Los Angeles]," where her two older siblings were already living. "We were six siblings." She explained:

> My sister had migrated months before I decided to migrate. But she got pregnant after being in Los Angeles for five months so that she couldn't send money anymore. My older brother, who had lived in Los Angeles for four years, also stopped sending money. My dad worked in farming but only made sixty *quetzales* per day, which comes out to about five dollars.

Camelia stopped attending school after six years to help her mother with housework, which included growing corn and looking after sheep and chickens on their small plot of land. She thought her decision to work would at least enable her three younger brothers to complete their schooling.

Camelia began seriously considering her migration on the day that her mother sent her to the local market to buy the family's food with one hundred quetzales—"which is about $8, maybe $7," Camelia clarified. "I told my mom that it would not be enough for everything we needed for that week and through the next week. She responded that it was all she had and that I should only get what is necessary, which she said was sugar, soap to wash the clothes, some fruit for my little brothers, and whatever other food I could bring." Camelia recounted in vivid detail that she returned home with "five pounds of sugar, three bars of soap, two pounds of beef rib, oranges, and some potatoes and tomatoes that I could manage to get. That was it." On that day, she realized "I needed to do something. We cannot keep on like this." She was concerned not only about herself but about her siblings, too. "It was so difficult for my little brothers," Camelia recalled, "because when you're a kid, you know, you want to have certain things. That was my childhood; I always wanted what other kids had. I just never had the opportunity. I knew that's how my little brothers felt, too. So, I decided to come here [Los Angeles]." Camelia felt morally obligated to care for her family, including her parents and siblings, and to make up for the support lost when her older siblings stopped remitting.

Camelia's parents, like Andrés's, resisted her departure, so she turned to her sister in Los Angeles to help persuade them. Her sister also declined, offering as her reason that "women are hard to take care of, and I don't want to be responsible for you," a dynamic I discuss in the next chapter. Still, Camelia persisted. "I told my mom and dad to please trust me, and I promised to send them money when I arrived here [Los Angeles]. I asked them if they could support me." Camelia's parents ultimately agreed to help her raise $3,000, borrowed from neighbors in their hometown and from family members and compatriots living in the United States, to secure her passage at age fifteen.

Intergenerational poverty made it difficult for the youth in this study to imagine their participation in youth culture and to contemplate prospects of belonging as they came of age. Yet youth's awareness of their impoverished families' efforts to make ends meet spurred them to take responsibility for attaining their personal social goals. Guatemalan Maya siblings Esmeralda and Patrick—two of eight children—were the second and third siblings, respectively, in their family to migrate. "There were eight of us in my family," Patrick said, "and my dad was the only one that worked. But because he drank a lot, there wasn't much work that he could do all day. He only worked when they offered him a few days, and that's where it got difficult because my mom was alone." Patrick described their family as "very, very poor," which both siblings attributed to their father's unemployability and spending habits associated with his alcohol addiction. Although the pair's mother occasionally worked, affording weekly expenses was a challenge.

Esmeralda grew up desiring to participate in cultural customs like her town festivals and religious celebrations but noticed from a very young age that her parents struggled to make ends meet. Her participation in local events would only worsen their economic burdens. At the age of six, Esmeralda stopped going to school after only two years of primary education to begin working so that she could "have [her] own things."

> I started working at six and a half years old. I started working, and my dad would tell me, "If you work, you will have money; you will have clothes." Every celebration there [in her home community], you buy

new clothes to change into the day of the festival. So, my dad would tell me, "If you work, you can have your things."

Esmeralda thought she could work to attain the items necessary to be social in her origin country's society while simultaneously alleviating the economic pressures these cultural expectations placed on her family's wages, but she achieved very little in terms of mobility. So, at age fourteen, after having worked in the fields for some time, she decided to migrate to the United States in search of new work opportunities. Esmeralda aimed to fully relieve her family of her living expenses through financial independence and to bolster the family's status by working to contribute to the household. Despite her efforts, she could not achieve these interconnected goals in the US (explained in the next chapter). Esmeralda's family continued to live in extreme poverty after Esmeralda's departure, prompting her brother, Patrick, to plan his departure three years later.

When I asked Patrick about his migration motivations, he talked about feeling a sense of deprivation throughout his childhood. He "was tired of seeing other people with more money treat us differently in school. Well, when I went to school, that is. My classmates would not get close to me because their friends dressed better than me." He felt rejected by peer groups at school and then by school entirely. Perhaps because he was the third oldest sibling but the oldest brother, who was now ascending into the provider role, Patrick considered how his migration could end child migration within his family. "I didn't want my siblings to suffer like I was, so I decided to come to this country," he said, hopeful that his displacement might enable his siblings' embeddedness.

Through his migration, Patrick aspired to earn money that would allow him, his mother, and his siblings to live better lives.[44] This mindfulness about the future of families and the expectation that remittances could improve a family's socioeconomic status when invested in children's education is typically associated with migrant parents.[45] In this way, when older siblings migrate to support their younger siblings' education, they assume adult and parental migrant goals and responsibilities. Once Patrick lived in the United States, he learned that his motivations were not unique and that "many of us come here with the same story."

Patrick's claim was echoed by Elías, who migrated at age sixteen. At the time, Elías had four siblings in the United States and four others in Guatemala. He explained:

> The truth is that when I was growing up in Guatemala, I never thought of coming here. I have always liked to study, and there came a time when my parents couldn't help me anymore, so it was then that I started to think, "What am I going to do? There is no one to help me. I don't have a house. I don't have anything." I didn't have anything. So, the first thing that came to my mind was that I needed to go to the United States.

Elías informed his siblings in the United States of his plans to join them. They responded, "And why would you do that? You're too young." "That's true," Elías agreed, "but I can't do anything here. You can't do anything, and I don't have money to keep studying." Elías felt discouraged and disappointed but did not want his younger siblings to be pushed out of school early because of their poverty as he had been.

> I didn't have anyone to support me there, though my siblings wanted to; they wanted to help me, but there were so many of us. There are nine of us. I couldn't continue going to school because no one could help me and my little brothers and sisters. That's why I came here. If I had stayed there longer, what was I going to do?

Elías's question illuminates the hopeless deprivation underlying his migration decision.

Youth often consider migration the only way to move themselves and their families forward. Far from passively participating in a culture of migration, these young people described encountering a moment of truth, a point at which they found themselves face-to-face with the inevitable. In choosing migration, youth consider their family's ability to get by in the short term and get ahead in the long term and their ability to belong in their local society in the present and the future. But even when migration is framed as a choice, it is forced, a response to untenable structural conditions that have disabled opportunities to survive and thrive.

Leaving Family Behind

Youth migration scholarship analyzes migration as a rite of passage to adulthood, as migration presents the point at which youth autonomize from their kin households and fictive kin communities. In this research, youth who decide to migrate within family units and who imagine collective family futures experience their departures differently, as they do so to become more integrated into family and community life. Establishing clear migration *metas*—whether they are as broad as ending suffering or as narrow as affording more groceries or a younger sibling's education—did not preclude youth from feeling the emotional strain of trying to sustain transnational family connections.

When I asked Usher how he felt when leaving his family's home in Guatemala at age fifteen, he said, "I felt sad because I had never left my house. I had never visited the capital or a major city in my state. I went from a small town [in Guatemala] to Los Angeles. I felt sad, but I knew I wanted to build a house, and I needed to get ahead, so I decided to come to Los Angeles." I followed up to confirm: "You came here to build a home?" Usher responded with a simple "yes" and a shrug.

Another interviewee, Jordan, said that although his mother cried when, at the age of sixteen, he announced to his family that he would be leaving home, the reality of his departure and the sadness that accompanied it did not set in until the morning that he left. "It's sad to leave your parents," he explained, "to leave your friends and everyone behind. It's really sad. It's sad to go from one place to another without knowing what will happen next. Many people leave their homes and end up dead." Young people were aware of the journey's dangers and that their fates upon arrival would be uncertain if they made it to Los Angeles.

Parents also knew of the dangers and, contrary to public depictions of parents complicit in their children's exposure to violence and exploitation of migration, many resisted their children's departure.[46] As Andrés planned his migration, his mother expressed her concern that they might never see each other again if he left. "You're the only son I have left here," she would say before pleading with Andrés, "Don't go, just stay here." On other occasions, she asked him, "What if I die while you're away? What if I die and I never see you again?" These words stung Andrés. "It was painful to hear that, but I asked her, 'What would you have me do? Stay here? There's nothing for me here. I can't do anything here.'" What my conversations with migrant youth made clear is that they weighed the material, physical, and emotional costs of their departure for themselves and their families and negotiated these before and during migration.

Migration as an Individual Escape

Reports of fleeing physical violence dominate narratives of youth's motivations for migration. In a prominent report on the contemporary era of child migration, the United Nations High Commissioner for Refugees concluded that children from El Salvador and Honduras were more likely than those from Guatemala and Mexico to report violence, including from drug cartels and domestic abuse, but that Mexican youth were more likely to say they were fleeing "recruitment into and exploitation by the criminal industry of human smuggling."[47] Exposure to violence contributes to youth's sense of exclusion in their origin societies and local communities and limits their opportunities to participate in a full social life. Because of this, they could not imagine futures of social integration and economic mobility, which scholars have referred to as "social death" that is often tied to physical death.[48] Youth who reported migrating to flee violence described a sense of resoluteness about the departure from their origin countries. In this way, youth set their sights on the United States as the place where they might find more permanent belonging.

In this research, participants reported experiences of physical violence ranging from direct exposure to state and domestic violence to quotidian violence of ethnoracial and gender discrimination. While poverty, as explored in the previous section, was indeed a form of violence that families faced, it is so normalized and widespread that when both parents were present in the family unit, most families dealt with poverty collectively. This collectivism might have buffered youth from the perception that they were experiencing violence, which then influenced how they talked with me about their decisions to migrate. Here, stories of violence were more specific, direct, and abrupt threats to youth's safety in the present and the future. Violence could fragment family units, or families could be the source of violence itself.

In El Salvador, youth faced multiple levels and coinciding forms of physical and emotional violence and abuse. In some cases, children were collateral damage when parents or other caregivers were persecuted and killed, resulting from generations of political perse-cution and the militarization of youth's origin countries that deny children and adolescents sources of care as they come of age and destabilize their sense of security in the community. After Álvaro was abandoned by his parents following their separation and move to dif-ferent cities, he witnessed the execution of his grandparents and his uncle in El Salvador. He described the scene during our interview:

> I was a little kid when I saw my grandma and grandpa, and they came; many came dressed. I don't know if they were Americans or Guatemalans, but they had different uniforms. They didn't have the Salvadoran uniform. They put all my family on their knees; they started giving orders. They put them on the side in a line and shot them on the side of the head. Everybody, everybody. In front of us. Two years ago, I barely got my family's death certificate and [infor-mation about] how they all died; they all got bullets in the head. They all died like that. No questions, no nothing, just like that. Everybody in a line, everybody on their knees. My grandma, my grandpa, my uncle, everybody, like that. In less than minutes, they eliminated the whole family.

At the age of nine, and with his three-year-old brother, Álvaro became homeless. A neighbor took pity on his younger brother but left Álvaro to fend for himself, as he was deemed old enough to work to support himself. Álvaro collected aluminum and glass recyclables from dumpsters and on the streets and sold these items for a few cents. He lived alone and in extreme poverty. He began sniffing glue to alleviate his hunger, thirst, and suffering. Álvaro described how desperate he was to distract himself from his grief:

> So, when you're on glue, over there, you're like the lowest, that's like the cheapest drug. You can get high with a dollar. Actually, no,

seventy-five cents of a dollar. It changes who you are; with seventy-five cents, I would get so messed up. I mean really messed up. I didn't have anything to lose. So, when you use glue, you forget about everything; you don't eat, you don't drink for days, that's why I got an ulcer; I've been having ulcers since maybe if I can remember, from eleven, yeah, eleven or ten. . . . I was thinking I was going to die before I was twenty.

Álvaro lived on the streets in El Salvador until he decided to migrate at age eleven. Like other youth throughout this chapter, his prospects for the future were so dim that, as he put it, "I didn't have anything to lose." Álvaro took the chance in the hope that something could be gained in Los Angeles.

Growing up in El Salvador, Valentina had envisioned her departure several times before finally making the journey north, "because, well, I didn't have a good relationship with my parents." Valentina endured mistreatment by her parents, who coped with poverty through alcoholism and, when intoxicated, abused her.[49] "They both drank," she said, "and then they would get mad at me for no reason. They would want to hit me for no reason. That's how they were with me, and I never understood why the people you think are supposed to protect you end up being the worst to you. That's how it was with them." Valentina remembered feeling frustrated and thinking, "I must get out of here. You could look around the country and see there weren't options to get ahead. It's so sad to see. I was so traumatized. I looked for other options but finally decided to come here [Los Angeles]." Her parents did not want her to migrate, but she insisted. "*Me venía o me venía,*" she said, using an expression that indicated that there was no other option—either she came (to the United States), or she came (to the United States). Despite Valentina's lack of prior work experience, she envisioned her life as an independent worker in the US. She called her uncle in Los Angeles and asked if he would help her leave her parents' home. With $7,000 secured, she left El Salvador.

Extreme poverty can also produce household violence through unsupervised child labor, parental abandonment, and severe emotional distress. Impoverished families are the most at risk of fragmentation because of the pressures of struggling to survive. Tomás, for example, grew up with his single mother and older sister Susana in the Guatemalan highlands until the age of nine. He explained that in his perspective, "Everyone, everyone [in Guatemala], most kids suffer a lot because of violence, abandonment from parents, from their mothers; and because they are abused so much; they hit them a lot." Tomás recalled that he began working as a two-year-old, accompanying his sister to shine shoes and sell trinkets on the street to supplement their mother's earnings. When Tomás was nine, his mother moved to a nearby town with a new partner who promised to take care of her without her children. Tomás's older sister Susana responded to their abandonment by migrating to Los Angeles the following year to support herself.

At ten years old, Tomás became fully responsible for himself. "I grew up in a town where there was so much poverty, the schools aren't [free]. You have to pay for everything," he said. I asked him whom he worked with, and he replied, "Me, by myself. I went to shine shoes, to clean them. I would go to the street to offer [shoe-shining] to people. When I started shining shoes, I would earn maybe twenty-five *quetzales* [less than $4]. I would earn that in one weekend after working all day." Tomás used his earnings to buy his necessities: "I bought soap, I bought food, things like that. I didn't have enough money." After four years of looking out for himself in Guatemala, he decided to migrate because he "needed clothes, I needed food, I needed somewhere to sleep. I needed a better life for myself. I saw that kids with parents [in the United States] would get clothes, sneakers, everything. I wanted . . . I don't know . . . I wanted that." At fourteen, Tomás left Guatemala in pursuit of survival and the security of opportunity and mobility he associated with life in the United States.

Youth are not equally affected by violence. Instead, society and circumstance wreak distinct forms of violence upon particular social groups. Youth imagine migration might offer an escape from the structural violence of gender, class, and ethnoracial oppression that has blocked them from opportunities for integration and mobility within their societies but also affected their everyday interactions and, therefore, their sense of self. Women were more likely than men to describe a gender-based exclusion that inhibited their ability to imagine a future of belonging and mobility. Young women envisioned futures with more significant gender equity, as they experienced cultural constraints reinforced in the family context, corroborating existing literature on adult women migrants.[50] Life in the US was perceived as an opportunity to overcome patriarchal restrictions in origin country cultures and societies. Women envisioned attaining more power and autonomy within their families and communities and often found autonomy in their home and work lives.[51] Serafina, aged twenty-nine, who arrived from Mexico at age seventeen, said:

> I came here because things were a mess. I came here because I didn't want to stay stuck with people saying, "You are going to get married to him, and they are going to determine your life." . . . Since I was little, I wanted to be a boy because my brothers—there are four men in my family—and I grew up with them so I would see all the privileges they had being men, and I didn't have as a woman. To start, they would scold me for getting dirty or ripping my pants [when I played]. So, they would make me sit and watch because my clothes were expensive. So, I wanted to be a boy. Well, not to be a boy but because of the same thing, for the privileges they have.

Serafina experienced her household gender dynamics as oppressive and exclusionary and understood that they reflected her position in society at large. She therefore migrated to the United States because she felt there would be "more opportunities," unconstrained by gender ideologies. While the women I spoke with more often told stories of the violence of sexism and gender discrimination, women across Latin America are targets of extreme gender-based violence and femicide that also spur migration.[52]

Guatemalan Maya youth, reflecting the anti-Indigenous legacy of colonialism that disproportionately excludes Indigenous communities from political and economic opportunity in their country, pointed to racism as the violence that motivated their migration. The young people in this study identified anti-Indigenous racism as one of the primary reasons they experienced diminished educational and employment opportunities, everyday discrimination, and low self-esteem.[53] Joel, for example, described life in Tacajalbé, a village in Totonicapán, Guatemala, as "bittersweet." Sweet because he was with his family, specifically his mother, who cared for him and his siblings, but bitter because he remembers growing up with low self-esteem and fear. Indigenous youth discussed growing up being ridiculed for their cultural practices and language; physical appearance, including stature and skin tone; and way of dress. Joel explained that many non-Indigenous Guatemalans treat Maya culture as "*del diablo*" (of the devil) and recalled painful childhood memories of being told "you're dumb" and "you're a dog" by children and adults alike, which seeped into his sense of self and future.

Other youth described being ridiculed, bullied, and even harassed for their Indigenous language and limited Spanish proficiency, way of dress, shorter stature, and dark complexion. They even noted their small, rounded teeth as a marker of Indigeneity and a source of everyday violence. Joel started to feel a sense of hopelessness about the future—"I'm Maya, and I cannot do the things that Ladinos (non-Indigenous Guatemalans) do"—which I took to mean that he and Maya youth were aware that they would be denied opportunities that non-Indigenous Guatemalans had access to, like education, jobs, and participation in social life. "You feel very small because of that," Joel said.

Several Maya youth attributed their mistreatment in Guatemala to Spanish colonization and the imposition of ethnoracial hierarchies used to justify Indigenous genocide, political and economic repression, and portrayals of cultural inferiority and deviance.[54] Joel could not envisage a social life in Guatemala in which youth could participate fully. Additionally, his low self-esteem, which resulted from daily ridicule and exclusion, diverted his expectations and spurred him to seek different and better opportunities in the United States. Joel would learn that Indigenous communities in the diaspora must navigate the "intersection of local, national, and transnational systems of power that shift, overlap, and hybridize in the process of migration."[55] This is one of the lasting legacies of colonial projects in Latin America and settler colonialism in the United States.

As with the youth who made decisions to migrate alongside families, those who made individual migration decisions did so in response to structural violence, marginalization, and exclusion. They did not anticipate migration but described it as an escape hatch. Their socioeconomic and socioemotional dislocation in their origin societies, which threatened their survival in the present and blurred their imagined future, pushed them to their destination: Los Angeles, California.

Conclusion

The Central American and Mexican teens portrayed in this book, who migrated between 2003 and 2013, like the unaccompanied children currently arriving in the United States, grew up in societies with long histories of dispossession and displacement supported by violent US intervention. This history of intervention has destabilized political and economic systems and repressed collective action; imported violent gangs that prey on vulnerable children and their families; heightened environmental degradation and the depletion of natural resources; and contributed to the rise of extreme poverty and debt, with few opportunities for safety, mobility, and well-being. Families and individuals in these societies—including children—consider their futures within the full range of institutions they participate in, such as the labor market, schools, religious and other community spaces, and available resources. Young people endure life pressures and forgo unattainable opportunities. Attention to the life stage at migration has revealed the futurity of young people's decisions within these violent and exclusionary contexts. In essence, teen migration is an agentic response to present risk as well as the long-term threat of the unattainability of their imagined futures.

Their micro-level contexts critically inform young people's departures—collective or individual—by foregrounding youth's migration *metas* and determines their social, economic, and emotional ties with left-behind families and communities. These ties shape how young people experience their migration to and coming of age in the United States and, as subsequent chapters show, their conception of success in young adulthood. Although youth's *metas* for their collective and individual imagined futures are formed within and shaped by their departure context, their arrival context, specifically the household context, moderates their ability to achieve them. I turn to unaccompanied migrant youth's arrival in Los Angeles next.

2 *Arrivals*

Tomás recalled his pueblo in the Guatemalan highlands as being plagued with *tanta pobreza* (so much poverty) and as a place where "most children suffer a lot because of the violence, because of their parents' abandonment, and because of the abuse"—a reflection of his experience. Recall that he and his sister, Susana, grew up with their mother until she abandoned them when Tomás was nine (see chapter 1) and that the two were separated after Susana migrated to Los Angeles one year later. When Tomás finally left Guatemala at age fourteen, he envisioned reuniting with Susana. Tomás's eyes welled up during our interview as he detailed the events that led to his remaining unaccompanied in Los Angeles.

Susana, an undocumented immigrant, welcomed Tomás into the home she shared with her undocumented husband and their two US-born children without hesitation when he arrived in Pico-Union. But two weeks later she grew fearful that her younger brother's presence and dependence on her and her husband would risk their household's financial stability and coherence. Susana was a homemaker and thus financially dependent on her husband. Tomás agreed to work to offset his cost of living. However, with Susana's two children enrolled in a local elementary school, she worried that a school official might discover that an unenrolled minor lived with her—a violation of California's compulsory education and federal child labor laws. Tomás described his final conversation with Susana in which she detailed her fear that a Child Protective Services official would take her children from her and put her and her husband at risk of deportation. As a wife and mother, Susana was expected to protect and maintain the integrity of her home. For her to do so, Tomás had to leave.

Tomás recalled his sister showing little remorse for her decision and justifying it in three ways. First, according to gender norms of manhood and masculinity that emphasize financial independence, Tomás, however young, was regarded as a man who should be responsible for himself. Second, Susana, a wife and mother, was accountable to the social expectation that she would prioritize her husband and children. Third, Susana did not tell Tomás that they could not see each other, only that she could not care for him. However, during our interview, Tomás asked rhetorically on what grounds he could see Susana again. Without a material and emotional connection to a long-settled relative, fourteen-year-old Tomás was suddenly unhoused and without a secure source of support. Moreover, far from finding reprieve from the emotional distress Tomás carried with him from his childhood in Guatemala and during his traumatic migration experience, his pain was compounded: he endured both abandonment in his birth country that prompted his migration and his sister's abandonment, betrayal, and rejection in Pico-Union, Los Angeles.

Tomás was able to weather this storm because he had already secured employment in a downtown Los Angeles garment factory. His only social connection was to his employer, who allowed him to sleep in the factory until he found a room to rent in an apartment with other young garment workers. He never saw Susana after he left her home and soon began crafting an independent life in Los Angeles. Tomás was one of the seventy young people I spoke with who encountered tenuous household welcomes with weak ties.

Much has been written about how immigrant youth's national, state, and local-level reception contexts—welcoming or hostile, political, economic, and social conditions—determine how they fare. There is less coverage of their receiving contexts at the household level. This might be attributable to the belief that Latin American-origin families maintain the "core cultural value" of *familismo* (familism) and are inherently sympathetic to children and welcoming to their newcomer kin. Consequently, scholars studying the effects of federal and state policies on undocumented young people's educational and occupational pathways and unaccompanied children's engagement with sociolegal bureaucracies tend to gloss over the household receiving contexts.[1] Tomás's arrival alone contradicts much of what we might assume about the receptivity of adults to children. However, his arrival experience corroborates the work of social network researchers that demonstrates the consequences of resource precarity and the power of gendered social expectations on family networks as they are beset by new tensions in a new context.[2] In the absence of parents, who are more likely to possess a higher sense of obligation to care for their children, ties to long-settled nonparent relatives are not always reliable, and support is not guaranteed.

Examining household contexts is important because families play an essential role in children and youth's development and well-being.[3] Household arrival contexts are particularly significant, given that all study participants arrived in the United States from disrupted family systems needing stability, improved well-being, and future security. Additionally, youth arrived with post-traumatic stress disorder (PTSD) symptoms stemming from prolonged exposure to the violence that displaced them and the harrowing experiences of unaccompanied and undocumented migration.[4] Securing access to material support is essential for newcomer migrants' survival but especially for youth with limited networks to call on once in Los Angeles. Youth need emotional support to navigate their simultaneous entry into a new society and transition from adolescence to young adulthood without the physical presence of a parental caregiver. Long-settled nonparent relatives play a critical role in unaccompanied migrants' trajectories, as they are the immediate and often only source of material and emotional support upon teens' arrival in the United States.

This chapter revisits and revises the nested context of reception framework by offering a micro-level theory of arrival that centers the household as the first social domain that migrant newcomers encounter.[5] The household arrival context has dual significance for unaccompanied migrant teens. First, it can offer material support, as familial ties are heralded as having mediating effects on being unhoused, food insecurity, and unemployment.[6] Second, the household can provide emotional support, as it is a place in which migrants first belong. Families can be a source of intimate and trusting ties from which youth develop a positive sense of self. The loss of family ties can have devastating socioemotional consequences for migrant youth who have endured multiple traumatic separations before and during migration.[7] Here I explore whether and to what extent households welcome unaccompanied teens and the dynamics of their household contexts of arrival.

I begin by situating youth's long-settled relatives within their nested reception context, recognizing that these individuals also negotiate the everyday tensions between structure and agency. Attention to the political, economic, and social contexts in which long-settled and mostly undocumented immigrant relatives have made their lives illuminates the material constraints families negotiated long before unaccompanied teens' arrivals. In the next section I outline the micro-level logic that relatives relied on to decide whether and to what extent they could and would support youth with their available resources. Regardless of relatives' altruistic intentions, they adopted behaviors that unwittingly replicated the "inequality regimes" that organize US society.[8] In some cases, even the most well-intentioned families strictly adhered to deep-seated gendered social expectations because they needed to justify the distribution of their limited resources without destabilizing their lives. I then offer the stories of two study participants who displayed the idealized receptive household dynamic that made way for their normative immigrant-youth incorporation and coming-of-age trajectories.

In the last two sections I analyze mechanisms determining unaccompanied boys' and girls' access to material and emotional support within households. I consider how youth are differentially received by men and women kin, who offer support according to the expectations of gendered cultural meanings of care. Women may feel compelled to support newcomers materially and emotionally, but marital status mediates women's decision-making autonomy. Regardless of marital status, men make independent decisions about their support of newcomers. They might offer boys material support like a room to rent or access to employment networks, but with few exceptions, boys are left feeling *solitos* (alone). Teen girls are more positively received, but ties can be dissolved when they are sexualized within the household. This chapter reveals how household arrivals serve as the proverbial on-ramp to incorporation processes and, for immigrant youth, to their transition to adulthood.

Latin American–Origin Immigrants' Arrival Contexts

Long-settled relatives originate from the same countries and unstable political and economic backgrounds that propel child migration, as outlined in chapter 1, and are likely to be undocumented in the United States. This means they are among the 11.2 million undocumented immigrants currently living in the United States. The fact that nearly half of Mexican and Central American immigrants in the United

States are undocumented prompts scholars to refer to the Latin American–origin groups' arrival context as one of legally and socially produced "illegality" that punishes immigrants and their descendants.[9] Moreover, because access to formal support that might offset political and social exclusion and economic immobility is dictated by legal status, Latin American–origin immigrants and their descendants are disproportionately affected. About two-thirds of undocumented immigrants have been in the United States for ten years or longer and have formed families within this context of illegality.[10]

Several immigration laws and policies have sought to remedy the situations of the vast number of undocumented immigrants in the United States since the 1980s, focusing on specific population segments. These have produced notable distinctions in social, economic, and political mobility opportunities across national origins and immigrant cohorts. In 1986, for example, the Immigration Reform and Control Act (IRCA) legalized nearly three million undocumented immigrants—mainly of Mexican origin but some Central Americans—and opened a family reunification migration and legalization pathway for more in the following decades.[11] In the 1980s the US government denied refugee status to Central Americans fleeing the region, which resulted in a patchwork of legal protections and the fragmentation of social networks that broke down in the face of resource impoverishment.[12] At that time, 97 percent of Salvadorans were denied political asylum. Thanks to advocacy groups' unrelenting pressure on the authorities, asylum seekers who arrived in the United States before September 19, 1990, were eventually offered Temporary Protected Status from deportation. In 1991 the settlement of the class action lawsuit *American Baptist Churches (ABC) v. Thornburgh*, which represented five hundred thousand Guatemalan and Salvadoran asylum seekers, reinstated Central Americans' eligibility for asylum applications in the United States. In 1997 the Nicaraguan Adjustment and Central American Relief Act provisions were extended to some Guatemalans and Salvadorans who had registered under the *ABC* settlement.[13]

There has been no comprehensive immigration legislation reform since IRCA. Yet punitive policies and approaches to immigration enforcement have risen to the level of legal and illegal violence against immigrants, who fear the threat of deportation, family separation, exploitation, and everyday racism and abuse.[14] Immigrant deportability has particularly devastating effects because it promotes a constant state of hypervigilance and fear in day-to-day life that socially, politically, and economically isolates and immobilizes individuals, families, and communities across generations.[15] Deportability was heightened when the federal government empowered state and local law enforcement agencies to carry out federal immigration law through the 1996 Illegal Immigration Reform and Immigrant Responsibility Act's (IIRIRA) addition of the 287(g) provision to the 1965 Immigration and Nationality Act. Once noncitizens are in state or local police custody, the Criminal Alien Program (2006) authorizes their identification and initiation of removal.[16] Later, in 2008, the implementation of the Secure Communities Program enabled state and federal enforcement database integration to streamline the transfer of custody from local to federal law enforcement agencies and expedite the deportation of unauthorized immigrants from the United States.[17] At the same time, the list of crimes that can result in a deportation order has expanded to include everything from murder and firearms trafficking through the Anti-Drug Abuse Act (1988), to theft and burglary through the Violent Crime Control Act (1994), to any crime that warrants a prison sentence of at least one year through IIRIRA and the Antiterrorism and Effective Death Penalty Act (1996).[18]

Research shows that punitive immigration policies harm immigrants' physical, mental, and emotional well-being, with developmental consequences for children.[19] These concerns notwithstanding, undocumented immigrant families continue to be disproportionately isolated from social services and health-care programs that could mitigate harms imposed by immigration law. For example, the Personal Responsibility and Work Opportunity Reconciliation Act of 1996 bans lawful permanent residents from participation in federally funded social service programs for their first five years in the United States and bars undocumented immigrants from public assistance entirely. In 2010 undocumented immigrants were blocked from the federally subsidized health insurance provisions of the newly implemented Affordable Care Act. Considering departure and arrival contexts together, it is evident how the US authorities create conditions for migration, as explained in chapter 1, then criminalize immigrants once they are in the United States while barring them from accessing public assistance.

Beyond undocumented immigrants' legally-produced illegality, however, is their socially produced illegality, wherein simply existing in a racialized body poses a threat to individual and family well-being, as anyone who "looks 'illegal'" is subjected to the negative repercussions of that classification regardless of their actual documentation status.[20] Someone can be marked as socially "illegal" based on characteristics like national origin or linguistic proficiency, with consequences for their job prospects, housing security, and treatment in everyday social interactions. Racialized legal status delegitimizes minoritized groups' standing in society and creates the specter of disposability through removal.[21] To minimize the threat of deportation, individuals and families resort to strategies ranging from changing how they speak and dress in public to remaining isolated from the public altogether.[22]

Experiences of exclusion and the availability of mitigating mechanisms are unequal. A long history of Mexican migration and the concentration of Mexican immigrant communities in the US Southwest has increased immigrants' interpersonal and institutional network density. At the same time, some legal protections have advanced Mexican immigrant community mobility.[23] Central American immigrants' departure contexts (chapter 1) and relatively younger migration history make coethnic ties and community support more tenuous. Furthermore, gender—in its correlation with employment opportunities and social network access, which are limited for women and expansive for men—obfuscates women's access to legal protection and economic mobility opportunities, which reifies their social isolation and the fragility of their social ties.[24] Likewise, language barriers compromise Indigenous-language speakers' ability to access the legal information and representation essential to acquiring legal protection that would broaden employment, housing, and social network stability.[25] Finally, men and Indigenous individuals are more likely to be stereotyped as undocumented. They are therefore more likely to interact with law enforcement officials, rendering men more vulnerable to deportation and women more vulnerable to becoming "suddenly single mothers."[26] Power conferred by class, gender, and legal status can make coethnic ties exclusionary and extractive and transform family relationships into what sociologist Deisy Del Real calls "toxic ties."[27]

Within a nested context framework, states are touted as potential buffers to the legal violence of federal policies as they establish and execute their political and economic agendas. However, they are limited in areas with minimal or ineffective oversight, like unauthorized labor in the secondary labor market. As explained in the book's introduction, California is a sanctuary state and does afford some buffers to total violence, such as refusing to link federal and local law enforcement and allowing eligible undocumented immigrant groups to obtain driver's licenses, receive Medi-Cal coverage, and pay in-state college tuition, to name a few.

Still, legally and socially constructed illegality and deportability render undocumented immigrants exploitable workers vulnerable to abuse, including underemployment, underpayment, wage left, and the threat of job loss for workers who express discontent, regardless of the state where they live.[28] Further, while California has implemented a wide range of laws, policies, and programs to protect immigrants' civil rights—including those of unauthorized immigrants—confusion about how federal and state laws interact, the stigma of receiving public benefits, and fear of the impact of such support on long-term legalization prospects, as well as the widely accepted neoliberal notion that being a "good" immigrant means *aguantando* (enduring) and *superando* (overcoming) one's oppression, can keep undocumented immigrants isolated from local and state-level systems of support and justice.[29]

These forces coalesce to place a disproportionate burden of poverty on Latin American–origin immigrants in the United States. Indeed, in the United States, 20 percent of Central Americans live in poverty as do 18 percent of Mexicans, compared to 14 percent of the total immigrant population and 13 percent of the US-born population.[30] Ultimately, long-settled relatives are experiencing life in the United States in ways set out by the federal, state, and local political, economic, and social structures that conferred or denied their opportunities for mobility long before the unaccompanied youth's arrival. Welcoming household arrivals are not made simply through ties to long-settled kin but in the strength of those ties. Arguably, unaccompanied migrant children who are apprehended at the US-Mexico border are released from federal custody to adult sponsors, who are mandated to care for and protect them. Although children's care is not guaranteed and the potential for conflict, mistreatment, or abuse is ever present, the unaccompanied youth who enter clandestinely and without inspection and for whom there is little attention to their arrivals remain more disadvantaged. These young people are outside formal support channels and entirely reliant on resources within the private household sphere immediately following their arrival and within local neighborhoods and communities as they settle in. I explore the dynamics of household arrival contexts in the following sections and return to their impact in the remainder of the book.

Intersectional Expectations in Household Arrivals

Despite the generalization of Latin American–origin families' *familismo* in the United States, households are spaces of dynamic interactions that rely on macro-societal hierarchies to make decisions about household roles, responsibilities, and resource allocation, not the least of which is gender.[31] As in society at large, masculinity and manhood and femininity and womanhood are sharply defined within households and families. Across Latin America, as in much of the United States, women are expected to be selfless and generous for the benefit of the family and to abide by the patriarchal gender norm of subservience to the authority of men.[32] Once women become mothers, they are charged with being the primary caregivers in the private sphere and entering the public sphere like the labor market when required to support their families.[33] Women are also expected to maintain moral superiority and practice self-sacrifice and denial. Conversely, men are deemed autonomous figures of authority and guidance. Unlike women's identities, which are mainly bound to the private sphere, men's identities are formed in the public sphere, and fathers are unburdened by obligations to self-denial and morality. Successful expressions of fatherhood are also more narrowly defined than those of motherhood, as the meaning of fatherhood is found in men's ability to provide families with financial security and physical protection.[34]

Socialization to these gendered expectations begins in childhood and is concretized and contested as individuals form their identities while coming of age. Teen boys are expected to learn independence, self-sufficiency, and risk-taking in their quest to develop masculine identities and become financial providers in their transition to adulthood.[35] Boys demonstrate patriarchal masculinity through sexual exploration and prowess. Girls are treated as dependent, vulnerable, and needing protection. They are expected to learn familial caretaking, primarily serving their fathers, brothers, and other male relatives.[36] Finally, women's sexuality perpetuates the burden of gender inequality, as girls are also expected to uphold a demure social posture devoid of expressions of sexuality that impugn their morality.[37]

Although kin ties in this study were not parent-child relationships, the age differentials between older, long-settled relatives and young newcomers recreated the dynamics of adult caregivers and children as care recipients. Therefore, gendered fatherhood and motherhood ideologies interacted with those of boyhood and girlhood to shape the sense of obligation among family members and to establish the roles and behaviors adopted within the household arrival context. These interrelational and intersectional dynamics resulted in a welcoming household arrival context for five study participants and tenuous household arrivals for seventy others.

A Welcoming Household Reception Context

When positively welcomed in a household, young people could adopt the role of children with varying degrees of dependence, putting them on an incorporation pathway through family and school. Long-settled relatives guided youth by overseeing their physical and material needs and nurturing their emotional well-being. As adult caretakers assumed normative roles as primary providers, youth assumed theirs as students.

There were distinct family dynamics that enabled this household arrival context. Marcos's reception was facilitated by two long-settled relatives who were older women—his aunt and his grandmother—and well-established in their communities. When Marcos left Guatemala at the age of sixteen, he entered the United States undetected, with a plan to find immediate work in Los Angeles. Instead, his aunt, uncle, and eventually his grandmother intervened to create a different arrival context by working together to offer Marcos support so that he might attend school. Marcos was twenty-eight when we met for our interview. By then, he had completed high school and had graduated from a public four-year university in Los Angeles with a degree in biochemistry, eleven years after his unaccompanied migration.

Marcos explained that he first arrived in Compton, a city in southern Los Angeles County, to live with his aunt and her husband. He remembered coming there and thinking, "Wow, this place is beautiful. You know . . . the green lawns, the houses, and air-conditioning and hot water." He began planning to find work in the area, but his aunt and uncle objected, insisting that he attend junior high and avoid exposure to Los Angeles gangs through informal work. Marcos initially resisted: "My expectation was, 'Okay, I'm going to work,' but they also expected me to go to school." After several months of refusing to attend school, Marcos was eventually relocated to California's Central Valley to live with his grandmother, where he was similarly expected to attend school. He recounted:

> When I moved with my grandmother, her expectations were the same. But I wanted to work, so I'd go to school in the mornings. But I didn't know that school was . . . like a whole-day thing since I'd never been to school [in the United States]. I thought you could show up anytime you want and leave anytime you want. But, so,

my grandmother just put me to work in the fields, so we would pick tomatoes in some of the fields in the farm area, to pick tomatoes. And then in the mornings, I would go to school from like . . . I would start like really early, early like, zero period like start like at six thirty [a.m.] to like two [p.m.], and then I would pick tomatoes from like two to five.

While Marcos worked alongside his grandmother as a tomato picker, he was not required to work or support himself, but once there, his contributions to his family were welcomed. As Marcos emphasized, his grandmother thought his education should be the priority. Her support and guidance allowed him to stay enrolled in school, learn English, and pursue other, less physically exhausting work options. He continued:

So, that was the expectation—that I would provide a little bit of income to my family. And eventually, you know, it's really funny because eventually I learned English, and then I was tired [of] working in the fields. So, I told my grandma, "I'm going to look for another job," and I started working as a dishwasher in a restaurant. To me, that felt like I was moving up, and instead of a dishwasher, I started doing some of the prep cook work and then from there busboy and then from busboy to waiter, and so I was moving up. I was moving up, and my grandmother was very proud of me, and I was bringing more income to my house.

Marcos described his decision to work as both individual—he worked because he wanted to—and collaborative—he worked alongside or in consultation with his grandmother. Although Marcos's adolescent trajectory is nontraditional in the Western context because he was working to supplement his household's income, he was not entirely financially independent, and he significantly benefited both materially and emotionally from his relatives' financial support. Such support enabled his work schedule flexibility and facilitated his school enrollment while buffering him from survival stress. This stressor weighs heavily on youth without support.

Marcos's regular school attendance, cultural capital, and growing English-language proficiency prompted him to leave farmwork and pursue a new area of work. Furthermore, his household context and family support allowed him to remain consistently enrolled in high school, exposing him to mentors who allowed him to develop his identity as a student. Teachers and peers enabled Marcos to access supplemental resources like tutoring and college application support. Because of Marcos's school attendance, he was set on a political incorporation pathway. When the government announced DACA, Marcos's supporters pooled all available resources to prove his potential as a member of American society. Marcos remembered feeling nervous about his DACA application and the intervention of his school principal. He recalled how his life changed after receiving DACA:

> It was a scary experience because I came a month before I was sixteen. So, I didn't know if I would qualify for it because I didn't know if I would get enough evidence to show that I was here before the age of sixteen. The only evidence I had was a letter from my principal at my school saying that [I] was here before the age of sixteen. That's all I had. And so . . . I put together my package on my own. I didn't have the resources to pay for a lawyer or anything like that, so I did it on my own, just like going through forms. And I got it. I got lucky. I've been in DACA for . . . this is my second time. I'm glad. It has changed my life, really.

Legal relief proved vital for Marcos's educational mobility. DACA represented an official welcome into US society that legitimized his presence. Marcos's pairing of DACA with his relatives' support allowed him to attend a prestigious public university in Los Angeles and participate in various community and work opportunities there. "I felt like America told me 'Welcome' for the first time," Marcos acknowledged. Despite knowing that DACA, because of its time limits, was not enough, Marcos recognized its impact:

> Even though, you know, it's not what we expect or what we want for our communities, but it's something, you know? And to me, as someone who had to deal with being undocumented—or I guess a lot of my young adult life—it's made a big difference. It allowed me to get my job at [the university]. It allowed me to pursue what I wanted to do, you know, without anyone questioning me for my Social Security number or anything like that.

Although Marcos migrated as an unaccompanied young person pursuing work, the intervention of adult women relatives afforded him educational and occupational mobility as he transitioned to young adulthood. He felt both materially and emotionally secure.

I met Valentina, who had migrated from El Salvador at age sixteen to escape alcohol-induced parental abuse and neglect, just two years after her migration. She knew she had a *tío* (uncle) who lived in the Los Angeles area and discovered he was married and had two teenage children—a son and a daughter. Perhaps her Tío Hugo saw his children in Valentina; he was sympathetic to her arrival and opened his home to her. Among study participants' relatives, only Valentina's Tío Hugo had protected legal status.

I interviewed Valentina at a Los Angeles immigrant community center, where her Tía (aunt) Marta—Tío Hugo's wife—accompanied her to seek information about Valentina's potential options for legal protection. During our interview, Tía Marta hovered protectively nearby. She was hesitant to leave Valentina alone with me—the first sign that Valentina was very much a child in Tía Marta's eyes. To alleviate her trepidation, I invited Tía Marta to join us. She sat across the patio table from Valentina and me and interjected answers to my questions from time to time.

Valentina enthusiastically detailed the unexpected support from Tío Hugo and Tía Marta, both material and emotional, upon her arrival in the United States, noting especially Tía Marta's nurturance. "I don't know," Valentina said, "my mind was traumatized. I can tell you, if it wasn't for her, I don't know how I would be right now! I'd never had someone [in my life] who cared for me as much as she did. I mean, never in my life, and that's why things are different now." Tía Marta proudly said, "I tell her, 'You must study. In my house, you will not lack a roof or food.'" This revealed her understanding that giving Valentina material security in adolescence related to her sense of emotional security.

Valentina agreed. "She always says that. She always supports me, telling me to do this or that." Tía Marta acknowledged that the financial resources come from her husband, Hugo: "Of course, she is supported by her uncle too." Through Tío Hugo's material support, which also signaled his emotional support, and Tía Marta's attention and care for Valentina, she could begin a new life that felt distinct from the abuse and neglect she had endured at the hands of her biological parents.

When I last saw Valentina in 2017, about three months after our first meeting, she was speaking at a community resource fair held at El Pueblo Los Angeles Plaza about her undocumented migration from El Salvador and her welcome in Los Angeles.[38] The fair was organized by a collaboration of agencies that were patchworking resources to create a safety net for unaccompanied children and their sponsors in the greater Los Angeles area. At the same time, the local government formalized a service provision pipeline. Valentina related how various people and organizations had come to her aid.

She asserted that current unaccompanied youth should feel confident knowing similar support would be provided by the people and organizations present on that day.

After Valentina's address, she interacted animatedly with community members; she looked no different to me than the undocumented students I had organized alongside during my college years at the University of California, Los Angeles, and who spoke at "coming out of the shadow" events.[39] I reflected on her final comments during our interview when she shared that she aspired to attend Harvard University to study science. After Valentina shared this aspiration with me, Tía Marta said, "And she is going to do it, you'll see." At that moment, watching Valentina make her speech and move across the crowd so confidently, I thought so, too.

To date, the household remains underrecognized as an arrival context critical in determining immigrants' prospects for incorporation in the transition to adulthood. Marcos and Valentina arrived in Los Angeles expecting to be entirely alone. Their long-settled relatives agreed on a plan for their incorporation and coming of age. Marcos's household arrival context, in which his aunt and grandmother assumed roles as elder caregivers and worked together to keep him physically safe and emotionally supported during his teen years, had a cascading effect on his identity and participation in family, school, and work. Significant to Valentina's arrival was her uncle's legal status, which gave the family some financial stability, and the presence of teenagers in the home, which likely softened her uncle's and aunt's sense of obligation toward her. Valentina's story showed signs of her being on an incorporation and a coming-of-age pathway akin to Dreamer youth and DACA beneficiaries.[40]

These young people's household arrival contexts allowed them to navigate their transition to settlement and adulthood with extended family financial and emotional support. Kin support bolstered their access to educational and even legal status mobility tracks—Marcos had DACA when we met, and Tía Marta was actively seeking pro bono legal representation to support Valentina's case. Their stories show that even among youth who enter the United States clandestinely, receiving full support from long-settled kin follows an expected reception context in a normative Western imaginary. Marcos's and Valentina's experiences evince how youth come to participate in a classic virtuous cycle: material, cultural, and emotional resources produce incorporation by making the markers of mobility attainable; achieving mobility, in turn, enables greater access to resources that facilitate incorporation.

The availability of these resources creates openings to experience childhood and the transition to young adulthood in a way that more closely approximates the traditional pathway. However, these trajectories were not normative among study participants. Most youth who migrated unaccompanied and entered the United States clandestinely encountered unpredictable support configurations. Resource impoverishment often forced long-settled relatives to make tough decisions about when and how to offer support, relying on gendered logic and social expectations to do so.

Receiving Unaccompanied Teen Boys

The perception of teen boys as independent young men intersected with perceptions of men's roles as authorities and financial providers and women's roles as nurturers; these perceptions shaped unaccompanied teen boys' household arrival contexts. Long-settled men more often provided symbolic support, such as allowing boys to rent a space in their apartment or introducing boys to their employers. However, they were reluctant to absorb the costs accompanying the young newcomer. Additionally, the length of time that men supported boys was unpredictable. Long-settled men might be less likely to provide long-term support to a newcomer boy migrant than women relatives, given that social norms dictate that both men and boys should demonstrate self-responsibility.

Fifteen-year-old Usher received a relatively warm welcome in Pico-Union, primarily because he was received by close kin—his older brother Gustavo, who was in his early twenties—but also because the brothers were close in age, which might have instilled a sense of camaraderie. Gustavo and Usher understood that the newly arrived teen would work rather than attend school, and Gustavo did what he could to guide Usher along that pathway. At the time, Gustavo worked as a floor manager at a downtown Los Angeles garment factory and agreed to help Usher find a job so that he could remit money to their mother. The factory owner initially refused to offer Usher a job, saying he was too young to work. However, the factory owner relented when Gustavo leveraged his reputation as a responsible worker to convince the factory owner that Usher would be an asset to the business. To Usher, that was one of the ways he felt his older brother supported him, by drawing on his resources to help Usher meet his goals. Furthermore, Gustavo was unmarried, which gave him greater flexibility in determining how and where to spend his resources. Usher recalled, "For me, when I got here, my brother told me, 'I will help you with what you cannot do, and you will do the same for me.'"

From the outside looking in, we can be critical of a referral for a notoriously exploitative job, but to Usher, this job was a tangible resource and a practical—and necessary—source of wages to pay his migration debt and to survive. Equally important was the proven assurance Usher gained that he could count on Gustavo, that the latter would follow through on what he promised, and crucially, that he was not alone. The material and emotional gains from his brother's receptivity were equally valuable for Usher.

In the bigger scheme of things, Usher's experience with Gustavo was rare in its material and emotional dynamics. More often, participants shared that when men received boys, the welcome was not guaranteed to be warm or consistent. Additionally, the physical presence of a settled male relative in the life of a newcomer boy does not guarantee that feelings of loneliness will be assuaged. That was Joaquín's experience when he migrated to the United States from his hometown in Guatemala at the age of sixteen. He had borrowed money from his older brother, who was already living in Los Angeles, to finance the journey and considered the gesture a symbol of his brother's support of his migration. When Joaquín arrived in Los Angeles, his brother—like Usher's brother—expected him to maintain financial independence while living with him. However, unlike Usher, who received the comfort of guidance from Gustavo, Joaquín and his brother spent hardly any time with each other despite living together. This dynamic solidified the reality for Joaquín that he lacked access to not only his brother's material support but also his emotional support. He struggled with feelings of loneliness and sadness.

> STEPHANIE: You lived with your brother when you first arrived?
> JOAQUÍN: Yes. We were together for four years. But almost not. We didn't spend time together, really. We were never together. We lived together, but . . .
> STEPHANIE: Was that because you work[ed] so much?
> JOAQUÍN: Well, yeah, we work[ed]. And, for example, sometimes he doesn't [work on] Sunday, Monday; and me on Saturday, Sunday. And he has separate friends. And I have different friends. We rarely would see each other, sometimes on a Monday. But sometimes, he wouldn't come home. We didn't spend time together.

Joaquín's and his brother's work obligations, low wages earned over long hours, and fragmented social lives kept the brothers on different schedules. The magnitude of Joaquín's loneliness became evident when he explained that even after moving out of the apartment he shared with his brother, "it didn't feel different. I went on the same way. Well, yeah, there are times when one feels alone, but what can you do?"

Married male kin were generally even less receptive to newcomer boys, providing some material resources but often only for the brief period following the youth's arrival in Los Angeles. Ander was fifteen when he arrived in Los Angeles. He spoke at length about his older siblings who lived in the United States before him. He anticipated living with his sister, but her marital status disqualified her from support expectations. Hence, Ander sought support from his brother. He imagined that having a brother already familiar with Los Angeles would benefit his settlement. However, upon Ander's arrival in Los Angeles, his older brother received him for only two days, citing the wife and children he had to care for. He offered Ander clean clothes, a shower, a bed, and food, but after two days, Ander was expected to be on his own. On the third day, Ander left his brother's home in search of housing and a job that would allow him to repay his $5,000 migration debt. However, as Ander was a minor, he could not quickly find a job on his own and was forced to amass even more debt. "I owed a lot of money, but here, there isn't anyone for you [on your side]," he lamented. Without support, Ander deviated from the goals he had imagined at the time of his migration: to pay his debt quickly, remit money to his left-behind family, and enroll in school. "Either way, I have to work," Ander said, "and I wasn't able to do what I wanted, you know?" Ander associated the lack of material support with the simultaneous absence of emotional support, saying, "I had my brother and whatever, but there isn't anyone really caring for you." Joaquín and Ander illustrated that sharing a residence does not always guarantee other forms of support, despite unaccompanied minor migrants desiring or needing multiple material and emotional resources as they settle in the United States.

Outside of their immediate family, boys were also received by uncles. Migrant boys like Gilberto described the callousness of their uncles, who were typically much older and felt even less obligated to provide care. I began recruiting interviewees at a Los Angeles adult English-language school in 2016, where I visited each classroom to explain my study goals and distribute flyers with my contact information. I met Gilberto in one of these English classes. At twenty years old, Gilberto had been in the United States for three years at the time of our interview. He explained that he came to the United States from El Salvador hoping to learn English, graduate from high school, and return home as a professional so that he and his family could escape poverty. Gilberto's goal was to start a business that would allow him to support his mother and two siblings. His grandfather and uncle, settled undocumented workers in the United States, offered him a place to stay, but promptly clarified their expectation that he should be financially independent. When Gilberto expressed interest in attending school, his uncle responded, "People come here to make money!" Gilberto was not expecting to take on so many living expenses upon arrival and soon realized that financial independence would delay his plans.

To help launch him into financial independence, Gilberto's uncle directed him to a neighbor who needed help with her business. At our interview, Gilberto was working at a swap meet for this neighbor, a woman whom he described as exploitative and verbally abusive. He nonetheless put up with the situation to repay his migration debt:

> She [Gilberto's neighbor and employer] doesn't pay me a lot, but since I can't find another job, I have to *aguantar* [endure]. Sometimes, I get mad, but I must endure. She's always mad or scolds me. I have to work to pay for my cellular and buy anything I want or any activity I want to do. I can't go out or buy anything if I don't work.

That's why I endure everything I do. But sometimes, yes, I leave with a headache. It's difficult, but I know I have to pay for everything.

This illustrates that, despite Gilberto having a designated place to live on arrival, he did not necessarily feel supported. His relatives provided him with items like groceries and deodorant when he needed a hand or a calling card to speak with his mother in El Salvador, but Gilberto felt emotionally disoriented.

Boys' assumed independence was mediated by the social expectation that older women kin provide nurturance, including material resources but also emotional care, a moral burden men did not bear. Reflective of patriarchal gender structures within the household, women's ability to warmly welcome newcomers, especially boys, was determined by their marital status. As such, long-settled relatives' marital status may have ripple effects on newcomer youth's arrivals and, ultimately, their incorporation and coming of age, as gender dynamics shift when married women are made subordinate to husbands in their households and defer to them the authority to make decisions about how household resources are distributed. Ander aptly explained this—and the circumstances that led him to grow up without familial support—as he noted that married women were regarded as living in and being dependent on their husband's household:

I thought I would live with my sister, but my sister got married, so she went [to live with] that person. That's how the family is in Guatemala, too. When a woman gets married, they go live with the man. It's the same here, too. When a man gets married, the woman lives in his home. That's how the family is.

Migrant boys described how cultural gender norms around marital status shaped their ability to call on their networks with women. If received by a single woman, newcomer boys might be granted material and emotional support. Long-settled women relatives, however, were often married and had limited autonomy over their individual and familial resources.

In this way, unaccompanied boys benefited from having more than one relative anticipating their arrival, especially when long-settled relatives were women, as in Marcos's aforementioned case. Ariel provided another example of this dynamic. When Ariel migrated at fifteen, he had three older siblings (one brother and two sisters) already living in Los Angeles. Since Ariel's brother was married, he knew his brother's obligation was to his new family and that their relationship would be strictly social. One older sister was a restaurant worker, but because she was also married, she could not agree to support Ariel financially. Although Ariel's sister's earnings were also strictly allocated to her husband-led household, she felt obliged to offer care for her younger sibling. She agreed to provide in-kind support instead, allowing Ariel to rent a room in the apartment she shared with her family. This arrangement worked well for Ariel, whose second sister was a domestic worker who could not offer shelter or food but could commit to paying his living expenses until he paid off his $6,000 migration debt. Ultimately, Ariel was not materially or emotionally alone. His sisters' combined support enabled him to delay full-time workplace entry until the age of eighteen.

During those three years of support, Ariel worked at a mobile car-washing service, then as office janitorial staff, and finally as a dishwasher in a Mexican restaurant. He worked by day and attended adult English-language school in the early evenings. Once he had learned enough English, he transitioned from dishwasher to busser. He eventually found work at a steakhouse, moving from back of house to front of house, earning tips alongside his hourly wage. He recognized how atypical it was for an undocumented teen to achieve such occupational mobility in such a short period. He also contemplated that his mobility transcended that of his brother and sisters, who had continued to work in the same occupations since their arrival. His arrival context was starkly different from theirs, and their disparate outcomes revealed the impact of that difference: his brother had been the first in their family to migrate, had married early, and was unable to support their sister when she arrived in Los Angeles, leaving her to find her own way. When the next oldest sister migrated, she immediately entered a live-in domestic worker job that isolated her both spatially to northeast Los Angeles and socially by limiting her ability to establish social ties. Ariel benefited from the number of kin already living in Los Angeles, his relation to them as a younger sibling, and the sense of obligation and social expectation to care that the two women siblings carried with them.

Having only one woman relative bound to the patriarchal logic of belonging to a man's family and home in the US could blunt boys' prospects of receiving support. For example, Theo thought he would live with his sister and attend high school in the United States but was not received by her because "she lived with her husband and her son. And another person lived there, so I could not stay with her." He went to live with his older cousin, who could not offer material or emotional support, which prompted Theo's entry into low-wage labor in Los Angeles:

> During those days, I cried a lot because, I'm telling you, my dream was to keep studying. I told my cousin, "I want to keep studying." I told him that, and he told me, "Look," he said, "I would like to support you, but I have my own family here. You have [responsibilities], too. You have to pay back the money you borrowed with interest. You have a family, too. Your dad isn't working, and you must help your brothers. They want to study too."

Unaccompanied immigrant youth acknowledge that married relatives cannot grant financial support to young migrant men. This corroborates the work of Pierrette Hondagneu-Sotelo, who argues that "patriarchal authority and constraints, as well as contention and resistance to patriarchy, shape family migration decisions" that contribute to the "creation of different types of gender relations once the families settle in the United States."[41] This finding also echoes Gloria González-López's findings of patriarchal privileges for *tíos* but not for *tías*, whose lack of matriarchal privilege and resultant inability to leverage financial support disadvantages their kin of origin.[42] In some cases, teen boys could continue to draw on the emotional support of women as socially designated nurturers within families. However, as we saw with Tomás, it was also the case that the conditions under which support was denied or withdrawn could rupture ties by inciting feelings of betrayal and abandonment in youth.

Receiving Unaccompanied Teen Girls

Because gender ideologies position girls as dependent, vulnerable, and needing protection, unaccompanied girls garnered more sympathy than unaccompanied boys initially following their arrival in the United States. This can be a double-edged patriarchal ideal, as girls might receive more protection but feel more significant constraints on their lives and opportunities for mobility within the household.[43] Still, girls benefited from their household position, as they were more likely than boys to feel emotionally supported. However, this emotional support had conditions, as families became tense when girls were positioned as sexual in, and in some cases as sexual threats to, the household.

Isabela provided an example of girls being given more welcoming household receptions, particularly emotional support, than boys. When Isabela arrived in Los Angeles at fourteen, she was received by her older brother and sister. She was nineteen years old at the time of our meeting. She recognized how her siblings attempted to alleviate some of her financial burdens so that she might pursue an education and how they encouraged her to continue working toward her goals. "When I came here, I started living with my siblings—one brother and one sister," Isabela explained. "I immediately felt comfortable living with them because they supported me in my studies, [and] I don't pay much rent. Yes, I am paying, but it is not much." Isabela's comfort within her home—where she lived with "a brother, my sister, my brother's wife, and my nephew. The five of us live in one house together"—made the cost of working to afford rent at the expense of full-time focus on school worth it. She elaborated, "Even though I work and study at home, we get along well." Isabela felt especially supported by her brother, who, although unable to alleviate the cost of living in the United States so that fourteen-year-old Isabela could attend high school, was emotionally supportive of her. Years later, she still felt emotionally supported by him, saying that her brother encouraged her to "keep studying. He tells me, 'I want you to keep studying, graduate, and have a career. I want to help you but don't have the means.' That's what he tells me." She spoke of the parameters of the support she received with some compassion, saying, "My nephew is studying. My brother has his family. I understand him." Isabela felt grateful for the companionship she received from her family and the encouragement she received from her brother.

Emotional support is important but insufficient to compensate for youth's material needs after arrival. Throughout my interview with Isabela in the library of a Pico-Union high school where she attended adult English-language classes, she commented on how tiring and difficult she felt her life was compared to what she had imagined before her arrival. However, her construction of a comparative framework helped her. She also drew strength to continue juggling multiple jobs and school from contemplating the emotional support and advice and moderated financial support she received from her older siblings—who, for their part, did not have supportive relatives to guide them when they arrived in Los Angeles. Despite Isabela's relatively strong welcome, which included partial material support, the opportunity to continue at least some form of education, and emotional support, she was unable to assume the normative childhood and student identities that full support garnered for youth like Valentina and Marcos, and she would therefore be set on a different incorporation and coming-of-age pathway.

Finally, it was only in the instances of young girls' arrival that I heard of the role of sexuality in influencing household dynamics. Young girls could, for example, face the suspicions of women in a household who felt threatened by the presence of a younger woman in their home and by her interaction with their male partner. Inés migrated from Mexico expecting to be received by her uncle in the United States. After arriving in Los Angeles, her uncle, unaware of the provisions of the *Plyler v. Doe* ruling, misinformed Inés that because she was undocumented, she could not attend school and needed to work.[44] The news disillusioned her. To exacerbate matters, she experienced a problematic settlement when her uncle's wife, Thalia, disapproved of the arrangement. Inés explained:

> Yes, I arrived directly [in Los Angeles] with my *tíos* [uncle and aunt] because I have a brother here who said I would live with him, but my uncle disagreed because he [Inés's brother] lived with only men. That's why I didn't . . . they didn't want that. So, what I did was I decided to stay with my *tíos*. They are a couple, but many things happened because I did not get along well with my uncle's wife. I suffered with her.

Inés described how Thalia became jealous of the attention and affection that she was receiving from her uncle. The fear that the relationship might become sexual incited suspicion around the pair's relationship and disdain for Inés's presence in the household.

Thalia began to abuse Inés by hitting her when the two were alone and denying her food. Inés, employed in food service, eventually left her uncle's home as a full-time worker and lost touch with him, followed by a series of abusive intimate relationships (chapter 5).

Left-behind parents, specifically mothers, were aware of these sexualized gender dynamics within families and warned their daughters to use them as guiding principles for newcomers' expectations and requests for support. Esmeralda's arrival demonstrated how household composition interplayed with girls' gender and age to place an expiration date on any potential benefits related to girls being perceived as dependent and innocent. She recalled, "When I came over here, my mom told me not to come because 'your sister is married, and you are a woman, and I don't want any problems.'" Esmeralda thought she had a workaround, explaining that she told her mom, "No, I am going to my cousin's [place]."

Esmeralda therefore prepared to live with her male cousin. She did not know what changed for him—perhaps it was simply the sudden financial pressure of supporting a newly arrived teen—but Esmeralda remembered that one morning her cousin told her that they were heading to Pico-Union to visit Esmeralda's sister, Priscilla. Unbeknownst to Esmeralda, her cousin had a plan: he would leave Esmeralda with Priscilla, which launched the family into a series of tensions, starting with that between Esmeralda and her fearful mother. "When they left me at my sister's," Esmeralda said, "I called my mom to tell her that I was with my sister, and my mom told me, 'See? I told you not to go with your sister. She is married.'" Wanting clarity on Esmeralda's understanding of the connection between a woman's marital status and her ability to offer welcome, I asked, "What is the problem with her being married?"

ESMERALDA: Because she has a husband, and the man might
take advantage of you if you are a woman. And it is true

because I lived with my sister, and my brother-in-law bugged me. He would greet me and touch my shoulder. We had problems because I would tell him, "When you want to greet me or when you want to say, 'Good afternoon,' it is not necessary for you to grab me or to touch me."

STEPHANIE: Did your sister notice his behavior?

ESMERALDA: I would tell my sister that I didn't like that he would touch me. My sister would tell me not to get upset, and maybe she felt jealous, but she never said anything. I would tell him not to touch me, but he still bugged me. I think it bothered my brother-in-law that I would ask him to stop.

The conflict between Esmeralda and her brother-in-law, Josué, continued and escalated when he kicked a soccer ball into Esmeralda's stomach, which she took as an act of retaliation for rejecting his advances. When she stopped acknowledging Josué, he became more hostile. Esmeralda explained that her sister eventually became suspicious that tensions were high because something had happened between Esmeralda and Josué, not because Esmeralda had rejected him. When Priscilla confronted Josué, he claimed Esmeralda had been suggestive toward him, which caused Priscilla to turn against Esmeralda.

For Esmeralda, just as for Inés, the potential for sexual attraction or relations among extended families is aligned with what Gloria González-López refers to as "sexual cultures of incestuous families," in which young girls may be sexualized and coerced into gendered servitude.[45] Esmeralda's mother's suggestion that there could be problems in her sister's household and marriage because of Esmeralda's presence demonstrates how the onus of male's sexual behaviors and infidelity is placed on women within the family and how the social codes of shame can disproportionately fall on women. Esmeralda's mother's comment, along with Priscilla's eventual blaming of Esmeralda, demonstrates how women are blamed for their sexualization by men and how such dynamics work to reproduce gender inequality in the home and society at large.

Esmeralda's experience in Priscilla's home left her unhoused for some time, but the most damaging consequence, according to Esmeralda, was losing Priscilla's trust without just cause. The emotional distress of being sexualized by Josué and experiencing assault was compounded by her sister's refusal to speak to her again. For the unaccompanied girls in this study, it was rarely incestuous sexual interactions within families that led to familial, social tie dissolution; instead, the perceived risk of such interactions left the young women without any networks of support from settled nonparent relatives. Because Esmeralda struggled to get on her feet after losing touch with her sister, she was in a precarious position when her brother, Patrick, migrated two years later. Her inability to offer him a place to stay or resources to support him caused her an immense sense of guilt—as his unmarried older sister, she was meant to be his caregiver. This weighed heavily on her as a perceived failure; she knew from her own experiences how challenging settlement would be for her brother.

These experiences contrast sharply with those of Valentina, who was not only financially supported by her uncle but also socially and emotionally supported by her uncle's wife. In Valentina's case, it was perhaps her uncle's protected legal status, Tía Marta's adherence to her normative gender role as homemaker and nurturer, and the presence of siblings, especially a biological daughter—a girl who might have buffered Valentina from sexualization within the family— that facilitated her household settlement. The differing household dynamics that the young women encountered complicate assumptions about Latin American *familismo* by demonstrating that newcomer youth are not guaranteed a warm welcome from female relatives despite the cultural expectation that women are caregivers.

Conclusion

This chapter introduced the household as the immediate arrival context and the first source of material and emotional support that contributes to shaping immigrant youth's incorporation in their transition to adulthood. In all, the receptivity to newly arrived youth—whether welcoming or hostile—is determined by the receiving households' position within interlocking systems of political, social, and economic (dis)empowerment. Latin American–origin immigrant communities' and families' condition of "illegality" shapes families' survivability and mobility prospects. When families are stably situated, children are received well. However, when families are precariously situated, social ties become tenuous, even for child migrants who are envisioned in the public imaginary as vulnerable and in need of protection. Long-settled relatives rely on gendered logic and social expectations to justify decisions about whether and what kind of support to provide youth when their capacity to welcome young people is constrained by resource impoverishment. Family composition (grandparents and children; aunts, uncles, nieces, and nephews; siblings; and cousins) mediates outcomes as the intersectional social locations that influence family dynamics (gender and sexuality, socioeconomic class and legal status, and marital status) shape expectations and feelings of obligation between long-settled relatives and newly arrived youth.

Household arrival contexts have critical long-term implications for youth's incorporation and coming of age, as households determine what other social domains of life—like school, work, and community—youth will participate in and how. Valentina and Marcos showed that, when receiving a warm welcome, migrant youth assume a child's role in the household, which enables them to enter schools and take student roles—two normative coming-of-age pathways. Long-settled relatives' complex migration and settlement trajectories and the gendered social expectations of support between long-settled relatives and newcomer youth might complicate the transmission of material and emotional resources. The lack of material support extended to youth—regardless of how much emotional support is received—can lead to their resorting to full-time work to survive. When youth receive partial material support (e.g., a room to rent) but no emotional support, it can result in their being materially independent but emotionally alone. In the event of youth receiving neither material nor emotional support, it renders them materially and emotionally vulnerable and can evoke feelings of betrayal for some. In all, household contexts can alleviate material precarity and emotional trauma for some and exacerbate it for others.

Important to recall here is that in the US, immigrants' deservingness of legal and social inclusion is often measured by their ability to demonstrate socioeconomic success and thriving (e.g., school completion, occupational mobility). But if, for migrant youth, the idealized incorporation pathway is only attainable through the preservation of normative childhood and transitions to adulthood in the US, we must interrogate the extent to which laws and policies bolster or suppress institutions', like families', capacity to fulfill their normative role in securing that pathway for young people. To legally and socially construct barriers for immigrant families to secure young people's mobility and well-being as they come of age, then weaponize families' immobility as the justification for their legal and social exclusion is nonsensical. What's more, it is cruel. The data reveal that in many cases families wanted to adopt the normative role as the material and emotional support system for unaccompanied migrant youth, but circumstances simply did not allow it, forcing young people to go it alone. In the next chapter, I turn to how participants embarked on their new lives with varying degrees of material and emotional support, which ultimately shaped how they defined successful incorporation in the transition to adulthood.

3 *(Dis)orientation*

During our nearly two-hour-long conversation about his life in Los Angeles, Patrick explained how his two older sisters' inability to support him when he arrived in Los Angeles at age fifteen affected him materially and emotionally:

> Crossing [borders] to get here is the most difficult [thing]. It is very difficult because you get separated from your family, brothers, and sisters. It's a journey where you don't know if you will make it stay there or if something will happen [to you]. That is why . . . for a minor, getting here is something very difficult. Then you get here and see it's something different than you imagined. It's different from what you think when you're over there.

He admitted that he believed he "would have the opportunity to do what I wanted and become who I wanted." Patrick wanted to enroll in school and pursue a professional career, but this was derailed by the unavailability of support upon arrival: "Sometimes you don't find the necessary support here. I know I can become someone [or amount to something] here, but only *if someone supports me*. I don't know where to go on my own."

The disruptive and even traumatic nature of migration to and arrival in a new society is magnified when it co-occurs with the transition from adolescence to young adulthood without the guidance of a parent or adult caregiver. Throughout my time in the field, even youth who did not know each other used the term *desorientación* (disorientation) to describe the nature of traversing these dual passages and identified their need for an adult figure who could offer them guidance, which they referred to as *orientación* (orientation). Youth like Alejandro stated outright that "we [unaccompanied teens] don't have *orientación*. We don't have anyone to talk to, to get guidance from," and Benicio explained that "you need people that can help you get accustomed a little bit. You need someone to say, 'Okay, here, you do this. Here, you don't do this.' I learned the reality that here, there is no one for me. I am [responsible] for myself." To Patrick, Alejandro, Benicio, and others, it was evident that they needed orientation as unaccompanied young people to get by and get ahead in Los Angeles.

Heeding this perspective, this chapter argues that orientation, or the process by which immigrants learn to navigate their destination society's unfamiliar institutional, social, and cultural realms, is the first phase in unaccompanied youth's incorporation following disorientation upon arrival. There are two kinds of orientation that unaccompanied young people undergo as they come of age. First, they encounter their social position as adolescents transitioning to adulthood. Those who are received by a supportive familial household are oriented to normative childhood, assuming social roles within institutions commensurate with their age. Others, who transition to adulthood without adult figures to usher them into life in Los Angeles and to buffer them from life's hardships, are oriented to independence. This means learning the institutions and norms that make up the social worlds typically reserved for adults, like entering low-wage workplaces and public life in neighborhoods where they negotiate resources within and across organizational and interpersonal social ties to make ends meet.

A second form of orientation is that to cross-cultural and cross-sociopolitical contexts. In some cases, immigrant youth are thrown into a set of cultural and social ideologies, norms, and values that may be fundamentally different from the ones they might have learned about as children in their origin countries. In others, they might encounter the persistence of ideologies, like gender discrimination and anti-Indigenous racism, that they sought to leave behind. Thus, young people's orientations can be to a system that exploits and oppresses them and reveals the falsehood of *el sueño Americano*, the American Dream.

Building on the assertion that household receiving contexts shape incorporation processes, this chapter begins by returning to Valentina's and Caleb's stories to show how household arrivals guided their orientation. I explore the more traditional orientation young people experience when they grow up among supportive family members in Valentina's story and the unexpected orientations youth encounter when they lack familial support in Caleb's tale. Evident from these divergent orientation pathways is that, on one hand, welcoming household contexts give youth the material security and the social and emotional belonging they longed for while growing up in their origin countries. On the other hand, youth who remained unaccompanied felt suddenly exposed to a new *sistema* without a sense of direction, reinforcing their disorientation and presenting unforeseen challenges for which they were often unprepared but were nonetheless required to navigate to survive.

The remainder of the chapter explores the orientation experiences of teens like Caleb. I first examine youth's orientations to material independence and their role as workers required to navigate the workplace, finances, and public life in Los Angeles. I then explore orientations to their social position as teens within adult roles as occurring through an emergent frame of reference, introduced earlier as the comparisons immigrants develop between their past and present living conditions and between themselves and their nonimmigrant peers in their origin society. Following this, I discuss the youth's orientation to agency, the ability to change the circumstances of their lives through a patchworking of resources accessed through interpersonal and organizational ties. These orientations are not one-time occurrences but are ongoing. They reflect immigrants' interactions with their local structure of opportunities, comprised of institutions, individuals and organizations, and the built environment.[1] Orientation progresses as youth's needs and knowledge about how to meet those needs evolve. In this sense, orientation is a material and emotional process, as unaccompanied young people must figure out how to get a job to pay their bills or how to find community, all while also making sense of what it means to come of age and build one's identity, even as that identity is discriminated against.

In the final section, I show how youth come to know significant adult figures and peers who guide their orientation by deepening their understanding of the US *sistema* and themselves. Beyond conveying knowledge, resources, and skills to survive within the structure of opportunities available to youth in the present, meaningful relationships can orient youth toward values and behavior that move them closer to their imagined futures. Here, I rely on life-course scholars' theorization of planful competence, or an individual's ability to plan for "opportunities and obstacles that are encountered in the course of adult development," which is argued as essential for adolescents' positive transition to adulthood.[2] Unsurprisingly, the nurturance of planful competence is typically attributed to watchful parents who present youth with "potential options [for the future] and who can raise thoughtful questions to help the adolescent identify important issues."[3] Parents' absence does not preclude youth from planful competence but urges alternative sources of it, like the interpersonal relationships and routine organizations in which immigrant youth participate in daily life.[4] Orientation to meaningful social ties and the planful competence they nurture can promote incorporation by advancing material and emotional adaptation (chapter 4). But without meaningful social ties that nurture planful competence, teens can experience perdition or the process of social and emotional maladaptation that occurs as immigrant youth adopt strategies that increase their material and emotional disorientation (chapter 5).

Divergent Orientation Pathways

Orientation among family members offers immigrant teens support to learn the new *sistema* they are entering. Moreover, it provides access to material resources like housing and education and age-based socialization to their role as children and teens in the United States rather than financially independent "adults."

Valentina was still young enough to live with her long-settled relatives two years after arriving in Los Angeles; they provided ongoing comfort and support. Recall that Tía Marta, Valentina's aunt, assured her that she would not lack housing or food and that Valentina's responsibility was to do well in school. When I asked Valentina to describe her family in the United States, she exclaimed that her family was "wonderful!" She attributed her joy to the feeling of closeness and the consistency of their routine:

> It starts with her [Tía Marta] and my siblings because I love them like my siblings. I have become accustomed here. I know when they get home, when . . . my brother gets home late. And now I know I can ask where he is and where he is going. Or my sister, Monica, who is around the house. Anytime I need anything, I have it there. Or even my uncle. I know he has a strange attitude, but I love him like that.

Valentina expressed a sense of security in her new family dynamic, a shared rhythm, and confidence in her place at home. At school, her cousins, who felt more like siblings, showed her the ropes: where her classes were, whom to make friends with, when and where to do homework, and what clubs and after-school activities she could join. Outside of school, Marta did what she could to get Valentina adjusted to Los Angeles geography, frequently taking Valentina on public transit around Pico-Union and the surrounding neighborhoods so that she could feel confident traversing Los Angeles streets independently. Marta did not anticipate this would ever be the case but explained that she did not "want her to be afraid if she gets lost."

Marta was attentive to Valentina's physical and emotional well-being and did what she could to foster her resilience "since the beginning." "When I noticed [Valentina] was depressed and had a lot of trauma," Marta explained, "I would tell her, 'You must overcome that. You need to have [a sense of] security in yourself. You are one of a kind. There is no one like you. You are unique.'" Valentina treasured these sentiments because Marta's demeanor toward her differed vastly from her biological mother's—the latter struggled with alcohol addiction and became physically abusive when intoxicated. Marta acknowledged Valentina's emotional stressors, increasing Valentina's confidence in her new home. Without referring to it as orientation, Valentina acknowledged Marta's patient nurturing as she navigated her new life: "I know everything because of her. She has shown me so many different things." It was from this material and emotional space that Valentina could imagine a future in which she would finish high school and attend college—Harvard to be specific.

Ultimately, Valentina's arrival context—a materially and emotionally supportive household—oriented her to her various new roles and responsibilities as a child within her family and a student at her school, and the norms associated with these institutions commensurate with her age. Although Valentina arrived in the United States as an unaccompanied child, she was no longer alone. Bolstered by the comfort of surrogate parents and siblings, Valentina was becoming oriented to a teenager's life in Los Angeles; she was becoming, as she put it, "accustomed." Valentina's family provided her with material and emotional security and cultural knowledge of family, school, and community life.

Valentina's case demonstrates that access to a present and nurturing adult figure helps craft a sense of stability in a new society. Additionally, she benefited from an arrival context characterized by several factors: the family's decisive intervention, her uncle's protected legal status as a permanent resident, her aunt's "othermother" role, and her aunt's suggestion that her cousins were her siblings.[5] Furthermore, Valentina's uncle solidified the family's sense of legal and financial security through his employment, which undoubtedly preserved the fulfillment of traditional gender and family roles, noting in particular his position as head of household and father figure. At the peer level, Valentina's two cousins played vital roles in welcoming her into their household and entering high school and the community. This positive trajectory is distinct from those of teens who could not secure support upon arrival and were materially, culturally, and emotionally independent.

Without a supportive household context and adult figures to rely on, unaccompanied youth enter institutions, take on roles and responsibilities that are not commensurate with their age in the US, and lack the social supports that might intervene in institutional and interpersonal marginalization. As a result, young people contend with cumulative disadvantages and disillusionment.

Caleb's orientation, which differed starkly from Valentina's, exemplifies how youth encounter and negotiate unexpected orientations. He had an older half brother living in Los Angeles at the time of his arrival, but this brother wanted nothing to do with him. Caleb was the first-born son of his father's second family and was resented by the sons his father left behind. When Caleb arrived at his uncle's apartment on a Sunday evening, he was aware that his first order of business was to find work to secure his survival and pay his share of the rent, groceries, clothing, and other daily needs. Caleb also anticipated that he would soon need to start remitting money to his family to repay his $6,000 migration debt, which accumulated daily interest. Eventually, remittances would transition into financial support for his left-behind parents and the construction of a new house he planned to return to one day.

The morning after Caleb's arrival, he went through the downtown Los Angeles Fashion District looking for a manufacturing job in a clothing factory, without success. "They wouldn't give me a job," he told me. "Because they would say I was too young—'You are a little boy; you need to be in school.' That's what they would tell me, but I needed to find work to take care of myself here." By 3:00 p.m. the next day, he had secured a job in a garment factory, sewing sleeves on blouses for sixty-six hours per week for around $200. Just as he got the hang of his responsibilities, Caleb's home life was upended. Unbeknownst to him and his family, his uncle's marriage was in disarray, and the couple would soon split. Caleb's uncle warned him that he would be moving to a new apartment within two weeks and that Caleb could not accompany him.

Caleb's estrangement from his brother and subsequent separation from his uncle intensified his loneliness, which became unbearable. While struggling with what Caleb identified as depression, he had difficulty focusing on his work in the garment factory, which paid piece rate (by the number of items produced). He was unhappy with the poor working conditions and low wages. His income was insufficient to pay his bills or to send remittances to his left-behind family; this ultimately led to his estrangement from his loved ones. His depression seemed to be soothed only when he distracted himself by joining his neighbors—all men in their twenties and thirties—on Saturday evenings at the front stoop of their apartment complex. "They would drink [beer], and things would get so fun," he told me with a wide smile. "They would crack up, tell jokes, everything, but all very drunk." Caleb remembered his parents' warning to avoid drugs and alcohol. He worried that if he were to get lost in addiction, he would disappoint himself and his family. Without his uncle, he would have to find his way but was unsure where to begin. Unlike Valentina, Caleb and others like him faced the arduous task of orientation, having to learn their adultlike roles and responsibilities outside of institutions commensurate with their age and the norms and values of their new society, without the guidance of parents or other adult caregivers. The remainder of this chapter explores how they did this.

Orientation to Independence

Most unaccompanied migrant teens in this study anticipated attaining financial independence following their migration through Central America and Mexico. Yet the degree of material and emotional detachment from long-settled relatives or known compatriots they experienced was surprising to many, especially when relatives in the United States lent money for their migration and offered an initial place to stay. In each interview, I asked participants to describe their greatest challenge upon arrival in Los Angeles. They unanimously declared that without adult figures on whom to rely, unaccompanied youth are thrust into the low-wage labor market to survive and to honor their moral obligations to provide care for their families.[6] As Danilo, a twenty-five-year-old Salvadoran man who arrived in Los Angeles at the age of fifteen, put it:

> Well, getting here is the first challenge. And then, once you make it here, it's a challenge to find a job. Really, as an immigrant, if you're

not legal in this country, everything is a challenge. Getting the job then keeping it because of your immigration status. Then, being able to cover your responsibilities in this country and your family back in your country is a challenge. Yeah, everything is pretty much a challenge.

Youth were disoriented by the reality that their age and legal status constrained opportunities for financial mobility, and exploitation of undocumented immigrant workers was commonplace. Like Danilo, most youth explained that they struggled to find work, and when they did, they had to make sense of their position as low-wage workers with little means to survive in hypercommodified markets. Twenty-four-year-old Rolando, a garment worker in downtown Los Angeles who had been paid three cents for every T-shirt he screen-printed since his arrival nine years before, had adopted a neoliberal ideology of work and survival. "You earn according to how fast you are," he explained. "Within a year, little by little, I started earning like $200, $250, $300, and yeah, like that." Rolando worked from 7:00 a.m. to 7:00 p.m. Monday through Saturday. I asked him how much he earned at the time of our interview, perhaps naively expecting reports of wage mobility. Instead, Rolando said, "I earn the same." On weeks when he also worked on Sundays, he made up to $450. Rolando used these earnings (about $1,200 per month) to cover rent ($300 per month) and his cell phone bill ($100). He estimated that he spent about $200 per week on food, public transportation, clothes, and other expenses. He also shared that he struggled to send consistent remittances to his left-behind family. This indicated that he either earned less than he suggested or was underestimating his expenses and living costs in Los Angeles. Study participants consistently described the near impossibility of making ends meet.

The hypercommodification of goods and services in the United States, including access to natural resources like water, was unfamiliar to immigrant youth, especially those from rural regions across Central America and Mexico, where agrarian lifestyles meant that "there isn't rent. You just don't pay rent."

Carlos laughed emphatically during our interview as he compared his life at home in Guatemala to that in Los Angeles. He began by providing context: "Over there [Guatemala], I had water, beans, and tomatoes. You eat what you want. My mom harvested so many things. You need a job to pay $50 for light or something, but water is free. Everything is free." This contrasted starkly with his life in Los Angeles, where, he exclaimed:

> I buy everything! Here, all you do is work to pay the rent, light, everything. I didn't know it'd be like this. I thought it would be the same as in Guatemala, but all I do here is work and work. I didn't know that work would be this hard either. But then I noticed everyone was working to pay their light bills, gas, everything. Everyone is paying for everything.

The "everything" included paying to wash clothes at a laundromat, buying food, tipping at a restaurant, paying basic phone bills and for long-distance phone calls, paying for light and water, and other unanticipated expenses.

Hypercommodification was disorienting for Carlos, just as it was for Elías. During our interview, Elías explained that he began working in a Los Angeles garment factory to support himself and his left-behind family at age sixteen. After six years of earning around $300 a week as a piece-rate worker, Elías moved into hospitality as a restaurant dishwasher. Despite Elías's occupational shift, he never made more than $400 per week, but he resolutely budgeted for remittances, albeit irregularly: "The first thing I pay is my rent. That's $270. Then, my phone bill, which comes out to $50. Then I pay [for] my food. Food is like $30 per week. Then, every fifteen days, I send my family $100." He continued, "Sometimes I can't send the $100," but he did whenever he could get the money together.

While learning how to make ends meet in the present, youth also had to learn to anticipate future expenses. Although Elías had other long-settled siblings living in Los Angeles, as the only unmarried sibling residing in the United States, emergencies and other unexpected familial expenses fell on his shoulders. For example, when his younger brother in Guatemala fell ill, Elías sent several hundred dollars to secure medical attention. Despite his US-based siblings' advice to try to save some money each month, this was impossible. When asked how much he had saved over his six years in Los Angeles, he replied, "I try. I've tried to save money, but there aren't any savings at the end of the day." He laughed nervously. "Everything changes when you come here," he explained. "So, you start over with getting accustomed to . . . you must get accustomed to making a new life here. You learn what you can and cannot do here. It is a total change." It was evident that Elías's efforts to go it alone reinforced his feeling of being alone.

Learning to navigate Los Angeles's built environment, such as how to get around the city and how they might establish a life outside of work, also required orientation. When Benicio first arrived, his long-settled siblings took him to garment factories in downtown Los Angeles to find work. Initially, he felt supported—oriented to his workplace and schedule—because one of his siblings showed up after work and took him to his apartment. Benicio recalled the sudden change and the resultant disorientation: "My first two or three days, they [my siblings] took me to work. But no one came to pick me up on my fourth day." He felt disoriented because "no one explains much about the street to you." Benicio said:

> [Newcomers] really must learn about the street by yourself. You must learn to cross the street because no one has time here. Everyone

works every day. If you start driving, no one tells you that you can turn [right] on red and green. They just say, "When the light turns green, go. Don't go on red, okay?" In my case, I learned Los Angeles by myself.

Benicio recounted his experience navigating the public transit system on his own on that fourth day without his siblings:

> I was left asking people, "Where do I find . . ." or, "How can I get to Olympic [a prominent Los Angeles street]?" I didn't know anything because people would tell me that the bus takes you to Olympic, but it takes you south of Olympic, down at Pico. That's where it leaves you, and you must walk. "But listen, I have to get to Eighth and Alvarado," I'd say, and they'd respond, "You must get on the Thirty. It leaves you on Pico and Alvarado, and you go up." You don't know, though. Or people say, "Take the Olympic [bus] and then. . . ." It's just like that, asking and asking. So, I'd say, "Okay, so you have to go to Eighth [Street], then get on the Fifty-Six [bus] and take it to the top," and I'd walk to the stop. That's how I found another person who was my neighbor, and I knew him a little bit in Guatemala. He told me, "Are you going over there? I'm also going there. I'll take you." And that's how he ended up taking me. I figured it all out like that on my own.

My conversation with Benicio reminded me of Valentina, whose Tía Marta accompanied her on buses across town to prevent the sense of spatial disorientation that Benicio felt. His account also highlighted the isolation that came with the realization that youth were truly responsible for their own survival and well-being, down to how they got around town.

As they traversed Los Angeles, unaccompanied youth learned about the city's racialized geographies, permissible behaviors (or not) in specific public spaces, and safety considerations—what colors not to wear on certain streets, what streets to avoid entirely to avoid gang territory, and at what stops it was unsafe to exit the bus.[7] Some youth arrived in the United States familiar with the choreography required to survive gang-riddled streets but imagined that Los Angeles would provide a reprieve from this traumatic dance.[8] Referring to the weight of responsibility for himself, Benicio said, "It's like, it's like, okay, you have everything on [your shoulders]. Everything I want to be, everything I want to do, that's all on me. You must help yourself. Everything is individual."

Gael was truly alone in his initial orientation. He was the oldest child and, at age sixteen, was the first in his family to migrate to the United States from Guatemala after his father passed away. Gael had no family or ties to community members in Los Angeles but quickly found work in the garment industry. However, his independence and isolation felt more real when he fell ill soon after arriving in Pico-Union. Gael reflected on the challenges of balancing work obligations and frequent hospital visits: "[I] would work two hours, half a day, something like that," but would have to "leave work to go to the hospital, hospital, hospital, with doctors." He worried that his low income was insufficient to cover his rent, food, and migration debt; his medical expenses—each hospital visit cost around $400—added to his debt.

Gael compared his arrival context—without material and social capital—with the experiences of other migrants with access to family and community networks. Unlike his situation, "[for] many people that have family here . . . it is easier to manage money that way" because "they give you $20." Gael soon discovered that he had to make ends meet independently, which meant working more to survive. He recalled: "I had to get little bits of money here and there to pay rent" and "didn't have money or clothes because I didn't have family here." He reflected on his disillusionment: "I thought I would always have something to eat here," instead, he realized, "Oh! I didn't have money." Gael aptly explained that this realization was shared by many young people, who "come here thinking that you are just going to earn money easily." He continued:

> Sometimes, people send photos, and everything looks good. Everything looks like you can live well. You come with an illusion. You think you're just coming here to easily take money back [to your origin country], to earn money quickly. You get excited. But the reality is that it's not what you think it will be. It's not at all what's in the photos.

Ultimately, orientation to a life of independence within low-wage labor and hypercommodified markets is characterized by disillusionment as youth come face-to-face with the myth of a better life in the United States.

Orientation to Childhood through an Emergent Frame of Reference

Youth growing up in origin countries facing extreme structural and community violence and poverty might engage in paid and unpaid labor early in life, leaving school and play behind to make ends meet for themselves and their families. However, unique to their lives as independent workers in Los Angeles was an orientation to the idealization of childhood, the treatment of children as morally priceless, and an emergent frame of reference through which they understood that children are expected to be students until they reach the age of majority.[9]

Many study participants indicated that before their migration, they were unaware of the dynamics of childhood in the United States, especially the relegation of children to K–12 schools. Because participants were workers in their home countries with either no schooling or inconsistent schooling and were surrounded by similarly situated peers, they expressed that *uno no sabe* (one doesn't know) that education is compulsory for children and adolescents in the United States and that full-time formal employment is uncommon among them. Compulsory education in many Latin American countries legally applies to a much younger age than in the United States. In addition, compulsory education is not enforced in practice, especially in rural areas.[10]

Twenty-four-year-old Andrés from Guatemala explained the phenomenon: "Over there [Guatemala], kids work. There is no age where you cannot work. Here, there is. It was tough for me to get a job. No one wanted to help me." Likewise, Juan, another twenty-four-year-old Guatemalan, recalled his first experience looking for a job. "When I got here, my mentality was to earn money. I came here at fifteen, and [during] the first month, I couldn't find a job." When I asked what job he wanted, he described his prior work experience in his origin country, where he sewed pants alongside his parents. Finding similar work in the United States was not easy.

> The bosses would tell me, "*¿Tienes experiencia?* [Do you have experience?]" I would say, "Yes." And they would say, "You are a child still. We can be sued [if we hire you]. You can go to . . . ." Basically, "Go to school." But I thought, "Yes, I would like to go to school, but no one will [financially] support me. Just me. Who else? It's me by myself."

Participants described their unexpected orientation to the reality that they were outside the bounds of normative childhood. Unaccompanied young people made meaning of their independence and exclusion from childhood and family norms in different social scenarios. That full-time teenage workers were outside the norms of adolescence was most evident at work, where they were surrounded by adults; in churches, where they met other teens who attended high school or were college bound; and in public settings like parks, restaurants, and stores, where participants noticed that adults typically accompanied other youth. This emergent frame of reference about the meaning of childhood created an unanticipated feeling of disadvantage.

These confrontations prompted comparisons between the everyday lives of teen workers and other immigrants growing up with caregivers, which could have detrimental effects on youth's emotional state and sense of self. Adán, who migrated from El Salvador at age seventeen, explained that growing up in the United States was "*cosa diferente*"— something different from what he imagined— "because a different picture is painted in people's own countries." Participants anticipated attaining financial independence and that they would need to *echar ganas* (put the effort in) to achieve their *metas*, but many did not expect the degree of their emotional independence or the various emotional challenges they would encounter. Adán chalked up the different trajectories to good fortune, saying, "There are people who come here and have more luck. They migrate with their families, and they feel supported. The family gives them [access to] education; they have somewhere to live. That's not me." Adán recognized that there are youth who, with the help of a caregiver or family member, can access the normative coming-of-age institutions and experiences, which contribute to their "feeling supported." Adán's identification of the luck of migrating with family as the starting point for this pathway and his indication that that was "not him" revealed his understanding that his exclusion from this pathway was rooted in his unaccompanied status and, ultimately, the absence of a caring adult figure.

Similarly, Jayson, who migrated from Guatemala at age fifteen, put his emergent frame of reference in plain sight as he shared that "*si mis papas estuvieran aquí*" (if my parents were here), he would have been kept out of the workplace entirely "because as your mom and dad, well, they . . . maybe they would have said I should go to school, and they would have [financially] supported me. Maybe then I would not have worked when I got here." Jayson firmly believed that "if [his] parents were here," he would have been buffered from labor exploitation and his nine years of struggling with alcohol and drug addiction to quiet the emotional distress he endured.[11] Dealing with the unevenness of family care between origin and destination countries is compounded by exposure to the uneven constructions of childhood across two societies. Tomás's emergent frame of reference, in which he compared his life to that of other youth in the United States, affected his mental and emotional health:

> You feel discriminated against, like, I feel like less than them. I would look at other kids and say, "Wow, why not me?" I would ask myself, "Why am I not a kid who was born here? Why aren't my parents here? Why is my life different?" I say, "Look, the ones born here go to school; they have their parents; they have everything."

Tomás compared his experiences with those of US-born youth, who had the capital afforded by their parental ties and did not have to work as he did. This heightened his sense of deprivation and fueled his hopelessness, low self-esteem, and feeling of being stuck. As a nineteen-year-old migrant, Tomás asserted that youth who migrate to the United States without their parents or familial support and who therefore grow up as workers "come [to the United States] to suffer."

(Dis)orientations to Enduring Inequalities

Unaccompanied migrant youth experienced the material and emotional stressors brought on by independence and deprivation of childhood unevenly; these stressors were stratified by ethnorace and gender. The young people's interactions in work and public community spaces oriented them to the persistence of the ethnoracial and gender ideologies that displaced them from their origin countries. Indigenous youth became aware of the racial stereotypes of their communities as backward and uneducated, affecting how they experienced work and community life. Indigenous youth encountered similar denigration in other spaces, for example in workspaces, where they were characterized as having no skills or as belonging on farms and not in factories or restaurants; in adult English-language schools, where Maya languages were described as unintelligible dialects (rather than languages); and in public life in general. Young people's experiences of being discriminated against by non-Indigenous groups engendered feelings of low self-worth, rejection, and humiliation before their non-Indigenous Latin American–origin peers. Participants reported initially preferring to leave their homes later in the day so that their darker skin tone would not be evident; they also adopted strategies like not speaking in public to avoid detection of their accented Spanish. Thus, unique to the (dis)orientation of unaccompanied Indigenous youth was their confrontation with the overlapping forms of anti-immigrant and anti-Indigenous discrimination and stigmatization that make up "hybrid hegemonies" across Latin American and US societies.[12]

Aarón, a Guatemalan Maya participant, was oriented to the persistence of ethnoracial hierarchies within the Latin American immigrant community, like those that marginalized Indigenous Guatemalans experience in Latin America. He said, "They used to tell me, and I was scared because they would tell me, 'Oh, you're also from a small town?' I would reply, 'Yes,' and they would say, 'Oh, you also speak a dialect.'" Anticipating the ridicule that would follow the acknowledgment of K'iche' as his primary language, Aarón denied speaking K'iche'. Attempts to cloak Indigenous identity could isolate youth, corroborating sociologist Sarah Halpern-Meekin's assertion that "feeling like an outsider across one's social groups can contribute to a sense of social poverty," further exacerbating material precarity and emotional distress.[13] Further still, as youth learned that Maya and other Indigenous cultures were looked down upon even in the US, they experienced physical manifestations of their anxiety and fear of being discriminated against, such as shortness of breath, chills, tingling sensations across their bodies, and panic attacks. This was the case for Andrés, who described that he "used to cry" because "that was the only thing I could do. I would lock myself in my room and cry when no one was around. It was the insecurity plus the fear. I would feel so insecure to talk to people; I just wouldn't talk." Without parents and adult figures to liaise with community organizations and act as buffers against discrimination, youth were independently oriented to the violence of hybrid ethnoracial and gender hierarchies and their consequences over time. Exposure to overt ethnoracial discrimination at young ages could worsen or prolong youth's disorientation.

Gender also acts as a mediator for experiences of orientation. The gendered patterns of public-sphere participation and private-sphere relegation informed the sample size and gender breakdown of study participants. It was more common to encounter men than women in public spaces where I recruited interview participants. It was also easier to secure after-work or weekend participation from men than women. Women were also more likely to have female-only social ties in public workplaces like garment factories. Outside of work, girls and young adult women were less likely to attend school, as adult English-language classes took place from 7:00 to 9:00 p.m. Following unspoken ethnoracial divides, Maya women tended to speak to other Maya women in their Indigenous language or Spanish. With limited social networks and proficiency in a language disparaged by non-Indigenous Spanish speakers, unaccompanied Maya girls and young women were especially disadvantaged in their coethnic community and the larger Latin American immigrant community. Delia and Annalisa, two Guatemalan Maya women, described feeling insecure when speaking in public, especially when their husbands were not around. Delia felt that people looked at her differently and ridiculed her behind her back because she is Indigenous. She knew it happened to others; her fears were enough to keep her home.

Maya men also openly discussed the abuses Indigenous women endure. Joaquín related that while working in a garment factory, he frequently observed that factory owners (typically White or Korean American men) and floor managers (typically non-Indigenous Mexican men) "took advantage" of Indigenous women who were timid in demeanor. Joaquín confessed that he and other Maya men often refrained from defending themselves against supervisors who called them "stupid" or "slow" at work. He surmised that women were even less likely to protect themselves against groping and sexual advances. On one occasion, Joaquín observed a Maya woman being pushed to the ground by a factory owner after she rejected his advances. He lamented not stepping in to defend her or helping her off the ground; yet, his fears and insecurity as an independent youth worker whose survival required that he maintain stable employment paralyzed him at that moment. Migrant young women are oriented to unequal power hierarchies that disadvantage them as Indigenous people and women. "These are the things you must endure," said Joaquín, summing up the precarity of undocumented young people's lives.

Orientation to Agency

Youth's orientation to independence and the isolating effect imposed by the urgency to survive made Los Angeles, with its nearly four million people, feel lonely. Hence, over time youth confronted their need to change their circumstances and were oriented to their agency. Many see the first step in this evolutionary process as finding an anchoring community in Los Angeles. Caleb was not the only teen to consider joining the adult men outside his apartment complex as a potential starting point. Ander explained that he felt sadness when he realized that life in the United States is "different" because of the independence and individualism that come with being an unaccompanied teen:

> *Aquí es cada quien* [Here, it's everyone for themselves]. I think that's why I got sad. Well, since no one over there can give me advice and no one here can provide me with discipline, it's just me by myself. I'm *solito* [alone] in my apartment. Sometimes, I'm just by myself. And sometimes, when you close yourself up inside, you get many things in your head. One day, I even thought of getting together with the people hanging out outside. I thought there was no solution to my life here. There were no jobs. There wasn't anyone to give me a job. I thought, "Well, if I join them, I probably won't work, and then I cannot pay my debt." I said, "I am going to be on the street with these people."

While Ander did not join the ranks of the men on the street, his logic reflects an orientation to agency as he contemplated how he might begin to change his circumstances through everyday interactions. Like Ander, Elías explained that being an independent youth worker meant that his day was spent almost entirely alone. First he was alone at work; then he was alone at home as others worked. He felt unsatisfied by this. "I realized that I needed friends," he said. "I need to have friends." He explained that without friends:

> I am locked up in my house after work. Imagine that? After being at work, I'm just locked up in my house without . . . and it's small, not

even a big apartment. It's only for me to sleep in. Then, you get home tired from work and don't have friends. So, the loneliness comes. It comes because it's full circle that when my brothers go out and they leave me alone, I don't have friends, and it's very sad. So, I get home, and now I get home, and I start to think, "Okay, I need to get out. I need to take a walk on the street." So, I got out and didn't have a specific direction without purpose in life.

What Ander and Elías described as loneliness and the need for companionship, Aarón described as "an emptiness" and a similar sense of purposelessness. "I didn't understand life," Aarón observed. "I didn't understand the meaning of life."

In Aarón's quest for the meaning of life, he turned to a local Catholic church. His decision corroborates an extensive body of research suggesting that religious communities, and Catholic and Protestant churches specifically, are often the first places Latin American–origin immigrants turn to when looking for material and emotional support.[14] This line of scholarship points to religious organizations' buffering and integrative roles in the settlement experience of newcomer immigrant populations. Immigrant churches are considered solidarity-enforcing institutions that promote ethnic retention.[15] These mechanisms are important as undocumented immigrants—especially undocumented Indigenous immigrants—face heightened racism and intragroup divisions along ethnoracial and legal lines.[16] They are even more salient for unaccompanied youth who are encouraged by their loved ones to turn to churches as primary sources of support. More simply, churches offered teens (and other churchgoers) an open-air space to gather away from workplaces, apartments, and busy city streets. Youth could gather with friends at church courtyards with patio furniture, water fountains, and small gardens that offered respite from their hectic lives. Once there, youth discovered that these spaces impart differential forms of community participation and capital and operate within their own rules and norms. Aarón found immediate relief in church. He recalled:

> I started going to church and said, "Wow!" It's like they would give me hugs; they would give me affection. That's when I started to enter a different world. They gave me hugs, and my parents never gave me hugs. My dad was an alcoholic. He would get drunk with his friends on weekends. So, the church changed everything for me.

Aarón gained companionship in the church through church-wide gatherings, small groups, and youth groups. Each one served its function and offered a space to gather nearly every night of the week. On weekends, churches offered prayer, worship, and Bible lessons centered on spiritual edification. During interweek Bible studies, people from the same origin country or towns gathered in small worship groups. Lessons focused on giving oneself and one's resources to God, knowing that God is watching and knows people's hearts and intentions, and trusting that God had a plan that would work in one's favor if they had pure hearts. These meetings also offered a chance to socialize. People often spent a few hours after a weeknight Bible study sharing food, stories, and laughter. Food sales were typically organized at these groups and included the sale of tamales, pupusas, and tacos—of which I enjoyed many. These were also social spaces to celebrate birthdays, weddings, and other life events. Immigrant teens also attended Friday and Saturday night youth groups that, like the small groups, had moments of prayer, worship, and a Bible lesson. Lessons typically revolved around faith, not giving up hope, and trusting God's plan. But these were also social gatherings. Here, and in typical teenage style, food consisted of snacks like Doritos and Gatorade, Snickers bars, and donuts. The meetings opened with games and activities, and the room rumbled with laughter.

Aarón's orientation to religious belief, faith, and the religious community was not without its challenges. Alongside his increasing awareness of ethnoracial discrimination in the church, there were further dynamics:

> I started to notice that it had been two years, and I was serving during those two years, and no one asked me what my goals were. No one said, "Look, you're in this country; you need to study." No one said, "You are in this country; you need to create something for your future." No, nothing. The ones that are in church are solely in church. "God loves you. God bless you. Serve, Sweep." That's it.

Aarón and others were clear that they were not only immigrants entering a new society but teens entering adulthood. He was oriented to norms and behaviors necessary to advance the church's mission; he was not oriented to the tools required by unaccompanied and undocumented teens and young adults to achieve their *metas* and access opportunities for mobility and well-being in the future.

Elías recounted a similar church-related experience: "At church, what they talk to you about is God, so yeah, that's good, and it's real and all of that. But in one's personal life, how people live, they [church leaders] don't always talk about that. Well, maybe they do, but it's not enough." What the youth described was their earnest desire to practice planful competence. They did not want to be consumed by the moment's needs, especially not those of any single organization. Instead, they were thinking about the future and how to leverage skills and resources within organizations to get ahead.

Some youth felt that their churchgoing did not propel them forward, while others felt held back. Usher joined a local Catholic church to make friends and establish community. He attended that church for several months before defecting because he felt constrained by the moral expectations of the church leaders and other youth. He explained, "Well, I don't have this experience, but I have heard that sometimes they don't let you go out. It's like . . . if you are in church, you always must be in church. You cannot go out, you can't visit with people, you can't go to parties." This restriction was meaningful to Usher, who was highly social and outgoing. He wore gel-spiked hair and sported silver chains like his favorite artist, Usher, whose name he requested I use as his pseudonym. He was among the first young people I met to ask me for dating advice—how to attract "American" girls and whether money, or the lack thereof, would make one undesirable to young women in Los Angeles. All this is to say, Usher enjoyed a robust social life.

Usher also felt that the church he attended centered its programming primarily on the organization's needs, serving the church's success over its members. It showed little concern for broadening the horizons of young migrant churchgoers who needed guidance as newcomer migrants and adolescents trying to make sense of the world. He expressed his frustration:

> I don't like that they give you rules. Like you have to stay here, and only God, only God. They don't think about us. They don't say, "Hey, you know what? Come to the church in the evening and go to work in the morning." No, they don't think about us. It's just about them. The reality is that I have to pay rent, light, *todo, todo* [everything, everything]. But to them, [the] church is everything. Everyone says, "Ask God for things." I know we have to ask God. I know we have to thank God. But for them, it's only going to church and asking.

Usher wanted more from the organization and the leaders he gave his limited time to. Young people were not against the imposed discipline; as Jayson expressed earlier, some unaccompanied immigrant youth actively longed for discipline and direction. Adán corroborated this when he asserted that not having a caregiver in

Los Angeles can lead to "low self-esteem." He was adamant that "not having your parents here, that's what you want the most. You don't have the discipline if you don't have your parents. You don't have someone to say, 'Wake up early.' You don't have someone to say, 'Don't do that.' And that's what's missing. Sometimes, that's what you miss the most."

It was particularly harmful to unaccompanied youth that religious leaders framed adolescents' need for orientation to their changing bodies or sex and sexuality as a weakness in their faith and moral character.[17] In Usher's view, the church does this by orienting youth to internalized shame related to teens' natural curiosities and their fear of making mistakes that could have lifelong (and afterlife) consequences. He elaborated:

> They didn't take the actions that they wanted, so I had to stop participating because that's what . . . if you do anything else, "[You] can't do this, you can't do that, you can't do that other thing." Everything is [deemed] a sin. And that can affect you and many things in your life because the *jóvenes* [teenagers] do something, and they hear that it's a sin—"That's a sin, that's a sin!" So then, there is always sin, but it's like 50/50. And for women who do things, too, that's where they get traumatized. Say someone steals something, and they hear that stealing is a sin; you get messages that you are a sinner and end up traumatized. That's what stays in your mind. That's what gets stuck, *y no se puede superar eso* [and you cannot overcome that]. That becomes very difficult.

Similarly, Delia went to church to get support in dealing with social isolation, which her increasingly abusive husband exacerbated (chapter 5). Instead, she felt judged and blamed, as the church leadership asked what she was doing to provoke her husband and insisted that she should respect him. Delia also attended a church youth group and mentioned to peers that she had joined a Zumba class, which made her feel good because she exercised and made new friends. Her peers admonished her and discouraged this social activity, warning her that moving her body to secular music was a sin and could awaken sexual desires within her and others around her. Delia's anxiety escalated, anticipating that God would punish her for dancing. She stopped participating in the Zumba classes and the church youth group activities.

Delia experienced trauma that led to greater social isolation, as Usher reflected during our interview. This does not imply that religion or religious communities are inherently wrong for unaccompanied youths' orientation or incorporation; instead, it demonstrates the power of organizational ties to orient (or disorient) immigrants toward specific roles and resources. Churches and other religious groups are often considered safe and welcoming for newcomers. However, given young immigrants' life stages and the complexity of their needs, the structure, dynamics, and messages that religious groups offer can have a different impact. The churches that the youth attended provided some supportive resources—such as a space to make pleas to God or a place to make friends—but some organizational norms were also harmful. Youth were oriented to both. A longer-term process of orientation required the young people to practice *desahogo* (unburdening) from these cumulative harms.

Activating Agency alongside Significant Adult Figures and Peers

I met dozens of young people who, through trial and error, were oriented to strategies of patchworking available material and emotional resources to foster a sense of stability in their lives over time. Common among them was that they established meaningful relationships with adult figures and peers across community groups and were oriented alongside them. A vital component of the effectiveness of patchworking social ties and resources is that youth have meaningful connections with adult mentors or guides who can orient their roles and responsibilities, norms and values, and the available structure of opportunities—what was referred to as the *sistema*. These ties were also meaningful to the unaccompanied teens as they provided the structure and discipline they longed for. Nonfamilial adult figures often did not provide direct material resources. Still, they offered emotional support by teaching youth how to decode the structure of opportunities, naming the isolation and hardship, making sense of disillusionment, and providing frames for thinking about and acting on these. Activating agency alongside significant adult figures produced planful competence—critical for youth to navigate their dual transitions as immigrants and adolescents in a new society.

The influence of a guide on youth's incorporation pathways became clear through my interactions with the Maya youth participants in Voces de Esperanza (Voices of Hope) between 2012 and 2018. During my six years with the group, it seemed that many unaccompanied Maya youth in Pico-Union, regardless of where I met them, had some connection to Wilfredo, the group's primary coordinator. Wilfredo, a former catechist instructor and refugee of the Salvadoran civil war, was a figurehead in the unaccompanied youth worker community in Pico-Union and MacArthur Park. He was often accompanied by Jorge, a Mexican American man in his mid-twenties from the Pico-Union area. Together they worked to encourage youth in seven distinct areas of their development: physical, intellectual, moral, emotional, spiritual, social, and sexual. Throughout my time in the field, it seemed that Wilfredo was well-known by many outside the group's membership. Although he was not the only mentor or significant other whom the youth came to know, he was an example of the influence that even a single guiding adult figure can have in the lives of unaccompanied youth.

We can see how youth came to meet Wilfredo and his impact on their orientation in Caleb's example. Caleb could not unburden with a trusted family member after ties with his brother and uncle dissolved. He dealt with these emotions in isolation. Caleb recalled, "I would isolate myself a lot. . . . I wouldn't tell my problems to anyone unless I thought it would help me, but that was hardly ever the case." He made friends, primarily with other youth workers living independently in Los Angeles, but he refrained from sharing his challenges with them unless they asked directly. Caleb adopted this stance "because I knew they would tell me, 'Just have a beer,' because that was the first thing they would do. So that's why I wouldn't tell them anything."

Caleb's isolation overwhelmed him with negative thoughts. This experience was "the thing that I [struggled with] the most." Sometimes these thoughts were related to the grief of family separation. Other times they were anticipatory stressors. "Sometimes I think about, for example, 'What will happen to me if I don't come to achieve my goals?' And sometimes I say, 'No, well, I know I can. Little by little, I can do things on my own.'" Still, he was not in the United States only for himself; he was here also for his family. Therefore he was anxious about his own and his family's future. "Then there are times," he explained, "that I think about my family. 'What will happen to them later on?' I ask myself. 'What will happen to my siblings?' Just things like that. Sometimes I start to worry, and sometimes it affects me. But I try to find a way not to think negative thoughts but to have positive thoughts." Without a clear orientation, Caleb felt financial and emotional insecurity about both the present and his own and his family's future. He resolved to do things "little by little" and "on his own." Indeed, Caleb was on his own until he sought help from organizations and individuals who assisted immigrants.

Caleb first turned to the church and, as other youth learned, noticed that churchgoing provided initial relief from isolation and overwhelming emotions:

> Being there gives me strength, like when I get depressed because my emotions go up and down, and I can't figure out what to do when they go down. Prayer helps me a lot. It gives me hope; it gives me strength. Sometimes, I cry, and then I start crying out to God. I begin to say a prayer, and I feel some peace. I feel free, and that helps me.

Caleb's church attendance afforded some emotional unburdening, but over time he did not feel he was obtaining tools to change his way of thinking or his way of life. Instead, beyond his ability to release his tears and cry out to God, he felt stunted by the messages to "rely on God" and "wait on God." His church provided him a safe space to release his emotions in private, but he wanted to learn how to manage them and to change the conditions that caused his emotions and those that resulted from his inability to control them. Caleb shared his challenges and desire to better understand himself and the Los Angeles *sistema* he was growing up in with friends he made at church, who then took him to meet an older Salvadoran man, Wilfredo. Caleb recalled:

> I told [my friends] the problems I was having. I told them I wasn't feeling well, had headaches, and would lose my breath. I told them I didn't know what to do anymore and felt *desorientado* [disoriented]. So, I told my friends that, and one of them said, "Oh, I know a man that might be able to help you. Let's see him now. I will call him to see where he is." That's when I met Wilfredo. We talked with him, and I told him all about my problems. Oh, there were so many problems to tell him about.

Wilfredo was known for gathering with youth every so often in one-on-one or small group meetings with a few youth at a time at a Pico-Union Starbucks. After a few months of meeting as a group, usually four or five people at a time, Wilfredo began coordinating what became Voces de Esperanza. Meeting once per week for two hours at a Starbucks coffee shop, the core goal of Voces was to support youth's *desahogo*. Wilfredo was particularly keen on Voces being a space of *desahogo* for unaccompanied Indigenous youth who were facing challenges other undocumented Latin American-origin immigrants faced, but which were compounded by their marginal status within the Central American or broader Latin American immigrant community.

The unaccompanied Indigenous workers were vocal during Voces meetings about feeling disadvantaged in three ways: as Indigenous Central Americans in Pico-Union specifically, but Los Angeles more broadly; as undocumented immigrants and working youth who did not qualify for such programs as DACA; and as unaccompanied minors who did not have parental material or emotional support of parents. Youth would express themselves to commiserate, find common ground, explore solutions through each other's stories, and develop intimate and trusting social ties. Wilfredo applied his extensive knowledge of structural inequality to point out the unevenness at all levels of society. He reminded the young people that their societal incorporation was distinct from those growing up with parental guidance and support. Hence, their outcomes could not be measured against better-resourced youth with normative coming-of-age experiences. He related his journey of coming to this realization:

> When I accepted that I was at a zero in everything, I started looking for things I could work on. Why am I going to compete with other people and feel bad? Imagine that. Imagine I am at a zero and want

to compete with Stephanie. At that point, I am in the wrong. I am going to feel [that I am the] worst. How will I compete with her if she started on her path when she was little and has never stopped working toward that goal [referencing educational attainment]? So, I must accept that I come from a different place. I have a lot to go, but that doesn't mean that I cannot get there. Of course, I can. It just means that is the area [in my life] that I must work on. What is most important is living the best [life] that we can. That is the key to life. We have talked about the value of life and that we are all the same. No one is bigger or smaller [than anyone else]; we are equally valuable.

Wilfredo contextualized the young people within their distinct social worlds, highlighting their diverse starting points of incorporation to increase their understanding of, and compassion for, their own lives and lived experiences. He referenced me, a US-born, English-speaking, and formally educated daughter of immigrants, as an example of an unreasonable comparison to make, even for himself. His comments also spoke to the role of *desahogo* in the orientation to his position in a profoundly oppressive and unequal society.

Wilfredo reinforced ideas of individual agency and capacity to access and patchwork resources and knowledge because he did not guide youth toward a specific decision or route. When Wilfredo and I spoke privately at least once per week during my six-year involvement with Voces de Esperanza, he reminded me that he wanted the unaccompanied youth with whom he spoke to remember that this country is not a refuge from pain or hardship and that the American Dream is a myth. Wilfredo was adamant that "the American Dream doesn't exist" but that this truth should not preclude youth from living and being well. He oriented Voces participants to their agency in achieving a sense of material and emotional well-being and to their ability to determine for themselves what that meant.

His orientation aimed to convert the pain of independence and the disillusionment that emerged over time in the US into the power of agency. He often gave the group messages like the following:

> You, each of you, with self-help and help from a group like this, can take new paths. If you feel lost and are asking yourself, "What am I doing here?" If you feel pressure from your family or your emotions getting away from you, look for a solution to feel better. You have the answer inside of you. *Animo* [have courage]. We only give you orientation here. It's you who must take the actions you need.

Wilfredo named the disillusionment that Indigenous youth felt with the falsehood of the promises of opportunity they imagined in the US and motivated them to see their capacity for action. He believed that to survive, young people must be self-sufficient. "*Tienen que superar*," he urged them. "You must overcome."

Of course, simply believing that young people can enact agency to overcome oppressive structures does not remove the constraints they face in accessing opportunities for mobility, well-being, and liberation from oppression. What was significant here was that they felt seen and cared for by a knowing adult figure, were encouraged to *superar*, and developed planful competence. Hopefulness enabled planful competence by informing new *metas* and the adoption of favorable decisions and behaviors to reach those goals.

Wilfredo acknowledged that many unaccompanied teens were carrying the weight of their futures, plus that of their left-behind families—illustrative of their transnational responsibility. To this end, he pointed out just how thinly they were stretched: navigating undocumented life in Los Angeles; struggling to secure employment; enduring unthinkable working conditions for exploitative wages; budgeting for sending remittances to left-behind families; suffering stress and anxiety induced by their families' worsening economic circumstances; and experiencing barefaced racism and discrimination, often at the hands of those professing to protect them. And all of this was at a significant cost to their own personal, financial, mental, and emotional well-being—as young people who had forgone their childhood to assume adult responsibilities. In this context, Wilfredo spoke directly, forcefully, and candidly to Voces participants, urging self-prioritization as a way of managing their limited financial, social, and emotional resources and imploring them to "take care of you":

> ¡Bichos! [Kids!] You must control your situation. Control your economy. Don't let yourself be pressured! I know you still have debts, and your family pressures you from over there. Alejandro [a young man in the group] keeps telling us. . . . I think he has opened himself up to us well. We can see how he gives and gives and gives to his family, and I congratulate you, but at the same time, I don't see where you are going. You, with your life, you. Where are you? We have seen you open up for your brothers and sisters and always look out for others. You are the youngest of everyone and the one taking care of them. Be careful. Take care of yourself. Be mindful, each of you, because even from Guatemala, you are getting a lot of pressure economically.

Wilfredo was by no means discouraging youth from sending remittances to their families; instead, he encouraged them to consider the sacrifices they were making at the expense of their mobility and well-being when they directed the money that remained after paying bills to left-behind families. This might draw criticism from transnational family scholars who analyze the intricate and intentional care networks that sustain migrant families across borders.[18] However, youth became oriented to an individualistic US society, including several long-settled family members who turned their backs on newly arrived young relatives seeking support. Wilfredo's message was clear: unaccompanied teens might have to do the same to survive in the United States. Failing to do so could be perilous. In many cases, these messages were well received precisely because unaccompanied youth longed for discipline and structure and for someone to help them develop strategies for achieving stability.

Supportive adult figures like Wilfredo also played a role in encouraging youth to develop positive self-concepts. Wilfredo's earlier role as a catechist instructor in Pico-Union sharpened his insights about the damage that guilt and shame could wreak on young people's lives. Hence his emphasis on the importance of the seven focal areas identified by Voces de Esperanza. "Why these areas?" he asked rhetorically, and answered, "Because these are the things they are dealing with the most." Furthermore, Wilfredo grasped the complexity of adolescence and the transition to adulthood, involving physical and emotional changes. Voces participants and their close friends confided in Wilfredo about their sexuality, their addictions to pornography or masturbation, and their engagement in premarital sex—taboo to discuss with adults and peers in most spaces.

Wilfredo related a conversation with a Guatemalan Maya teenager, Vicente, who confessed, "Don Wilfredo, I am embarrassed to say this, but I am bisexual, and my family in Guatemala will kill me [if they find out]." Wilfredo detailed the ensuing conversation as follows:

> I asked him, "What? Do you know what bisexual means?" He said, "No, the truth is that I think I am homosexual." So, I told him to tell me why, and he said, "It's because I have a girlfriend but only to be in front of my family. I don't love her; I only use her. The truth is," he told me, "The truth is that I have more [physical] contact with men than I do with her, but my family says that if someone in our family

is homosexual, we will kill them. Don Wilfredo, what do I do?" And that made me think, "Wow, sexuality [really matters here]."

This orientation contrasted starkly with young people's experiences in religious communities, where they were shamed for expressing curiosity about their changing bodies and relationships and where discussions of sex and sexuality were taboo.

Establishing a positive self-concept requires that youth accept themselves. In September 2014 I observed how Wilfredo reassured youth that it was okay to make mistakes; mistakes were not evidence of immorality or a personal deficit. During that September meeting, the youth discussed the approaching school enrollment deadlines. Some young people contemplated whether the sacrifices of money and time were worth it, given how little progress some participants had made through the English-language class levels. Matías indicated that he did not pass his level-one class in the summer term, had to reenroll in the same level for the third time, and was feeling down about it. Modeling how youth could accept their mistakes and continue to move forward, Wilfredo responded:

> That's how life goes. What is essential is to learn to accept it. Learn to accept that we make a ton of mistakes. How will a kid not make mistakes if they don't have the orientation? Of course, you will get into strange things; you've lived through strange things. But that's what happens. It causes pain, it causes trauma, and you aren't prepared to manage it because of where we are from and where we live [currently]. We have all heard that the people here have an education that may be in the second or third grades. So that is where we are working, step-by-step. That's where the change will start to happen. So, this isn't about "Why me?" That's why we are here. That is, that's what this group [Voces de Esperanza] is for—to listen to each other. And thank you to those of you that share your story. Everyone has

a story; maybe some are more or less difficult, but we are all here. And like I am telling you, it is not about resolving everything that has happened [in our lives]; it is about accepting ourselves and understanding where we come from [in terms of place and experiences].

Right now, you are okay; you have your feet, you have your hands, you can work, you can smile. You have what you need. But if you latch onto one thing that is happening, you have thoughts that go in another direction, and that's when you will not be fine. Instead of living in the present, your mind will be focused on something else that is difficult. So, you must have courage, which is why we have this space. There are things you can bring here to share, and you can share with a friend. That is the only way to heal.

Wilfredo's creation of a collective space in which once-isolated youth could encounter shared experiences and learn how to express their emotions equipped them to better participate in their communities. Wilfredo's message was unambiguous:

Échale ganas [put in effort]. That is the key that we have. We must heal our wounds, accept them, and then work on different areas in our lives. We have seven areas that we talk about here. We have talked a bit about the physical, intellectual, moral, emotional, psychological, spiritual, social, sexual, and what is important is to accept.

Wilfredo could not see a future in which US society would embrace and actively support immigrant communities, including unaccompanied youth, but especially Indigenous youth. Instead of youth considering their marginalization and unaccompanied status a deficit, they should approach it as an opportunity to develop self-reliance. Being independent in the United States did not have to be an occasion for loneliness; it could signal strength and individual capacity. They could at least count on themselves if no one else was on their side.

The immense value of such messages notwithstanding, they did not solve the very real structural and material problems that participants confronted. But they did provide youth with a framework of self-compassion, acceptance, and worth. Wilfredo encouraged youth to view themselves as active agents in their lives and futures, capable of changing the direction of their lives. In short, Wilfredo encouraged them to value their own lives, skills, and experiences—a lesson more often imparted by parents as their children come of age—so that youth could become the community leaders and guiding figures in the future that Voces participants hoped for in the present.

Despite Wilfredo's lack of formal education in child and adolescent development, psychology, or relevant fields of expertise, and without material resources, he was committed to listening to unaccompanied teens' needs and providing context-specific orientation that allowed them to understand themselves better, and I repeatedly witnessed Wilfredo's impact on individuals' lives. I often wondered if he knew just how rare a figure he was for unaccompanied youth and just how meaningful he was in the lives of those we mutually knew—youth like Caleb who, when I asked him to reflect on his time in Voces and Wilfredo's role in his life, spontaneously exclaimed, "Wow!" He elaborated:

> I started to learn so many things. I began to learn about socializing and how to balance my emotions. I am learning how to understand other people when they are doing well and when they are doing poorly. I understand now. I am adapting to how people are in different situations. I am learning so much about life and spirituality. I am learning about what we must do and what is necessary; spirituality is essential but must be balanced. We always need the spiritual, but we also need to socialize, talk about our problems, and talk to our friends—*me libero de mis problemas* [I liberate myself from my problems] with Voces.

These lessons, perhaps usually associated with a parent's or extended family's guidance, were learned in a public space and within a group context.[19] Caleb concurred, "What I like about the group is that I have the freedom to express myself to overcome my fears and more. That's what I like about the time that I get to speak. I can get everything I have inside of me out because there's nowhere else that I can do that." The stigma and fear of being misguided had once led Caleb to isolate himself; hence, speaking about his emotional distress in the group, he began to destigmatize the destress and expand his social world.

Crucially, the group also helped participants discuss their feelings and experiences while simultaneously hearing about those of others—and in so doing, learn that they were not alone. "In my case," Caleb explained, "I started to express myself more when I heard that there were other *jóvenes*, even more *jóvenes* that had the same problems that I did." A new frame of reference emerged, in which he noticed that other youth were in more trying situations: "There are some that have even more problems—they are in even worse situations than I am." He continued his self-reflection, realizing that his condition was not unique but shared by other unaccompanied youth who also had "problems": "When someone has a problem, it's necessary to express yourself so that you can find a solution. That's what Voces is. But because we can't express our emotions, we can't express ourselves to people. I am discovering more now. I am learning more things about life."

When Caleb's peers introduced him to a mentor and support group, he became oriented to "expressing" himself, "figuring out what to do," and "finding a solution to [his] problem": planful competence. His experience of several compounded hardships and delays in establishing stability in the United States motivated him to support other youth in similar situations. Ultimately, Caleb's orientation to his community; to understanding how to direct his time and effort; and to the knowledge that different forms of support existed and that he, too, had the power to support others revealed to him "that things could be better, and that life has a purpose."

Conclusion

Life in the United States is not what youth imagined while in their origin countries or expected upon arrival. Instead, there was a complicated misrepresentation of life in the United States, which caused feelings of material and emotional disorientation once they were there. The concept of orientation prompts us to recognize the unique nested institutional, spatial, and social contexts that immigrants occupy in the US. There is not a singular orientation experience, as immigrants' orientation is a reflection of their distinct social location(s). While I have relied on the categorical comparison between undocumented immigrant youth who arrived in the US as unaccompanied minors but were welcomed by adult caregivers and those who remained unaccompanied as they came of age as a launching point to understand how household contexts of arrival shape orientation, the stories shared here demonstrate that intragroup differences in orientation experiences exist.

Unaccompanied youth's survival in Los Angeles is contingent on their orientation to the structure of opportunities available to them, including institutions; the built environment; organizations; and their agency in patchworking knowledge, skills, and social ties to those who can support their material and emotional well-being and guide their use of their limited resources. The orientation of unaccompanied teens who did not receive the material support of a long-settled relative began with learning the urgency of finding employment to afford debt repayment, housing, food, and other essentials, as well as the structure of opportunities available to them to survive in the short term. With time, unaccompanied teens were oriented to Los Angeles life: the city's streets and how to navigate them, the institutions and individuals that make up their local communities, and inequalities and interactions between groups.

Though unaccompanied by an adult caregiver, young people were oriented to the possibilities of community participation. Engagement in the local community might orient youth to the helpfulness or harmfulness of neighborhood organizations as they faced the disillusionment of their oppression and marginalization in the United States. As they sought to build community and companionship, young people approached organizational participation in ways that reflected agentic patchworking—building resources within and across institutions—of newfound skills, social ties, and emotional resources to achieve their *metas*.[20] Some young people established meaningful social ties to adult figures and peers that promoted their planful competence and staved off social isolation and feelings of loneliness, which promoted adaptation. Others remained isolated from meaningful social ties, leading them down a pathway of perdition. I turn to these pathways in the following two chapters.

4 *Adaptation*

Caleb wore a red Nike T-shirt, a red Chicago Bulls hat, and baggy blue jeans when I met him at a Starbucks patio near Los Angeles's Mid-City in late 2018. Over the six years we had known each other, Caleb and I came to feel like friends. Like many other teens in Los Angeles, Caleb carried a JanSport backpack over his shoulders and had a pair of earphones hung over his ears. I had not seen him or other youth for a few months after graduating with my PhD in the spring of 2018 and moving to Texas to start a new job. When he asked me how my transition to my job and life in Texas was going, I told him how hard it was to be away from my family. I shared that it was my first time not living in California, and I could not imagine how he and others felt being entire countries away. "You adapt, you become accustomed," he responded with a shrug, perhaps to console me.

In the seven months since our last meeting, Caleb's English had become more proficient. He was even learning some Japanese at the sushi restaurant where he worked first as a dishwasher, then in food prep, then as a line cook. His new job paid him more money, which meant he could work fewer hours. But the distance between Pico-Union and the San Fernando Valley was over an hour by bus. To make this work, Caleb left the adult English-language school he attended off and on for several months. His newfound knack for learning English from English-speaking coworkers alleviated the pressure to attend school. Where previously Caleb had rushed to shuttle from work in a downtown Los Angeles garment factory to the adult English-language school in Pico-Union near his home, he could now practice his English at work, saving him time, money, and grief.

But now Caleb was facing a new challenge: his cousin had left Guatemala some days earlier and was on his way to Los Angeles. As Caleb anticipated his cousin's arrival and the responsibility that receiving him would entail, he remembered his sense of abandonment and loneliness because of the absence of support when he arrived. This motivated Caleb to find ways to offer his cousin support to ensure he would not have the same experience. I wondered how this would affect Caleb's progress toward his *metas*. Caleb often talked about how he wanted to return home to Guatemala, if for no other reason than to see his mother again. Sitting on the Starbucks patio, I smiled at Caleb and asked, "Do you still think about returning to Guatemala someday?" "No," he quickly responded. "Well, I don't know. Maybe only to visit." As in Caleb's response to my sharing about my transition to life in Texas, he continued, "Sometimes I feel like I am adapting. So many years have already passed, and like . . . I don't know, *ya me acostumbre*. I am used to it now." His tone struck me. He was coming to terms with the possibility of a new future because he had become "used to," adapted to the routine of his everyday life and his lifestyle in Los Angeles. It seemed he had achieved stability.

Caleb grew up without parental supervision and outside of K–12 schools, which might have set him apart as someone destined for downward mobility.[1] He had not reached the traditional socioeconomic markers of success at his life stage, including educational completion and degree attainment, but he explained that he had adapted to life in Los Angeles. At first it was largely a matter of surviving within the context of an unexpectedly unwelcoming household and limited opportunities for mobility. But as he transitioned to young adulthood, he experienced orientation toward his employment and educational options; interactions with more diverse groups of people outside of the immigrant community in the immediate Pico-Union neighborhood; and agency in deciding how he would spend his time and resources, including preparing a welcoming household for his cousin. Caleb's adaptation to these colored his imagined future, including a potential permanent settlement in Los Angeles in adulthood.

This chapter examines how, for some migrant youth, orientation can be followed by experiences of material, social, and emotional adaptation within and across societies over time. In adaptation, youth activate their agency and leverage the interpersonal and institutional resources acquired through the orientation phase to establish material and emotional well-being within limited structures of opportunity. Like orientation, adaptation is ongoing, as adjustment to one social domain of interaction (e.g., work, school, family, and community) impacts immigrants' subsequent orientation to and adaptation within another. Unaccompanied teens must adapt first, as a matter of survival, to life as an undocumented low-wage worker and thus to a nonnormative childhood. Financial insecurity makes work, especially low-wage work, the central organizing institution and feature of young people's lives. I refer to this as *work primacy*—the inevitable result of unaccompanied teens' premigration *metas*, postmigration unaccompanied status, and dependence on themselves to meet their material needs.[2] The youth who migrated with financial obligations to their left-behind families and transnational communities carried an added responsibility. With strong familial financial obligations in the origin country and few initial attachments in the receiving country, youth have little to do but work.

I also analyze how youth's work lives and work primacy shape their adaptation to the roles and responsibilities, norms and values, and aspirations across their multiscalar social context of school, community, and family within local and across transnational societies. Notably, while unaccompanied immigrant youth must work to survive the present, they maintain *metas* for their adult futures, including what they will do and who they will become, as Patrick put it in chapter 3. Thus, this chapter shows how orientation and adaptation work together and how youth's strategies to patchwork information, skills, and material and social resources move them closer to those futures. While I cannot account for the entire spectrum of adaptive strategies, I detail the most frequently observed ones, like job jumping and on-the-job reskilling, participation in informal learning groups, and using communication apps and technology across borders. I also attune to the distinctions between material and emotional adaptation, highlighting the experiences of young people who developed emotionally adaptive strategies to and through community such that they relied on meaningful relationships with adult figures and peers to achieve *desahogo*. In the next chapter I explore the strategies deployed by young people who were bereft of meaningful ties and unable to adapt emotionally.

Adaptation to Work, the Workplace, and Work Primacy

As previous chapters show, many of the young people included in this book were oriented to their role as workers in their home countries, as they worked alone or alongside parents and siblings and envisioned engaging in similar or better work once in the United States. Although prospective employers initially questioned the youth's work experience, expressed hesitation because of their age and stature, or raised concerns about their being out of school, persistent youth were still able to obtain employment as minors. In the secondary labor market—the segment of the dual US labor market associated with low wages, job instability, and poor work conditions—the characteristics that render someone exploitable, such as lack of English-language fluency, undocumented status, limited knowledge about work opportunities, and exploitative work conditions, increase their employability, which creates significant mobility barriers.[3] While undocumented workers share these conditions in the United States, unaccompanied young people's status renders them more vulnerable, with few, if any, social ties and negligible human capital. Living in this scenario, participants in this study transitioned to a new *sistema* of living, working, and surviving while supporting left-behind families. Young people assumed full responsibility for their well-being yet remained committed to helping their left-behind families, albeit within a new framework.

Teens' financial obligations and resource constraints are distinct forces that make work the central organizing institution in their lives as they navigate survival and coming of age. Carlos's earlier comparison between life in his rural, agrarian town in Guatemala and Los Angeles is revealing in this regard (chapter 3). In Guatemala, "the only thing is that you pay the light—fifty *quetzales* [about $7]. But only the light. Water? Free." In the United States, "you work to pay rent, water, light, everything." Unaccompanied youth did not anticipate how quickly expenses would accumulate in Los Angeles. The reality that "you pay for everything, everything" required migrant youth to work longer days and for more time than they desired to meet their daily needs and attain their migration goals. Furthermore, teens had often incorrectly calculated the interest on their initial migration costs. This resulted in added expenses that their low income earned in the secondary labor market could not absorb, which invariably diminished the young workers' ability to save money or to remit adequate sums to their families.

What's more, the industries in which youth worked were unstable, complicating matters further. In the garment industry, where 43 percent of youth workers in this study were employed, market influxes caused an annual decline in factory work during the holiday season.[4] Tomás explained that "there are moments where there isn't work because the work slows down in the garment industry. It's good for six months, then it slows down, then there isn't work. We will work for one day, maybe two days per week, but it isn't enough." Like garment workers, hospitality and domestic workers experienced a slowing of work during end-of-year holidays when families traveled, or parents had time away from work to look after their children and homes; car washers and construction workers felt the pinch during the rainy spring months. Learning these patterns took time. After several years of moving through financial ups and downs, the young people adapted to working more hours or multiple jobs during the busy months of the year to have a cushion for the drought months.

At work, youth adapted to workplace violence, including subjection to dangerous work conditions. Throughout my time in the field, I met teens and young adults who described chronic ear and eye aches, migraines, and numbness in their limbs. One participant even described a numbness in her spine that she equated to the feeling of "tiny giraffes running" after hours of bending over a sewing machine in a poorly lit and ventilated factory. Youth who worked in construction, maintenance, and auto services discussed chemical burns, frequent cuts and scrapes, strained muscles, and broken bones.

Although the violence of labor and wage exploitation and workplace abuses that youth endured was a shared experience, the degree of violence that they were exposed to at work was often shaped by ethnoracial and gender discrimination. Indigenous immigrants, for example, were subjected to the violence of hybrid hegemonies that relegated Indigenous teen workers to the lowest rungs of intersecting citizenship, ethnoracial, and gender hierarchies.[5] Indigenous youth described being talked down to at work as if they were children at best or animals at worst. They were assigned the most undesirable and lowest-paying jobs. Likewise, gender ideologies influence how undocumented women experience work primacy. Women's position within the gender hierarchy intersects with their position in legal and ethnoracial hierarchies to determine access to work and wages and their treatment in the workplace.[6] With their more constrained social networks, Indigenous youth and women were less likely to have alternative employment options or the opportunity to work additional hours to supplement their earnings, especially if working in a private residence. In addition, navigating work and work primacy demands even more resources from native Indigenous-language speakers as they simultaneously navigate Spanish- and English-language learning, which can slow social and economic mobility.[7] Research points to long-term consequences, such as being unable to complete education, participate in broader community life, cultivate social capital with peers, or access health and social services.[8] This in turn reinforces the primacy of the low-wage workplace in unaccompanied teens' lives.

Despite their injuries and ailments, limited financial resources and time caused youth to avoid institutions that could drain their resources, even when such avoidance risked their health and well-being. This was evident as I spoke to Tomás about his financial obligations and how he spent his earnings. Like other participants, Tomás detailed how wages and work schedules determine whether unaccompanied youth go to school, which I return to later, but he went a step further, elaborating on how these factors can also shape attitudes toward health and seeking medical care:

> You can attend school if you earn well, work a few hours, and aren't *bien matado* [translated directly as "very killed," meaning overworked]. If you get sick, you can go to the hospital. But if you have nothing, you earn little and work a lot, then no. I'd prefer not to even go to the hospital *aunque me estoy muriendo* [even if I am dying].

The precarity of being both unaccompanied and undocumented is clear in Tomás's repeated references to death and dying. He described how exploitatively low wages created temporal and financial resource constraints in accessing even medical attention. He also alluded to the financial burden of falling ill, which can be so heavy that youth imagined that it would be better to avoid seeking medical attention at all costs—even at the expense of their own lives. The young people's narratives demonstrated that work-related physiological and psychological ailments were nearly unavoidable.

Adaptation to work also meant becoming accustomed to workplace violence, low wages, and exhausting schedules. The work conditions and the ailments they produced constrained the teens' participation in nonwork activities—like attending school and improving their English-language proficiency—that could propel their job and wage mobility. Even when youth found ways to participate in nonwork activities, their physical adaptation to their work environment further limited their engagement. Participants' descriptions of their daily routines revealed the physical and psychological effects of their unhealthy and unsafe work environments. Paulina, a garment worker, detailed some of these effects:

> Sometimes I'm so tired, I get sleepy at school. It's true. It's not that the teacher or what they are teaching is boring. No, I don't see it like that. I always want to learn, but because I am so tired, I get sleepy. . . . I feel so tired. You also feel mentally exhausted. It's twelve hours of the same sound in your mind.

Paulina's description of her experiences at school after work corroborates research that shows that poverty, hunger, housing instability, and violence can distract young people in the classroom, diminishing their educational attainment.[9] Here, Paulina also reflected on the large number of hours spent "just sitting"—primarily at work but also at school:

> Then you get to class, and you still hear the same sound. You spend twelve hours [at work], then another two hours sitting [in class] aside from the twelve hours at work. If you count what time people start [work] at 6, 7, 8, 9 [a.m.], [and then you spend] another three hours at school. You spend twelve, thirteen, fourteen, sixteen hours [just] sitting.

Similarly, another participant said, "You get home tired and just go to sleep. You wake up and do it again." These narratives show that the teens' physical, psychological, and emotional labor during their workday hampered their class attendance and ability to remain engaged in learning. Under these conditions, teenage migrant workers made little to no advancements in their formal education. Inconsistent attendance inevitably resulted in students enrolling in the same level of English-language class multiple times—a sure financial burden—or discouraged them from enrolling altogether. I return to this point below.

Negotiating Financial Mobility Constraints through Job Jumping

Young people's agency in the process of adaptation to the primacy of work was evinced in their efforts to change their work conditions and advance their mobility opportunities. For example, when youth described moving up through the ranks of garment manufacturing or restaurant work, they were engaged in "on-the-job reskilling," a process by which workers learn through interactions and "exchanges of knowledge" between "coworkers and supervisors."[10] Unaccompanied migrant youth observed how reskilling offered mobility pathways to immigrants with low levels of education and engaged in this practice—either intentionally or by virtue of time in the industry. Caleb's experiences of learning English and some Japanese words at his restaurant job exemplified this. Reskilling, in turn, can enable "job jumping," which is "a strategy developed to escape bad jobs or those with limited advancement opportunities and to demonstrate newly acquired skills to prospective employers."[11]

Julian, a twenty-year-old non-Indigenous man from Guatemala offers an example of successful job jumping. Julian arrived in Los Angeles at age seventeen and began working for his uncle in a carpet installation company. He worked installing carpets from 9:00 a.m. to 7:00 p.m. each day for $100 per day. Simply put, he "didn't like that. Installing carpets is bullshit. Most people would be happy. I was helping somebody, and it was my uncle, too. I was like, working for his fucking company, and they called it his money, but I was doing most of the dirty work," and he decided he was "going to go do something else." He switched to clothing sales near downtown Los Angeles, only to discover that it was "a worse situation because I was getting paid $50 a damn day for about nine hours of work, no breaks in-between. It was basically a sweatshop." Despite such terrible conditions, young workers like Julian stayed because they were constantly promised that things would improve—eventually:

> I never experienced such lying and all this shit. This is an example of the donkey with the carrot: "We'll start paying you more, don't worry, you're almost there, you're almost up to the money you want. Oh, give us more time. Show us more, this and that." You just keep putting in time.

Julian persisted because the reskilling seemed worth it, but the process was disillusioning:

This is where I perfected my salesman skills. I wanted so hard to make money, and they were like, "Don't worry, you'll make it." It was just always something like the next day, they would say, "Don't worry, you'll make money, just keep practicing. You're not there yet." I worked nine-hour shifts for $50 per day. And they would tell me, "Hey, don't take thirty minutes for lunch. Nobody does that." I can't do anything [with $50 per day], and I guess that depressed me for a while. I was pretty depressed for a bit, like, man, this life sucks.

Julian recalled feeling "useless" at that time and despaired that he had "burned bridges with my uncle. I couldn't go back with him because he was angry." But feeling as though he had acquired sales skills, he next found work in a fabric store, where he was "selling a lot and not getting commission." He recounted:

I was getting $60 per day, and I'm like, "This is still bullshit." I quit that, and now I'm at this job where I'm getting paid $370 a week. I've been working at it for six months already, or four to six months, I don't know. Basically, I've been switching jobs around. Now, I work at this fabric warehouse. They hired me to do computer and tech things on a third-party seller store on Amazon, answer phone calls, and [provide] customer service. I get to talk to people. That's why they hired me initially. First, because I spoke some English, and my boss [a Korean man] did not. I basically don't do anything. I just kick back.

In this way, Julian acquired job experience in Los Angeles that helped him get the next job and the next until he could "kick back." Julian achieved relatively fast-paced job mobility, partly because he benefited from Spanish-language fluency at arrival, on which he built his limited English-language proficiency. Speaking more English than his Korean employer was enough to set him apart as capable of answering phones and engaging in customer service. Indeed, expertise in youth culture and technology, as evidenced in the reference to Amazon, facilitated his ability to manage an online store. Julian was not trained in warehouse sales but patchworked knowledge and resources and deployed them in his job, jumping into occupational mobility and a sense of dignity in his work.

Danilo offers another example. When Danilo left his initial job at a grocery store, he started working as a cook at a Japanese restaurant. After a few months, he realized that he "didn't have much time to socialize," perhaps a pronounced situation for a teenager who wanted to develop friendships and have fun. He recalled that his loneliness at work "was fine at first because I was putting in a lot of hours, but then I somehow got tired of it. Not physically, but mentally. I got stressed. It got boring. So, I got a different job in party rentals, which is where I'm currently at." This job involved teamwork and provided socializing opportunities. "We get to go out," Danilo explained. "We set up events and parties, which is great." Danilo earned less at his new job but paid this price in exchange for increased social ties and connections with other Spanish-speaking teens and young adults. "I don't make as much as I used to, but I like the people that I work with. . . . I get along with everybody and have been there for six months now." Danilo still spent most of his time at work and accepted lower earnings for that, but he gained emotional and social mobility through job jumping. Danilo's experience exemplified that young people's mobility was defined not merely by increased material earnings but also by increased emotional support.

Like Julian, Danilo benefited from being a Spanish-language speaker who could immediately begin learning English. Indigenous Maya-language-speaking youth were limited in their ability to practice job jumping across occupations due to the more complex language-learning processes that nested their adaptation within language ecologies.[12] Indigenous youth typically had to learn Spanish (and cope with language stigmas) to engage with the immigrant community before eventually learning English to navigate life outside the ethnic enclave or with non-Indigenous and Spanish-speaking people. Therefore, their labor and workplace adaptation could take longer and expose Indigenous youth to exploitation and violence in undesirable workplaces—which they described as "backbreaking" and compared to working "like a slave"—for longer periods than non-Indigenous peers.

While men promptly found employment by "jumping" into new industries, women had fewer opportunities to job jump. This might have been due to their limited access to information-producing ties in light of the cultural expectations that women's social lives are mostly lived in private, making them less likely than men to participate in community-based organizations or other recreational and educational spaces.[13] Indeed, several women I met throughout my fieldwork were live-in domestic workers and could not enroll in school, as they worked around the clock, Monday through Friday or Saturday. Their workarounds could ultimately slow their adaptation.

This was the case for Camelia. Camelia considered herself a resourceful homemaker, particularly because she helped her mother around the house in Guatemala when she assumed the task of running the family's errands after her older sister migrated to Los Angeles. Thus, when Camelia migrated years later, she began working as a live-in domestic worker for a couple and their two children in an affluent Los Angeles neighborhood. Having never established her own place to live and without coethnic and community-based ties, she felt powerless when she was dismissed from her job after the couple separated. To exacerbate matters, Camelia's employers reneged on their arrangement to pay her final wages—perhaps knowing that she could not resort to any legal measures against them. Camelia was rendered vulnerable, bereft of income and accommodation.

With no place to live, Camelia's older sister offered her accommodation and provided her basic needs on credit. By the time she secured employment as a live-in nanny, Camelia was indebted to her sister. Thus, as Camelia's wages over the next few months were committed to repaying her sister, she centralized work and the workplace in her life. Her survival strategies as a domestic worker in the private industry were limited, which ultimately tightened the grip of work primacy in her life. This was not unique to women in domestic work. I also observed young women who worked in the public sphere reinforcing work primacy through their labor market survival strategies, attempting to compensate for labor-force disadvantages by taking on multiple jobs or working more hours.

Adaptation to Los Angeles's Spatial and Social Landscape

Early in my fieldwork, as I was getting to know the various activities unaccompanied youth engaged in outside of work, many explained that despite their increasing orientation to Los Angeles geography and navigating it via public transportation, there were few places they felt comfortable venturing to alone. Some young men and women experienced verbal and physical harassment, which discouraged their curiosity about neighborhoods outside of their own. Still, over time most young people adopted adaptative strategies. To avoid potential gendered harassment, women learned to walk in pairs or in groups, regardless of the time of day. Youth, especially young men, knew not only how to use public transportation but where to deboard to avoid confronting gangs or gang members. Specifically, when moving from east to west in Los Angeles and crossing through MacArthur Park along Wilshire Boulevard, immigrant teens would deboard busses either before reaching the park or after, never at the MacArthur Park stop. Getting off too close to the park could result in being jumped or getting one's backpack, purse, or phone stolen, as happened to several young people. Indigenous men discussed feeling as though they were targeted by gangs like

MS-13 or those they identified as "*morenitos* (Black people)" because of their darker complexion. Indigenous youth were thus especially cautious when engaging with non-Indigenous people for fear of targeted harassment.

As young people entered adulthood, they adapted through more autonomous mobility strategies. This included relying on a network of private shuttle vans, colloquially referred to as *taxi piratas* (pirate taxis), that functioned as an informal ride-share program with designated pickup points throughout their neighborhoods. *Taxi piratas* offered the convenience of charging teens only one dollar per person when they traveled as groups across Pico-Union, MacArthur Park, Westlake, and downtown neighborhoods. Owning a car became possible with wage stability over time and was essential for young people's social life engagement. After purchasing cars, two young women—Camelia and Bianca—who worked as domestics and felt isolated from the community began driving from the San Fernando Valley or the west side of Los Angeles, respectively, to Pico-Union on Friday nights. With access to her own car, Camelia attended church youth group meetings on Saturday nights and Mass on Sunday mornings before running errands and eventually returning to the San Fernando Valley home where lived and worked full time. In mid-2016 Bianca, a Salvadoran woman, began occasionally dropping into Voces meetings on Friday nights, where by that time she was typically the only woman present besides me. She explained that she often spent weekends accompanying her older sister on errands and attending family or community gatherings. This enabled her to make friends whom she kept in touch with throughout the week via Facebook and WhatsApp, a virtual community-building adaptation strategy I discuss later.

As 2018 approached, I observed more young men in their mid- to late twenties purchasing their own used cars as well. Some youth had become frustrated with their reliance on public transportation, while others were explicitly in hot pursuit of romantic relationships. Usher was among the most vocal about his hopes that owning his car would make him more appealing to women. Owning a car required a new orientation, as youth learned the rules and norms of driving, parking, and avoiding law enforcement in Los Angeles.[14] Parking tickets, towing fees, and the fear of drawing attention to oneself by having one too many passengers in the car became new concerns for car owners, but youth adapted to the rules of the road by learning the meaning of painted curbsides, adhering strictly to the number of passengers permitted in each car, and minding the speed limit. During my research, several youth had accrued parking tickets, typically for missing street sweeping days, but no one had been pulled over. I did not hear from study participants about direct interactions with law enforcement officials while in the field. Still, spatial orientations and adaptations would introduce youth to new experiences and expose them to new responsibilities, norms, and emotions, including the stress of encountering law enforcement.[15] In all, youth's adaptative strategies to spatial mobility gave them access to new social spaces and places as they transitioned to adulthood.

As their social worlds expanded, youth were oriented to the need for language proficiency and the ability to communicate with non-Spanish-speaking people. They were required to adapt once more, this time linguistically. Many young people, regardless of ethnorace, gender, or age, described feeling a sense of insecurity in public spaces where Spanish was not the dominant language. Spanish or Maya languages sufficed within the Spanish and Maya linguistic communities in the Westlake/MacArthur Park neighborhoods, where this research was conducted, but venturing outside these neighborhoods required some English-language proficiency. Hence, youth widely perceived English-language learning as necessary to participate in their local communities and Los Angeles society. Ander agreed that "you always need English [because] there are always people who solely speak to you in English." Ander maintained that the inability to speak English could lead to isolation:

> Sometimes, the Americans ask questions, right? And I don't know the response. In stores, on the streets, for example. I walk here, and people will ask me what time it is or, "Where is this or that?" I don't know [how to respond], so I stay quiet and don't talk because I cannot respond to what they are saying. I realized that if anything happens, say I have to go to the doctor or anything like that, it's all English.

Ander and others adapted to the importance of multilingual proficiency by setting new goals around language learning that ensured more, or at least more confident, community engagement.

More precisely, Indigenous youth who initially struggled to understand others when they were in public—including in confrontational situations—described how learning the Spanish and English languages made them feel more confident in public and helped them avoid harmful situations.[16] As Ander adapted to the importance of proficiency in different languages to navigate space and place in Los Angeles, he said that he "decided to learn English" and would "make an effort" by enrolling in school and learning independently. The discursive strategies teens and young adults adopted to navigate Los Angeles better demonstrated their keen orientation to the power dynamics that shaped their ability to experience full inclusion in their local communities as they came of age.

Learning in the Shadow of Work Primacy

Youth's interactions at work and in public demonstrated their need to maintain multilingual proficiency to secure their financial mobility, safety, and sense of belonging. In their orientation to independent work and social life, however, unaccompanied teens constantly came up against the reality of their nonnormative transition to adulthood that denied them K–12 school enrollment. Instead, they adapted to learning in the shadow of work primacy through adult English-language schools and alternative learning spaces. Of the seventy study participants who grew up as full-time workers, twenty-two (31 percent) had enrolled in adult English-language schools, two completed the full sequence of English-language development (ELD) courses, and only one had plans to obtain a general education development (GED) certificate. The other 69 percent developed alternative learning spaces to resist their linguistic marginalization and adapt to multilingual Los Angeles.

Entering English-Language Night Schools

There were two potential pathways to enter ELD night courses. First, posing as being eighteen years or older—the permissible age for enrollment—some teens enrolled in adult English-language schools on the advice of coworkers, neighbors, and peers shortly after arriving in Los Angeles. Several participants said that administrators at these schools rarely believed the minors. However, when I discussed this with a school administrator and a Pico-Union high school principal, they explained that there was an unspoken understanding that work schedules constrained unaccompanied youth, and like employers who would hire minors, school administrators would allow their enrollment.

Given their resource constraints, participants who entered adult English-language schools knew that the learning curve would be steep and that prospects of attaining a degree were slim to none. If they attended class consistently and passed every learning level (e.g., English 1A-C, English 2A-C, English 3A-C) in a timely manner, they could attain their ELD certificate after three years. With a language certificate in hand, young people could then begin independent study for the GED assessment, which, if passed, grants test takers the equivalent of a high school diploma. The GED assessment comprises four exams: reasoning through language arts, mathematical reasoning, science, and social studies.[17] The assessment could take up to seven hours to complete. These steps were daunting. Even if immigrant teens and young adults attained their ELD certificate, they were only minimally prepared for the GED, discouraging many young people from this aspiration entirely. The cost of adult English-language schools ranged from $30 to $60 per month. These conditions produced bumpy schoolgoing and unsuccessful completion of the early English class levels.

In the early years after arrival, as youth were still orienting and adapting to independence, hypercommodified markets, and agency, the negotiation was clear: either work or attend school. Tomás explained that attending an English-language school was nearly impossible without financial support because "no one helped me. I had to pay rent, I had to pay [for] food. Okay, so, either I go to school, and I don't have money for rent or my food, or I don't go to school and have money for rent and to eat." Similarly, Uriel described inconsistent school enrollment for financially independent undocumented youth, whose energy and focus were drained by financial precarity:

> Well, not going to school has to do with the fact that when you come here very young, and you don't have support, you are working. You try to study, but your mind does not have sufficient energy. You only think about work. "I have to pay this; I have to pay that; I don't have enough money."

As with other poor and working-class groups, the youth's decision to attend school to advance their economic and social position often conflicted with the urgency of meeting everyday survival needs. At the same time, not attending school meant it would be "difficult to speak [English]," and speaking English secured young people better jobs, higher wages, and a more promising future because "the bosses like when you can talk with them." Julian's narrative, introduced earlier in the chapter, exemplified this as well.

Oriented to the importance of the English language for any prospect of wage and occupational mobility, most study participants underwent the second pathway into ELD courses: enrollment after several years of orientation and adaptation to life in the United States. When Serafina arrived in Los Angeles from Mexico, she wanted to attend school right away but had to work instead. She connected with two older women from her hometown who allowed her to rent a room in their apartment. Through them, she found employment at a Pico-Union hair salon. Serafina's initial close relationship with the salon owner turned toxic when the latter began exploiting her. She had to work longer hours—from 6:00 a.m. to 8:00 p.m. on most days and some nights until 10:00 p.m.—without additional pay.

Despite her long hours, her employer "told me that I could not earn more than $200 because I didn't have my papers. On top of that, she took out another $50 and said it was taxes." Serafina did not protest because "*Yo no sabía* [I didn't know]." Serafina soon learned that her fellow workers were not "taxed"—her wages were effectively being stolen. Serafina stood her ground, confronted her employer, and successfully reversed the situation, resulting in her receiving higher "untaxed" wages.

Serafina's low wages, her long working hours, and the high cost of school enrollment—$30 per term—proved unworkable for her. Going to school "was a dilemma," Serafina lamented. "My options were to eat or go to school. I know $30 is not a lot, but at the time, $30 was a lot for me. I had to pay rent; I knew that. And I needed to eat; that was necessary." An opportunity arose for Serafina when she secured cheaper accommodation. However, "the reality was that I was alone. I cried. I thought about my family a lot." Serafina's material mobility did not guarantee her emotional well-being. In particular, she missed her family in Mexico.

Additionally, she felt guilt-ridden that she had promised to send them remittances but had not yet been able to do so. Serafina found relief from her loneliness when she met other unaccompanied youth workers at a local church. "I met some friends," she said, "and I started to feel good here."

Serafina's social relationships oriented her to new opportunities for adaptation. She learned about an adult English-language school—the same school that many of the youth in this study also attended. Her increased earnings, fewer work hours, and a lower monthly rent payment enabled her to enroll in school. By the time I met Serafina, eight years after her arrival, she had been attending school for one year. When I asked her if she still had to choose between attending school, paying rent, and eating, she replied, "No, it's easier now." "In what way?" I asked. She proudly responded, "Well, I've paid off my debt, and I am supporting my family. I feel good." Her material stability created new opportunities to reengage in the social relationships most meaningful to her. Serafina's orientation to and agentic navigation of the workplace, and her patchworking of social ties equipped her with skills to overcome the barriers to attending school and making her way through English-language classes. This was the relationship between orientation and adaptation in which youth experienced increased material and emotional mobility over time.

English-language classes, and indeed the English language itself, promoted youth's adaptation by increasing their sense of belonging and confidence in their ability to achieve their mobility *metas*. When I spoke with young adults who had enrolled in ELD night classes, I learned that in the shadow of work primacy, unaccompanied young people set distinct education goals that reflected their primary role as workers. The youth who attended ELD classes adapted their expectations around education and assigned pragmatic meanings to English-language learning. They needed only enough English-language proficiency to boost their economic position, make way for employment opportunities, and enable them to engage in public social settings.

The undocumented workers' English-language acquisition cleared the path for them to get better positions within an industry or enter a new industry entirely. Furthermore, given their primary role as workers, participants developed their own measures for education and their own understandings of what it meant to be educated. Specifically, growing up as workers prompted youth to frame their English learning goals within the social domain of work as entrepreneurial aspirations.

Assigning pragmatic meanings to education helped young migrants envision the application of their learning to their futures as workers, which informed their choice of classes. Twenty-one-year-old Matías also wanted to learn English to become an entrepreneur. Matías, a native Maya K'iche' speaker, learned Spanish as a second language and was adamant about completing ELD courses. For several weeks, he asked that I meet him on Thursday evenings before his classes to review his homework due that day.

One evening Matías asked, "*Chep*, do you know what idioms are?"[18] Unable to make out his pronunciation of *idioms*, I replied, "I'm not sure; give me an example." "Well," he explained, "today I learned what 'cool as a cucumber' is." Matías had passed beginner's English in his adult education program. When given the option of either moving on to advanced literacy or taking a conversational course, he chose the latter. Matías explained that in the short term, he wanted to be able to talk to people in public, but that English would be useful for his long-term plan of owning a business.

Matías often indicated that learning English would allow him to return to his hometown in Huehuetenango, Guatemala, where he planned to open a flower shop near a cemetery just three miles from his parents' home—equidistant from the cemetery to the west and a market to the east. His business location would alleviate the need for his target clientele—burial parties, visitors to the cemetery, and the town's tourists—to walk six miles from the market to the cemetery. He proposed to apply his knowledge of floral arrangements and sales from his work in the downtown Los Angeles flower market and his budding English-language proficiency to build a successful business. His business would initially employ him and his parents and be expanded to a second location, employing his siblings.

In 2018 Matías graduated from his English-language classes with a certificate of completion and posted a photo of himself and his fellow ELD course graduates to Facebook, saying, "I'm so happy because i graduated from ESL (English as a Second Language). Thank you Jesús for helped me."[19] When I last spoke to him in 2020, he was still living and working in Los Angeles. Matías navigated his local and transnational community in a way that opened the possibility of different futures in adulthood, reflecting his life stage and transitions through the life course. This case demonstrates how education—and education as English-language learning—was a means to increasing his status as a worker and caregiver for himself and his family. Even as Matías adapted to life in the US, his *metas* continued to be collectively motivated.

Resisting Linguistic Marginalization

The young people who could not or did not want to attend school recognized the importance of language learning for their mobility and well-being in English-dominant Los Angeles and found alternative ways to resist their linguistic marginalization. This is evidence of orientation and adaptation to the available language-learning mechanisms—formal and informal—within their local community. Given that education became synonymous with language learning, some youth relied on more readily affordable and accessible learning strategies, such as listening to English-language music, podcasts, radio programs, and audiobooks (typically religious) through their earphones while at work. Youth leveraged an array of tools at their disposal to achieve their learning goals.

Aarón, for example, was adamant about his belief that adaptation required gaining linguistic proficiency to communicate "with other cultures." He spoke K'iche', Spanish, and English at different proficiency levels and often enjoyed showing off his English-language skills in conversations with me. Aarón prided himself on being trilingual, especially because he grew up with a stutter that drew the ridicule of his peers and affected his self-esteem. Aarón stopped attending English-language classes after four years because he felt proficient enough to discontinue his enrollment.[20] With the skill he gained, he wanted to share his linguistic ability with others, particularly youth facing enrollment challenges. To this end, Aarón hosted a Saturday afternoon book club in a local community garden. Starting in late spring 2014 and continuing through that summer, a group of five to seven youth would gather between noon and 2:30 p.m. on Saturday afternoons.

The initial focus was on reading and discussing the same book, which elicited a poor response. Aarón changed his approach and invited friends to the garden to read a book of their choice, in whatever language they preferred, and eliminated the discussion component. More young people showed up each week, coming and going as they pleased. Some sat on picnic tables in the center of the garden, while others stretched out on benches in the sun and held books over their faces to shield their eyes from the light. A napper was spotted every now and again, but for the most part, participants appeared to read. One afternoon, as 2:30 p.m. approached, Elías sat beside me at a picnic table and chuckled, "I'm reading a book in English, and I don't know what it says, but I'm hoping the words will stick, and I'll learn something." Another day, a participant shared that he was reading very slowly and did not know if he was sounding the words out correctly in his mind, but like Elías, he hoped some words would eventually become familiar. Whether or not English was learned in this way, youth attempted to advance their proficiency and felt at least somewhat assured that they were not giving up on themselves.

Another creative adaptive learning strategy was a reading group established in 2015 by Zacarías, a Maya man in his mid-thirties. Zacarías was a native Maya Q'anjob'al speaker who learned Spanish in Los Angeles when he arrived as an unaccompanied teen. He later learned English through adult English-language classes. I met Zacarías through Wilfredo in 2014. He rarely spoke—in any language—but when he did, he spoke slowly and softly, which caused his listeners to become quiet and still.

In 2015, Zacarías had the idea of offering an informal reading class, specifically for Maya youth in Pico-Union. Given that many Maya youth worked in the garment industry and that the garment industry's typical schedule was 6:00 a.m. to 6:00 p.m., Monday through Friday, and Saturdays until noon, Zacarías scheduled the gathering for Saturday afternoons. This group, built around youth's needs and availability, contrasted with more formal programs with established curricula and schedules. Instead, it offered youth the manifest function of English-language learning at their pace and the latent function of providing a physical and social community space to participate and belong.

I chose not to attend the Saturday afternoon class meetings for several reasons. I learned through the course of my fieldwork that Maya youth confronted a great many linguistic insecurities. Learning from an older and longer-settled Maya-speaking man likely presented a safer learning environment than the classrooms where youth were ridiculed for their accents. Also, by 2015 the youth I had become more familiar with had begun to refer to me as "teacher" upon learning that I hoped to be a sociology professor one day. I was also aware of Zacarías's shyness; hence, I was reluctant to distract people from his role as their learning guide. Instead, I relied on the youth's descriptions of the group, which they eagerly shared.

The group began meeting in the late winter of 2015, lasted through spring, and tapered off in the summer. In total, about ten people participated in the reading group. Zacarías began his lessons by giving each participant a pocket-sized Spanish-to-English dictionary and explaining how the dictionary worked. He encouraged participants to carry the dictionary with them throughout the week. And they did. I encountered several people with dictionaries on hand and who described using them in conversations. Later, Zacarías introduced the book *Alice in Wonderland*, which had a side-by-side, Spanish-to-English translation. He first read the book in Spanish, allowing the Maya youth to become comfortable with their Spanish-language reading comprehension, and then introduced the English-language translation. Admittedly, the group did not meet long enough for the participants to finish reading *Alice in Wonderland*, which I attributed to the fact that the English-language reading had likely become challenging to complete as the summer days called. These were teens and young adults, after all, and after a full week's work, Saturday afternoons were meant for leisure.

Coincidentally, as I heard about Zacarías's group slowing down, another group of youth garment workers asked me to meet them for biweekly English-language tutoring classes for nearly three months in the spring of 2015. They suggested that our class could serve as a review of material they were falling behind on in their adult English-language school and a learning opportunity for youth who could not enroll in school. Prepared to discuss worksheets and perhaps read together as the other groups had, I was surprised to find that the group was less interested in reading comprehension than in learning to translate and properly pronounce the phrases they used in everyday work and public interactions. The young people's desire for everyday conversation also showed a socioemotional interest in developing a richer connection to life in a new place.

To ease workplace interactions, the group asked to practice phrases like "I have to leave [work] early today" and "I am sorry I'm late." A young man who often saw people leaving a local Starbucks with a whipped-cream-topped frozen drink and wanted desperately to try one asked to practice the question, "Can I have a vanilla bean frappuccino?" Others who relied on public transportation brought questions such as, "What time is the bus coming?" and "What is the next [bus] stop?" Women who joined the Saturday morning meetings asked how to request fitting rooms and "*otras tallas*" (different sizes) in retail stores.

Outside of the classroom, translation requests came in real time. Youth who attended our weekly gatherings regularly called and texted me to ask that I translate words or phrases throughout the day. One example is when a young man messaged me saying, "Hi Stephenie, I have A question. *Que quiere decir* this sentence (What does this sentence mean?). I neglected to tell my boss that I would be late today."[21] The phone calls and texts proved that I had become a mobile resource for youth in uncertain situations outside of the classroom.

After about three months of biweekly meetings, the group slowly ended. One of my greatest disappointments during fieldwork was not securing interviews with the women who attended. However, unlike their absence from formal classroom spaces, their mere presence in the Saturday afternoon group reinforced the gendered nature of community participation. That the women joined the group to learn how to ask for fitting rooms, for different clothing sizes in stores, or how to get directions demonstrated their longing to participate in cultural spaces, enjoy leisure time, and explore their interests through fashion or short trips around town. They desired a more robust social life. Perhaps their attendance had something to do with the flexibility of the space itself, which was not tied to curriculum, exams, or general assessments of competence; perhaps it was my gender that had something to do with their comfort in participating in the space and asking me the questions that might be taboo in public classroom settings. Regardless, the organization and eventual dissolution of the group demonstrated that they, too, were adapting.

As our meetings grew more infrequent, I thought back to one of my first times hanging out with unaccompanied youth workers at a coffee shop in 2012, when a young man left the group and walked to his apartment three blocks away to use the restroom rather than ask an employee for the restroom door code. Adapting to public community life as youth came of age included learning enough English to communicate basic needs and desires and have them met, as well as leveraging any and all resources to do so. Time, social orientations, and linguistic adaptations would allow youth to resist marginalization.

Ethnolinguistic Adaptation in Multicultural Los Angeles

Language learning, and especially learning how to patchwork multilingual Maya-, Spanish-, and English-language skills, was central to young people's adaptation to their expanding social worlds as they were coming of age. Indigenous teens, when navigating hostility toward them, sometimes adapt by dampening or cloaking their Maya identity.[22] This adaptation, scholars find, can take the form of denying one's identity, adopting another ethnic group's cultural practices, or brightening one's ethnic identity and engaging in cultural practices that evoke pride. Maya youth in this study displayed a pattern in which they initially dampened their ethnic identity as they were oriented to the persistence of anti-Indigenous racism in the US. Over time, and through interactions across multicultural Los Angeles, they adapted by brightening their Indigenous identity and culture. As one participant explained:

[Maya youth] arrive with a lot of fear. We do not know if we can speak our language, K'iche'. We think we are inferior to people who are born here. We feel inferior because, well because we are afraid. We are ashamed of speaking K'iche'. People tell you, "Don't speak K'iche'," and then I became accustomed and stopped speaking it.

Because concealing their identity and refusing to speak their native language could isolate youth from their already limited coethnic ties, orientation to multiethnic and multicultural Los Angeles facilitated adaptation by creating opportunities to reclaim and reveal one's ethnic identity. Indeed, time in Los Angeles and exposure to other groups' cultural expressions, including Korean and Korean-American factory owners and non-Indigenous Latin Americans who take pride in their language, food, and celebrations, helped Indigenous youth to openly practice their culture and feel less compelled to cloak their language, food, way of dress, and other cultural expressions.[23] As a researcher, I learned much from this pattern of linguistic adaptation, which provided insight into how active group membership and pride in group identity increased individual confidence and sense of self—especially for adolescents transitioning to adulthood without primary caregivers.

In 2017 I observed instances of ethnic and linguistic pride in the days leading up to Thanksgiving. A group of Maya-speaking young people sat around a table, discussing their plans for that night; I was the only non-Indigenous person present that day. As people discussed the foods they planned to eat, someone mentioned the word *chuchitos*. Since I was familiar with the terms *chucho* (dog) and *chuchito* (puppy), I teased the group about the conversation being mistranslated to mean that some people planned to eat puppies. "It's like *tamales* for Guatemalans," someone shouted through the eruption of laughter across the table. The conversation turned to how distinct Central American cultures used different terms for foods, such as the various

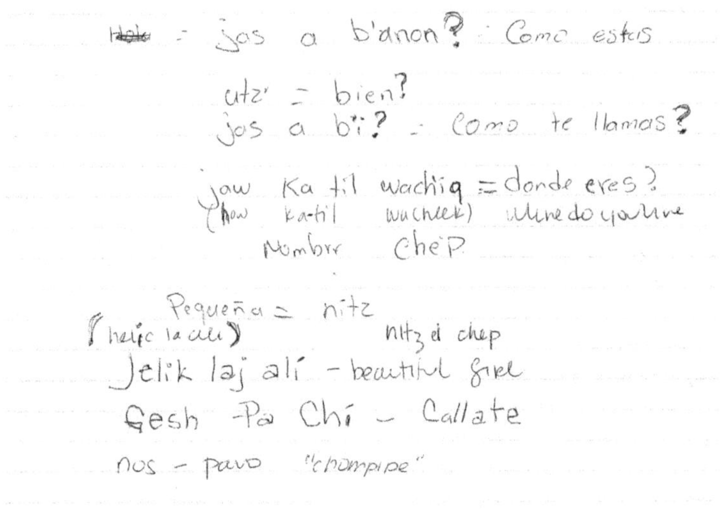

FIGURE 1. Legal pad sheet on which participants wrote phrases for the author to practice K'iche'. Photograph by author.

translations of *turkey*. "We use *pavo* in my family," I said. Youth shared that in Guatemala, their families used *chompipe*, or in K'iche', *nos*.

This conversation prompted one young man to take a yellow legal notepad from his backpack and take notes as the group collaboratively provided words and phrases that I could practice in Spanish and K'iche' (see figure 1). At the end of their lesson, which included the phrases: "How are you?," "Where are you from?," and "Where do you live?," and playful descriptions of me as *pequeña Chep* (little Chep), a young man who had grown fond of me suggested *Jelik laj alí* and said "beautiful girl" with a proud grin on his face. This prompted another to shout "¡*Cállate!*" (Spanish for "be quiet!") from across the room as others roared with laughter. Someone added this phrase to the list of words I should study. As the lesson wound down, I jotted at the bottom of the list the term that had started the conversation in the first place: *nos-pavo-chompipe*.

Participants' ethnolinguistic adaptation reflected their orientation to when and where it was (un)safe to engage with others in public spaces. Perhaps the five years of relationship building leading up to this interaction had something to do with the confidence Maya young people demonstrated in the interaction and the playfulness of the moment we shared. Still, the interaction demonstrates how adaptation to ethnolinguistic diversity within multicultural communities allowed teens who were developing their identities as immigrants and young adults in Los Angeles to establish a sense of ethnic pride. This was critical for Indigenous youth who might have previously experienced social isolation or the stunting of social ties for fear or shame at being identified as Indigenous.

Adaptation to and through Community and Family

Community participation is critical for immigrant adaptation, as it is through community networks that immigrants establish ties that offer material and emotional support. The social ties unaccompanied migrant teens develop through community groups can formulate and affirm their sense of self, identity, and hopefulness for the future in their transition to adulthood.[24] As the previous chapter illustrated, teen workers embodied agency in and through their choices for how to participate in community. Still, youth's patterns of community participation reflected the primacy of work and their role as workers in two ways. First, youth rationalized the cost of nonwork activities and affiliations based on the benefits of their participation in their work activities. Second, they reacted to the limitations on time and resources but abundance of social and emotional gaps in their everyday lives by engaging in groups and activities that met specific needs.

Nicolás's and Patrick's experiences speak to these patterns of adaptation both to and through community. Nicolás was a warehouse worker who adapted his community participation to work. Nicolás joined a martial arts class for $40 per month that offered him a recreational space and opportunities for exploration and discipline. These classes also provided skills that he believed made him more productive in the workplace:

> I practice [martial arts] and have been advancing. Right now, we are training with other youth. We motivate each other. . . . I take that back to work. For example, with that . . . I started earning [more], I think, because of the speed I had in working. . . . I earn more now than I did before [the classes].

Nicolás justified spending time and money on martial arts classes because they enhanced his financial position. He engaged in a recreational activity that promised mobility by increasing his working pace, coordination, and stamina.

Like Nicolás, Patrick also described his interest in martial arts, explaining that he was initially interested in karate as a self-defense tool but became passionate about the sport because "I used to feel, you know . . . less than other people. [Karate] helped me because when I had a problem, I would start to exercise or practice." After practicing karate for three years, Patrick was excited to work at the karate studio and potentially become a karate instructor. Unfortunately, his inability to speak English with other students impeded his aspirations, and an eventual injury forced him out of the sport altogether. Patrick joined a local church youth group in which he developed a new social community called a "family." However, like other youth, he felt the church group did not provide the support he needed.

Nicolás's and Patrick's shared interest in recreational sports led to forming a group that met their social and emotional needs. Patrick described the group as one that "gets together on weekends, and we go to the mountains. We go for runs. We go to the beach and go for runs. It's a group of *jóvenes* that support one another. We teach each other ways to have good, clean fun." Young people resisted the social and emotional disorientation brought on by their household, workplace, and community contexts through establishing peer-led groups. The option to have "good, clean fun" was especially important for unaccompanied, undocumented young men, who, as we will see in the next chapter, might otherwise spend time after work with older adult men who can introduce them to alcohol and drugs, which might then lead to the use of other harmful substances and eventual addiction.

The study participants learned that initial adaptations to community that focused on advancing their material and social position could change over time as they came of age, experienced material adaptation, and developed new interests and *metas* that they were curious to explore. The young people adapted to their changing social and emotional needs by reconfiguring how they participated in their community. Diego, for example, struggled to maintain full-time work and consistent school attendance during his teenage years. He reconsidered juggling these responsibilities after a severe bout of bronchitis, likely caused by hours of steam pressing screen prints onto T-shirts after being soaked by rain on his bike ride to work one morning. Diego weighed this as a near-death experience and was no longer interested in pursuing academic achievements. He wanted to focus instead on attaining a meaningful life, and he adapted accordingly.

Diego left school, joined his local church, and honored his "second chance at life" by playing the piano in a youth group band. Diego's serious illness oriented him to the brevity of life and the value he placed on pursuing his interests; it also heightened his appreciation of the meaningfulness of life alongside a community of peers. The church was a supportive place for him because he entered the church community with a targeted purpose, to learn to play an instrument, and he did so. Even though Diego was not in school, he had a new musical skill, was surrounded by friends, and considered these changes worth it. Sure, he would not gain wage and occupational mobility, but he would fulfill a personal need that bolstered his sense of self and well-being. The opportunity to pursue a path like Diego's may be more accessible for youth without transnational familial ties—in particular, young women—and therefore more liberty to participate in recreational community spaces. Therefore, the more fortunate youth can dedicate their earnings and other resources, including time, to pursuing newly established individual *metas*.

The relationships that young people forged in Los Angeles to and through community, which provided them with material and emotional support—from information about jobs and housing to events in their neighborhoods—and companionship were significant during the times of year most people spend with their loved ones, including on holidays. These relationships notwithstanding, Andrés reflected on missing his left-behind family and the pain induced by loneliness:

> The most difficult times that I've spent in this country are when Christmas and the New Year come. I feel alone. It's not the same to be away from your parents, to not be able to hug them or to share gifts. It's not the same sending money. I feel pain when these moments come. I feel alone.

Referencing his fraught relationship with his brother, who also lived in Los Angeles, Andrés's disappointment was palpable. "I call my brother, and he doesn't answer. That's when I really feel the pain. In those special moments," he said during our interview. Youth with similarly painful experiences established fictive kin ties that granted pleasure, joy, and play among peers who gathered on birthdays and holidays like Thanksgiving, Christmas, and New Year's.

Some years later, during a group dinner organized to celebrate Christmas at a Pico-Union Guatemalan restaurant in December 2016, Andrés shared with the group of nineteen youth gathered: "Before coming to this dinner, I felt very emotional. I felt bad. But I thank you for your friendship. I feel good about myself being with you. I feel happy that I am here." Another young man stood up across the room and said, "We spend our weekends and holidays together to support each other. We miss our families, but we are here and can offer support." Others around the table nodded in agreement.

When young people could not gather in person, they created virtual community spaces. Youth's adoption of digital media corroborates research that found immigrants rely on technology to "maintain complex spatial attachments to both homeland and host country on various different scales of locality" by engaging in "everyday uses of digital media that make them feel physically and emotionally situated with relation to the physical spaces they inhabit and move between."[25] The importance of technology in adaptation processes became more observable over time. Along with using translation apps or websites to communicate in public or accessing podcasts, radio programs, or audiobooks to learn English, young people across field sites used social media apps, which dominated youth culture during my fieldwork.

Throughout Los Angeles and across national borders, young people relied heavily on apps like Facebook to share photos, videos, and updates about their work and school lives and to access information about others. For example, when Matías graduated from his ELD classes and posted a photo on Facebook in 2018, Bianca commented, "*Cuando fue??*" (When was your graduation?), to which Matías responded, "*Ayer fue*" (It was yesterday). Bianca wrote a few minutes later, "*Si wow ayer no vine*" (Yes, wow, I wasn't there yesterday).[26] Despite being an in-home domestic worker on the west side of Los Angeles, Bianca kept up with her community in Pico-Union through Facebook throughout the week. The pair's Facebook interaction shows how youth adapted to the tools available to participate in the community and maintain their social ties to resist isolation and support one another.

For undocumented workers who could neither legally nor financially afford to travel to their origin countries and securely reenter the United States, communication technologies and social media apps became ever more important for adapting to transnational family and community life. Just as migrant teens transitioned to adulthood in the United States, so too did younger siblings in their origin countries. These transitions often called for celebrations like birthdays, weddings, and the birth of new children, which young immigrants from the United States participated in via WhatsApp videos or Facebook livestreams on their mobile phones or laptop computers. There was an emotional toll on immigrant teens who missed out on these family milestones, as well as some financial costs for those who now added new expenses to their remittances list. Meanwhile, parents and grandparents also transitioned out of the workforce and into their older adult years, often experiencing injury, illness, and in some cases, death. The current technologies were especially essential in times of crisis and grief when teens and young adults longed for closeness with family members from whom they did not anticipate prolonged separation.

Smartphones, tablets, and social media technology provided lifelines in times of crisis and grief when teens and young adults longed for closeness with family members they had not anticipated prolonged separation from. I observed this when Gabriel shared news of his father's passing with his Facebook community in mid-2015. Some days later, he gathered with kin and fictive kin to watch his father's procession and burial via Facebook Live and uploaded photos of his father's burial the following day. Two of the images depicted his father's casket being lowered into the ground while at least two dozen people, dressed in traditional Maya clothing, gathered around with heads lowered to honor him. Another photo looked out to the cemetery where his father was buried, with people gathered around crosses and tombstones. In the album's cover photo, an older woman placed white roses over his father's gravesite. Beneath the cover photo, Gabriel commented, "I left my country and said goodbye to my father one day. Today, my dad is underground. How the years have passed. Only a few bouquets of roses to thank you for everything."[27] The words "Rest in Peace Antonio" were set as the album's caption. Like most youth who migrated with *metas* tied to collective imagined futures (chapter 1), Gabriel had not anticipated being in Los Angeles so long that he would not be able to see his father again.

The growth of media technology meant that communicating with families across Central America and Mexico became more frequent. For example, in 2016, when I attended a funeral for a young man who had lost his life to suicide in Los Angeles, young people organized themselves to broadcast the ceremony to a radio station in Totonicapán, Guatemala. And just as Facebook and WhatsApp were prominent means of communication in Los Angeles and with origin countries during my early fieldwork years between 2013 and 2015, toward the end of my fieldwork, youth also started joining Instagram and Twitter. Unaccompanied, undocumented youth and young adults were no exception to the social media culture that researchers have noted as prominent among young people described as millennials and Gen Z in the United States.[28]

While technology offered immediate strategies for adaptation to transnational family and community separation, teens came to be involved in hometown associations—organizations formed by immigrants of the same hometown—as a long-term strategy to collectively cope with the material and emotional fallout of the loss of a loved one. This simultaneously increased embeddedness in their local coethnic immigrant community in Los Angeles and their transnational communities across Central America and Mexico.[29]

Social and emotional adaptation appeared in teens' transition to adulthood most apparently in forming local fictive kin communities and agentic strategies to maintain intimate ties across Los Angeles neighborhoods and transnational borders. Youth's patterns of community engagement effected their primary role as workers, but as workers who are also adolescents transitioning to adulthood who want to have fun, explore interests, feel intimacy, and, in some cases, as youth who are celebrating milestones or grieving the passing of time and the loss of loved ones across borders.

Conclusion

Immigration scholars have long studied youth adaptation and adaptive strategies while coming of age within families and schools, social domains commensurate with the Western normative expectation for their age and life stage. That these are the spaces migrant youth occupy has remained largely unquestioned, empirically and theoretically. This chapter shows that how and to what immigrants, including migrant children and youth, adapt depends on the institutions, social roles and responsibilities, and norms and expectations to which they are oriented. Migrant youth who are oriented to the role of unaccompanied and undocumented, low-wage worker experience adaptation through behaviors, beliefs, and practices that bolster their material stability and emotional well-being as such.

Growing up outside of parent-led households and K–12 schools set youth up to transition to adulthood in various public spaces. Their intersectional social positions as unaccompanied teens and undocumented workers, along with their ethnoracial and gender identities, inform the resources and opportunities youth have access to once in those spaces. Teens' entry into the secondary labor market uniformly produced the condition of work primacy in their everyday lives, but the nature of work primacy was different for Indigenous youth and women, given the ethnoracial and gender hierarchies that intersectionally disadvantage them. Young people's adaptation to life in Los Angeles during their transition to adulthood required adjustment to work primacy through negotiations of work and the workplace and nonworkspaces to make material, social, and emotional ends meet.

Adaptation is thus the stage in migration and incorporation in which knowledge, skills, and resources acquired through orientation are activated to increase material and emotional well-being and the pursuit of belonging. Through ongoing orientation and adaptation processes, youth learn the architecture of their structure of opportunities, from which they set new *metas*, make decisions, and adopt behaviors that allow them to achieve those goals. This was evidence of budding planful competence to agentially negotiate opportunities and limitations in transitioning from newcomer to long-settled immigrant and from teenager to young adult. Teens and young adults demonstrated their flexible adaptability as they deployed financial, cultural, and emotional labor in community spaces, across social ties, and in their multicultural environment to survive in Los Angeles. The teens who could not participate in community in ways that offered meaningful support, however, did not experience social and emotional adaptation. In the next chapter, I show how this threatened teens' material stability and prompted them down pathways of *perdición* (perdition).

5   *Perdition*

I met Adán in an east Los Angeles coffee shop in 2016. He was in his late twenties and cut a striking figure: tall, immaculately dressed, and with well-kempt hair. His cologne was pungent, which made sense when he explained that he sold perfumes and colognes from the trunk of his car as "a side hustle." We chose to sit at a counter near a window facing the parking lot so that Adán could "keep an eye" on his car with his merchandise.

Adán had arrived from El Salvador at age seventeen after his dream of becoming a lawyer was cut short when he became a target of forcible gang recruitment. As threats of violence against him escalated to threats against his mother if he did not join the gang, his fear and shame grew for the danger he and his family were enduring. He decided to migrate to Los Angeles, where he initially lived with his uncle, hoping to work and remit money to relocate his family to a safer neighborhood away from the gangs. To Adán's dismay, his uncle separated from his partner, and the household disintegrated. He was suddenly rendered materially and emotionally independent and underwent orientation to life as an unaccompanied migrant teen.

When I asked Adán what that was like, he relayed many of the themes discussed in chapter 2, including the challenges of finding work and housing, enrolling in school, learning how to manage money, taking public transportation, and making new friends. Without probing, he went a step further. "Depression really affects you a lot," Adán said, "because you don't have anyone looking out for you. I know that the depression that I've experienced in different stages has come because . . . well, it's the same type of depression that different people can feel, but then you pair it with the loneliness [of not having your family here]. I think, more than anything, it's *la soledad y agonía* [the loneliness and angst]." Adán's narrative spoke directly to the deep distress young people feel in the absence of someone to materially and emotionally "look out" for them as they come of age and the interconnectedness of the two forms of care. This starkly contrasts with much of the literature that treats migration as an act of autonomy and individuation from family and parents.

As Adán spoke, he relied on his emergent frame of reference to detail how unaccompanied youth's orientations were qualitatively different based on their household context of arrival. Young people who received a longer-term warm household welcome experienced orientation and subsequent adaptation to a teen's life within an adult-led household and as a student in school. Adán referred to these youth as having *suerte* (luck) as they grew up feeling embraced by their long-settled relatives. This embrace included the material support that enabled educational attainment and the emotional support of *desahogo* from the pain of their childhoods as displaced migrant youth. Some were even orienting to the legal system and adapting to a life of legal protection and social belonging, as observed in Marcos's and Valentina's migration and coming-of-age experiences in prior chapters.

Young people without the *suerte* of having an adult caregiver faced distinct incorporation processes, as they were (dis)orientated to the materially, socially, and emotionally arduous life of an unaccompanied and undocumented worker. In these cases, the difficulties of youth's premigration lived experiences were met with the reality of labor exploitation, the unforeseen stressors of hypercommodified markets, and the material and social constraints of work primacy. The comparisons unaccompanied teens drew between the lives of immigrant and nonimmigrant adolescents growing up with parents or other adult caregivers and their own magnified their sense of deprivation and even feelings of discrimination against them.

Young people like Adán, who maintained transnational ties, worried about their left-behind families who originally motivated their migration but felt increasingly disconnected from them. Sometimes the phone calls, WhatsApp texts, and Facebook posts went only so far. Without intimate connections to loved ones, relationships with parents can become stale, as youth assume the role of financial providers but do not receive a reciprocal exchange of social or emotional support from those they left behind, negatively affecting youth's sense of self and hope for their futures. Adán expressed this, saying, "I felt that I was never going to be able to see anyone in my family." This made relationships feel transactional: "Sometimes you feel like you don't belong to a family. You're only sending people money. It's like, 'Okay, here, here's your money.' That alleviates some stress, but you must keep yourself motivated constantly." Feeling motivated was particularly important for immigrants moving from adolescence to adulthood, who might not be oriented to planful competence in a new society without adult figures and peers to guide them.

Adán elaborated, "If you don't have anyone, then you just don't care. There are so many people that live here alone, and they say, 'No one is watching me. My parents are over there.' You feel a void." Many youth had social ties—to relatives, coworkers, neighbors, or romantic relationships—but these ties did not provide meaningful support and did not mediate psychological and emotional distress. Youth who remained outside of mentor, peer, or other community networks of support lacked the socializers, guides, disciplinarians, and other adult figures introduced in prior chapters who bestow socio-cultural ideologies and values, advice, and care upon children as they come of age.[1] In this way, the void "doesn't only mean, 'Oh, I'm alone,' and then you start to cry. It's also that there isn't anyone to see your accomplishments [and] there isn't anyone to motivate you," Adán clarified. Research shows that these desires are shared by working-class young adults in the United States, regardless of immigrant status, who require witnesses to their lives to validate their achieved adulthood status as a "normative and socially recognizable transition to adulthood" disappears.[2] Ultimately, and as previous chapters showed, for migrant youth, feeling cared for included receiving material support (e.g., having someone "looking out for" you) as well as the social and emotional support of having a witness to one's accomplishments and motivation to pursue one's imagined future.

In the absence of care, "you get depressed," Adán said, "even when you don't want to[;] you fall into a cycle to fill the void." This cycle is one in which the practices youth adopt to quell loneliness and angst in the present and sinking feelings of hopelessness about the future exacerbate their material insecurity and social and emotional isolation. Since adolescence is a period of goal setting and the establishment of behaviors, beliefs, and values that propel youth toward achieving their goals, the potential loss of goals for the future means losing sight of the future itself. Under such conditions, the United States, and Los Angeles more specifically, became what Adán called "*un lugar de perdición*" (a place of perdition).

This chapter relates the stories of unaccompanied migrant youth caught in *perdición*, a phase in the incorporation process born out of persistent social and emotional disorientation—that is, born out of the void of *soledad y agonía*.[3] Without meaningful social ties with which to *desahogar* and establish social and emotional orientation, young people confronted overwhelming feelings of deprivation, precarity, and hopelessness in isolation. To cope, they relied on practices that unwittingly reinforced their material insecurity, emotional distress, and ultimately, the void itself. This feedback loop is where *perdición* occurs. *Perdición* is not sudden but unravels slowly and over time. What's more, it is not an end state but a process that can be reoriented to positive adaptation through the intervention of meaningful material and emotional support from adult figures and peers. Through the support of his peers, Adán was eventually reoriented away from *perdición* and toward adaptation. Many others were not.

In the following I analyze how teens' and young adults' intersecting identities determined their options to fill the void of *soledad y agonía*. Specifically, how sociocultural expectations about men's and women's relationship to their emotions shaped each gender's ability to express their social and emotional needs as well as the social contexts in which their emotional expressions occured.[4] And, because gender mediated youth's participation in public and private spaces, it inevitably also determined what resources—like relationship quantity and quality—young people relied on to fill the social and emotional voids they felt. Young men were more likely to limit their emotional expression and adopt void-filling behaviors and practices that they were exposed to in the public sphere, typically by older single migrant men. Women had more flexibility in their emotional expression but were limited to coping strategies available within the private sphere.

I detail three practices that young people relied on to "fill the void": (1) substance (ab)use, (2) romantic relationships, and (3) suicide and suicidal ideation. I analyze these responses to profound structural disadvantage as reflections of the sociocultural expectations around each gender's emotional needs and acceptable forms of expression. I show that substance (ab)use, for example, was most often discussed by young men who felt deep loneliness but had few options to acknowledge the pain that became a mainstay of their daily lives and *desahogar* from it. Men and women alike sought out romantic relationships to quell their loneliness, but women's disadvantaged social and economic position made them more susceptible to intimate partner violence. Women's attempts to secure companionship often left them more materially, emotionally, and physically isolated and harmed. In the case of both genders, suicide and suicidal ideation were observed among youth who reached a point of extreme isolation and despair, realizing that their efforts to fill the void were futile.

What's clear throughout this book is that the presence of social ties is not enough to promote a positive incorporation process from material and emotional (dis)orientation to adaptation; their quality shapes youth's life chances. I show this in the final section to demonstrate that access to meaningful social ties can intervene in *perdición*. The line between *perdición* and *adaptación* is thin, and positive orientation can alter youth's fate by providing material and emotional resources that offer a sense of companionship, care, and hope for the future.

Sampling Teens and Young Adults Experiencing *Perdición*

Research with teens and young adults in *perdición* was challenging, for several reasons. First, this study relied on recruitment in community groups and participant snowball sampling, which inherently excludes any young people isolated from these networks. Second, periods of *perdición* might have been associated with feelings of shame that they did not have stories of successful material and emotional adaptation to tell. These young people might have avoided me to save face. Hence, to tell this side of the incorporation story, I rely on a select set of stories from young adults, like Adán, who had experienced *perdición* but were reoriented to adaptation through meaningful relationships over time. They also included young adults I observed through ethnographic fieldwork but who were not interviewed, those I knew about only through secondhand stories from key study participants, and others I did not meet whose lives I learned about after their deaths.

Across these experiences, even when not referring to the process of *perdición*, teens were aware of its conditions and expressed
a desire to escape it. This aspiration was often unattainable because
they had few to no resources. In fact, in many cases, teens' *meta* was
to survive *perdición* itself. In *perdición*, in short, youth lost their sense
of self and their sense of hope in the future as migrants and as teens
transitioning to adulthood.

Gendered Options to Fill the Void

Even while optimism exists among immigrants, the forces of origin-
country displacement, acts of migration, and experiences of settlement in a new society ignite feelings of grief and loss of home
country, family, and community ties as well as fear and uncertainty
about the future.[5] Unaccompanied immigrant teens faced an erosive
soledad y agonía—the same heavy emotions other immigrants face
once in the United States. However, young people in this study met
them without supervision and guidance from a parent or adult caregiver—often the first teachers of emotion management—and without
witnesses to their trials and triumphs.[6]

Emotions shaped youth's decision-making and coping strategies
to "fill the void" (e.g., substance (ab)use, romantic partnerships, and
suicidal ideation), behaviors that reflected their orientation to the
sociocultural contexts and milieus in which they were embedded.
These contexts determine scripts about who can feel and express
emotions and where. In Latin America, as in the United States, gender prominently defines emotional expression but is framed in the
former around notions of *machismo* and *marianismo*.[7] In *machismo*,
men ascribe to hegemonic masculine traits, including the expectation that they are unemotional and dispassionate in their expression and do not require emotional nurturing. In *marianismo*, women
are entitled to feelings of longing and sadness, and femininity is

associated with nurturance and interdependence. Women are also expected to act as moral pillars and demonstrate emotional strength within families and romantic relationships.

Sociocultural ideologies around gendered emotional expression leave little room for men outside of trusting social ties to communicate the distressing emotions they feel.[8] In both the origin and destination countries examined here and in countries across the globe, substance abuse provides working-class and immigrant men an outlet for inexpressible emotions and offers disenfranchised men an embodied practice of hegemonic masculinity.[9] With strict parameters on which emotions are permissible for men to feel and where they can express them, research with Latino men has found that as a demonstration of toughness, they commonly engage in substance abuse when navigating trauma and emotional distress.[10] Alcohol and drug use, as this study shows, offers only a temporary remedy and can exacerbate financial insecurity, intensify work primacy, and ultimately worsen isolation.

Conversely, women, who are afforded more emotional expression in private relationships, are discouraged from public behaviors such as substance use when coping with emotional distress, ostensibly to protect their purity and to uphold their position as a source of familial and spiritual strength.[11] Women might enter romantic relationships to stabilize their material circumstances and emotional condition through partnership with men who are better positioned in the labor market, although this outcome is not guaranteed.[12] Painfully, young women who are dependent on romantic partners to fill social and emotional voids are vulnerable to financial, emotional, and physical abuse, which can perpetuate their isolation. Experiencing violence at a young age, lack of legal status, un- and underemployment, and linguistic marginalization, as many of the women in this study did, can make immigrant women more susceptible to intimate partner violence.[13]

When coping strategies are ineffective, and feelings of disorientation persist, young people might attempt to end their pain altogether through self-harm. In sociologist Émile Durkheim's theorization of social integration and the threat of alienation, he concludes that deep emotional distress emerges from "melancholy detachment . . . [in which] the individual isolates himself." [14] Combined with fear and uncertainty about the future, social alienation produces "incurable weariness," perhaps the equivalent of participants' *soledad y agonía*. During the life-stage transition between adolescence and young adulthood, when individuals contemplated their futures, suicidal ideation and suicide itself arose for those who felt overwhelmed by the cumulative pain over their lifetimes and who struggled with their inability to see an end to loneliness and angst in the future. These young people had previously engaged in drug and alcohol use or pursued romantic relationships to remedy the social and emotional voids they felt, without success. After extended periods of social avoidance and withdrawal, the risk of suicidal ideation grew. [15]

Substance (Ab)use as a Pathway to *Perdición*

Substance (ab)use is common among young men of all backgrounds in the United States who are traversing the transition between adolescence and adulthood—an experimental life stage in which addictions can be formed. [16] In my study, instances of substance abuse were most observable among the young men participants. In some cases, substance use was moderate, entangled in recreation and leisure. In others, it led to addiction. Addiction was often tied to teens' and young adults' feelings of being overwhelmed by their emotions. When I spoke to young men who had lost several days or weeks at a time while being in a drug- or alcohol-induced state, they explained that their actions were means for *desahogo*. Indeed, those facing high levels of financial insecurity, such as poor and working-class people, might engage in substance use to cope with such emotions as fear. Drug use among immigrants and refugees might be an effort to medicate symptoms of PTSD and acculturative stress.[17] The financial and emotional stressors of being low-wage, undocumented teen workers in a new society without parents or caregivers to provide orientation or adult figures and peers to provide companionship exacerbated their already precarious situations. But far from being healthy or helpful forms of finding relief from loneliness and angst, such coping strategies created cumulative harm.

Earlier in the chapter, Adán spoke candidly about the social and emotional void unaccompanied teens felt and the strategies youth developed to fill them because he dealt with substance abuse for nearly six years. When Adán lost touch with his uncle after moving into his new apartment in south Los Angeles, he spent his nonwork hours with the three older men he lived with. These men tipped him off to a job as a door-to-door vacuum cleaner salesperson. He did not sell many vacuum cleaners and thus earned very little. He returned home each night exhausted and disillusioned and found his roommates drinking beer to pass the time and to destress from their workdays. He joined them, which corroborates research that shows that adolescents who engage in extensive periods of unstructured peer socializing are more likely to adopt risky behaviors.[18] Eventually the weeknight habit spilled over into the weekends, as the men visited a local bar and nightclub to drink and dance. The distraction and company felt good in those moments, but on Monday mornings Adán felt physically unwell and had depleted his meager earnings. The stress he felt about his inability to make ends meet for himself was compounded by the guilt of not being able to remit money to his mother, whom he had set out to protect.

Adán looked for another job that would increase his wages—and feed his addiction—and eventually found one in construction. These wages were not commensurate with his grueling physical labor as a construction worker, so he accepted an offer to do janitorial work at the nightclub where he and his roommates spent their weekends. While at work, Adán observed firsthand the very cycle of depression, attempts to fill the void, and *perdición* that he was in, and he was oriented to his need for change. During this time he also made friends who shared an interest in music, DJ-ing, fashion, and entrepreneurship. He explained that he and his friends began selling cologne out of the trunks of their cars, typically to other young men who enjoyed nights and weekends out on the town. Such ventures were exciting, kept him "motivated," and allowed him to set a new *meta* of opening his own business. He also learned to mix and produce his own music at home, eventually moving from being a janitor to a resident DJ at the nightclub where he was employed.

Even as Adán broke his pattern of alcohol addiction and income depletion, he watched others struggle to "fill the void" every weekend. "I work *en un lugar de perdición* [in a place of perdition]," Adán said in a concerned tone. "I work in a nightclub, and so many people come there that I always see that they crave the weekends. They work Monday through Friday and party and want to enjoy themselves on the weekends. People want to drink and dance and get drunk, and a lot of them do that." "Another part of it is the money," Adán observed. "They spend money, and it's easy for them. That's why they do what they want. So, I think the depression influences a lot of things." Substance abuse acted as a numbing agent for distressed workers' loneliness that affirmed their masculine identities as risk-takers and adventurous within networks of other men. However, seeking *desahogo* through alcohol or drug use provided only temporary escape and often created more financial pressures, which in turn incited greater emotional distress.[19] Migrant youth were no exception.

Numbing the material precarity and emotional stressors of unaccompanied and undocumented statuses became a mechanism for survival. Samuel, who lived with his brother for three years when he arrived in Los Angeles at the age of seventeen but was left behind when his brother moved out of state, resorted to alcoholism *"por la soledad"* (by the loneliness). He shared that he was *"perdido"* (lost) in alcohol and drugs for seven years. I asked Samuel how he spent his money during that time. He responded, "I would get paid on Fridays, and on Fridays, all my money was gone. I would wake up on Saturdays with ten or fifteen dollars," a pattern that posed challenges in meeting everyday needs over the next week and ultimately exacerbated his emotional distress, causing him to drink more.

Samuel found some relief when he borrowed rent money. "Since I lived with my brother's brother-in-law, he [the brother-in-law] did me the favor of lending me rent because they were family." Although this got Samuel by for the month, he became indebted to his brother's brother-in-law. This added a financial stressor—especially as families felt the social pressure to "maintain a positive reputation" across families and borders. Samuel used the same language of *perdición* as Adán when he said, "Here, you lose yourself. *Es un lugar de perdición* [It's a place of perdition]. People lose themselves." At the time of our interview, Samuel was completing his first year of total sobriety and becoming more involved in his local community church.

Even when youth have social ties to community spaces and individuals within them, the quality of these ties matters in their ability to mediate loneliness and angst. For twenty-seven-year-old Ignacio, membership in a youth group focused on spirituality and morality caused him to feel an increased sense of shame related to his *perdición* in Los Angeles. When I met Ignacio in 2015, he had lived in Los Angeles for eleven years. For two years, I observed him sporadically attend but then disappear from youth group meetings. Each time he rejoined the group, he described either days or weeks lost in alcoholism, saying, "I must start over, friends. I don't know where I have failed." He acknowledged the benefits of consistent attendance at group meetings and participation in its practices, like prayer and worship and reading the Bible. He also recognized that these activities could be the starting point for overcoming his alcohol addiction.

The last time I saw Ignacio, he was sleeping under a bench at a Pico-Union bus stop wearing a soiled white T-shirt, sky-blue denim pants, and white sneakers. When I caught up to the others I was meeting that afternoon at a nearby community garden, they asked, "Did you see Ignacio?" I said yes and that I had never seen him like that before. In response to my surprised expression, one participant said, "We see him like that every few weeks. He's not always there [at the bus stop], but he falls asleep on the street when he's been drinking." Ignacio's loneliness caused him to drink, which reinforced his financial precarity as he was spending his limited earnings on alcohol to "fill the void." This resulted in greater stress and led to more drinking, isolation, guilt, and shame, which he could quiet only with more alcohol consumption.

Surprisingly, Ignacio continued to work in the garment industry each day to ensure his survival and, at least in part, to sustain his addiction. He had not entirely lost his sense of self or his imagined future. His participation in the youth group and his modest participation in his local Catholic church seemed to keep him afloat. Here, Ignacio demonstrated his intention to one day redirect his limited finances to support his left-behind family. Unfortunately, his inconsistent engagement did not move him beyond his addiction as he was not being effectively oriented to the material resources and emotional support that he needed to progress from *perdición* to positive *adaptación*.

Romantic Relationships and the Gendered Risk of Intimate Partner Violence

Romantic and sexual relationships begin in adolescence and grow more serious as young people come of age. In the United States, romantic partnerships and cohabitation are gaining prominence as markers of the successful transition to adulthood, while home-ownership and wealth attainment decline in accessibility.[20] Poor and working-class young adults particularly rely on romantic partnerships to reclaim their dignity and signal a sense of responsibility, morality, and belonging. They might also enter relationships earlier in life.[21] In their longing for intimate attachments and to soothe their *soledad y agonía*, unaccompanied migrant young people often enter romantic relationships with people they meet in the workplace or through local community spaces.

Adán pointed to the prevalence of romantic relationships as a coping strategy. "Sometimes," Adán began, "people come here, and they partner [up] very quickly." He understood the phenomenon as tied to the need for intimate care: "It's because of the same thing[,] because they are trying to fill the void. And then you are without your mom and dad; you need that affection." Relationships can have social benefits, as they affirm young people's gender and age identity and desirability; they also serve as substitutes for the witnessing and motivation lacking from adult caregivers. In Adán's view, men in particular benefit from relationships in this way because "once you have someone that sees you, seeing your accomplishments, then you start to feel like you are doing the right things." This might promote their adaptation, as it allows men to perform their masculinity and gendered social role as leaders and protectors. Few young adult men in this research study were able to maintain long-term romantic relationships, either because men's legal and class statuses hindered their economic mobility and therefore positioned them unfavorably in the dating market or because they kept the hope of returning to their origin countries, where they could partner with someone of shared origin culture and values.[22]

Women experienced relationships differently, as they described romantic relationships that produced *perdición*. Women's disadvantaged social and economic positions, which affect their prospects of legal protection, make them materially dependent on men, increasing the allure of partnership as a source of material and financial security.[23] And because women's social lives are often expected to remain in the private sphere of the home as they are assigned the gendered expectation of household and familial care, women are similarly dependent on men to participate in their community's social life.[24] Once in romantic relationships, young women's material and social dependence and limited orientation to the public community resources available to them increase their vulnerability to potential abuse by limiting their options for escape.[25] Without parental or other adult supervision, unaccompanied girls become hypervulnerable to intimate partner violence compared to women who migrate at older ages or alongside other family members.

Being in an abusive relationship created feedback loops between material and emotional needs and financial, physical, and emotional abuse that reinforced women's isolation and material and emotional needs. Matters were worse for women who had prior experiences of abuse, including sexual assault. I observed this with Delia, whom we met in chapter 3. Delia left Guatemala after being raped in adolescence by a group of men.[26] Later, while migrating to the United States, she was violently raped again. Delia felt unsafe when she arrived in Pico-Union because, as an Indigenous woman, she spoke neither Spanish nor English and felt unsafe in everyday life. In the Los Angeles garment industry, Delia struggled with the pressures of piece-rate work and her inability to make ends meet for herself, repay her migration debt, and send remittances to her mother and younger siblings in Guatemala. Furthermore, Delia feared interactions with men in the workplace and public. She felt trapped and frequently overwhelmed by nearly every social interaction.

Delia suffered from PTSD and found self-responsibility in the United States to be a crushing psychological burden. She related that when she met a young man in the factory where she worked, he convinced her that life could get easier for her once she was married. But not just to anyone, to him. As her betrothed, he promised to assume their everyday living expenses and free up her finances so that she could remit more to her family in Guatemala. Instead, after they married he became possessive and controlling. Their relationship soured, which added tension to the relationship between her and her left-behind family. When Delia unexpectedly became pregnant, her husband discouraged her from working in the factory where they had met. Already fearful of men given her previous experiences of sexual assault; uncomfortable in public spaces given her Indigeneity, dark skin, and accented Spanish; and stressed by her fast-paced piece-rate job, Delia agreed to quit. Her husband had effectively reoriented Delia to isolation from community and family by pressuring her to become a stay-at-home mother.

It took me nearly a year to earn Delia's trust, but she poured her fears out without hesitation once I did. She longed for a caring companion. Whenever I met her at a Pico-Union coffee shop, she had her two-year-old son in tow. She explained that she could not leave their apartment, have friends, or even take her child to activities or play-dates without her partner's consent. Meanwhile, time in isolation caused her to grow more afraid of being in public and interacting with others. At home, her husband had become physically, verbally, and financially abusive. She also struggled with the guilt of having to distance herself from the family she had left behind, as she no longer had personal wages from which to send remittances. Not only was Delia unable to provide the financial resources she had promised, but she also carried a sense of shame and helplessness about being in an abusive relationship, a circumstance that she did not want to share with her mother and sisters. Delia was locked into a cycle of abuse, of *perdición*.

Delia's roles as a wife and mother and the gendered behavioral expectations of those roles, including remaining silent in cases of domestic abuse, created new situations from which she needed to *desahogar*. When a neighbor invited Delia to attend Zumba classes, she found at first a place of unburdening, but even this unburdening was stifled and suppressed with more shame and guilt when peers at church told her that the activity was sinful (chapter 3). Delia's orientation to the sinfulness of her unburdening strategy pushed her back into the privacy of her home, where the abuse continued.

I noticed a similar situation with Inés, who grew up with abusive parents and an extended family that was forced to migrate to survive extreme poverty. Once in Los Angeles, Inés was disoriented by her need to work and the abuse by Thalia, her uncle's wife, at home. Discouraged by her tiring work schedule, unfulfilled educational dreams, and departure from her uncle's house, Inés sought comfort through romantic relationships. By the age of eighteen, Inés was living on her own and in a relationship with a man twenty years her senior who repeatedly physically abused her, leaving her with bruises on her arms and chest and sore muscles across her back and abdomen. During this time, Inés also began to face health complications, including dental issues that caused migraines. On one occasion, she recalled, she "got very sick. My molar was infected, and I had to have it treated. I spent like $1,200. That's the bad thing about teeth: they are very expensive. Now I have another molar that hurts. It hurts a lot. I must start saving money again, but I always work to help my family." Financial obligations and the search for higher pay eventually led Inés to a fruit-packing factory in Los Angeles, where she met other unaccompanied young people from Central America and her home country of Mexico. Among them was a Guatemalan young man whom Inés described as "gentle" and who made her feel calm.

Inés could not control her tears at work one morning after a fight with her partner. The young man she befriended insisted on knowing what was wrong. She remembered his saying, "I want to help you, but if you don't tell me what is wrong, I can't do anything." Inés responded, "It's just that I feel empty inside. I don't know what's wrong with me; it's just how I feel." Her friend offered to give Inés a ride home from work that day, saying, "Calm down, rest tonight, and we'll talk tomorrow." She explained what happened next:

> He left me. He left me there, and I couldn't stop crying. When I got to my house, I kept crying. I felt so bad and didn't know what it was, but it happened to me a lot. I would get to my house, and I would feel something. . . . I don't know . . . I would feel like, like, no . . . like, someone took a piece of me. I was in pain, but I didn't know why. It was inexplicable, but it always happened. Something I did know, though, is that *quería desahogarme* [I wanted to unburden]. I wanted someone to listen, and I would be content with that.

Inés articulated her pain as an emptiness—a void—which she described as overwhelming and inexplicable, and her need to unburden from it. She longed to unburden with her parents, whom she felt physically disconnected from. For Inés, this disconnection was compounded by the fact that her relationship with her parents was strained.

> I think that's what I wanted because the next day, when we [Inés and her friend/coworker] talked, I told him, "It's because I don't get along well with my parents. . . . Take advantage of the fact that you have a good relationship with your parents. If I were you, if I had my parents, I would take advantage. I would give my life for them. You have really good parents. They love you. They are always looking out for you. They always try to support you. I don't know what else you could want. I don't have that. I miss my parents." He asked me, "If you miss your parents, why don't you go back [to Mexico]?" I told him, "I can't go back. I miss them, but I don't get along with them.

That's the difference between me and you. Why would I go if I always fight with them? I feel dizzy when I am with them."

Inés described similar conversations she had with her boyfriend, who often responded by offering to buy her airfare to return to Mexico. She responded to him by saying, "No, I can't go just because I miss my parents. Who will take care of me? Here, I can take care of myself. I can't do that in Mexico."

Inés's story speaks to several interrelated processes that lead to *perdición*. First, the dislocations that prompt youth's migration from origin countries persist in the United States. Despite Inés having educational migration *metas*, her arrival in Los Angeles did not provide an educational incorporation pathway but an entry into work. Second, and relatedly, youth's (dis)orientation to available material and emotional resources significantly shapes their well-being by determining their ability to respond to present needs and plan for imagined futures. Inés felt financial strain, physical pain, and emotional distress that overwhelmed her, but for which she had few outlets. Finally, family separation and social isolation contribute to emotional suppression and instability that keep youth in holding patterns, wherein they seek immediate relief that might cause more harm. Inés's emergent frame of reference—the comparison she drew between herself and her coworker—made her disconnection from family more vivid. Her emotional deprivation, social isolation, and a deep desire to *desahogar* pushed her into dependence on anyone who made themselves available to her. The men she connected with only worsened her feeling of being misunderstood and alone, making her more dependent on those around her for relief. Neither Inés's coworker nor her boyfriend provided viable solutions, but while her coworker was gentle, her boyfriend was violent.

Inés's case also demonstrates how women's relegation to the workplace out of financial need and to the home during nonwork hours in accordance with social norms can limit women's social ties and thereby restrict the flow of information and guidance they receive. Inés's experiences reiterate that it is not just the presence of social relationships but their meaningfulness that determines their potency in leading undocumented, unaccompanied immigrant youth out of *perdición*. Women might more specifically need strong same-gender relationships to offer orientation to women's structure of opportunities and potential gender-specific adaptation strategies, given the constraints on their financial, social, and physical mobility. For her part, Inés relied primarily on men for support: her uncle, her boyfriend, and her male coworker. Misinformed by her uncle and mistreated in his home, abused by her boyfriend, and misunderstood by her coworker and friend, Inés remained emotionally disoriented. She tried to look for help in church, and a friend recommended seeing a therapist to "leave those [feelings] behind," but she struggled to maintain consistent participation in these groups. On her worst days, Inés thought of taking her own life.

The issue here is not so much that women pursued romantic relationships, as this is a normal part of the life stage for this age group and of the life course more generally. The desire for intimacy is a fact of life. And of course the pursuit of romantic relationships is not restricted to women. But because they have less social support and are more financially dependent, unaccompanied and undocumented women may stay in harmful relationships longer out of material and emotional necessity.[27] Moreover, while the legal reforms made possible through the Violence Against Women Act could have been pathways for these women's protection, their isolation from social networks that might have introduced these women to this legal route put the option out of reach.[28] Ultimately, young men like Adán may have more opportunities to participate in the local community to offset the loneliness and reliance on a romantic partner in a way that women, such as Delia and Inés and others in the study, were unable to do.

Suicidal Ideation and Suicide as an End to Loneliness and Angst

Inés was not the only person to discuss suicidal ideation during interviews and fieldwork conversations. My first encounter with an unaccompanied youth's suicidal ideation came from a Voces de Esperanza meeting in February 2013, when Gabriel was called on to greet the group and guide the day's discussion. He described Voces as "*un lugar de honestidad y mente abierta*" (a place of honesty and an open mind), a stark contrast to places of *perdición*. He volunteered to share about himself first, candidly saying that when he arrived in Los Angeles, there were several months when he could not control his emotions. He was overcome with anxiety and depression, and the flood of these emotions triggered thoughts of self-harm. He walked to a freeway overpass in downtown Los Angeles and contemplated letting his body fall over the edge. He recounted that as he stood on the ledge of the freeway overpass, he thought about how miserable his life was, then about his mother and her words to him: "No matter how bad it gets, always fight. Never stop fighting." These words moved him away from the overpass ledge.

In a conversation we later shared in my car as we drove across Pico-Union from one youth gathering to another in 2015, Gabriel told me that he had contemplated suicide a total of three times, always returning to the same freeway overpass. But his obligation to take care of his mother kept his feet grounded. "I could not leave my mom," he said. "She's fought all her life in Guatemala." He thought of how she fought to take care of her eleven children and of his desire to be able to repay her—"If I take my life, who will help my mom?"— powerfully demonstrating the extent to which immigrant youth remain collectively oriented and see themselves as familial caretakers across borders and over time. Even though Gabriel's mother was not in Los Angeles, Gabriel was motivated by her sacrifices for him and his siblings and infused his experiences with similar meaning. He remembered and continued to live by his mother's mantra: "Everything is possible." Gabriel's moral obligation to his mother kept him from following through on his suicidal thoughts. His subsequent participation in Voces grounded his social attachments to the local community in Los Angeles, in which he confided.

The devastation of the pain of separation, the reality of exploitation and poverty, and the disappointment of not being able to fulfill promises made to left-behind families combined to compel some youth to rely on deadly actions to assuage or end their suffering. These forms of distress mounted to the point that three young men in support-group participants' kin and fictive kin networks died by suicide within two months. I attended two of the vigils, and as family and community members told stories to honor their lives, I repeatedly heard people say that life in the United States was not what young people had envisioned for themselves. Unfortunately, the *desahogo* Gabriel experienced was not available to his cousin, who in 2016 died by suicide. Gabriel did not speak about his cousin's passing except on one occasion, when he expressed remorse for not realizing what his cousin was battling through. Yet given Gabriel's history of suicidal ideation, the fact that the two young men had not spoken about their shared struggles likely reflects a gender ideology of male independence and emotional valor that can isolate men and the normalization of suffering within immigrant communities and the paucity of opportunities to escape it.

This point, that the presence of social ties does not suffice to soothe loneliness, was made clear on April 23, 2015, when I attended the memorial gathering of Esteban, a twenty-eight-year-old Maya man. Esteban lived with his brother, his sister-in-law, and their two children.

That afternoon, Esteban's sister-in-law returned home from work and knocked on Esteban's bedroom door and remembered that he had been drunk the two preceding days and missed work. She thought perhaps he was sleeping. Five or six hours later, she returned and knocked on the door again. She used a master key to unlock the bedroom door and, to her horror, discovered Esteban hanging from a hook in his bedroom doorway with a scarf around his neck. I would not learn about this until later that night.

At 9:00 p.m. I received a text message with an address and the note that "one of the *jóvenes* died, and we are going to be with the family." Without asking questions, I went to the address. Upon arrival, I was ushered into the bedroom where Esteban had died. A man to my left leaned over my shoulder and whispered, "We have the custom of honoring the person in the place where they died for twenty-four hours." This was a sacred time for those left earthside to share their joyous memories but also their grief. The room was crowded, humid, and dark, illuminated only by a collection of candles at the center of the bedroom floor. I sat quietly, listening to Esteban's brother and other family members in the room discussing Esteban's loneliness and desperation to be reunited with his family in Guatemala and his drug and alcohol consumption habits. They confessed that they had little help to offer. Esteban was a garment worker who spent his nonwork hours in his bedroom drinking beer and passing the time by watching television and scrolling on Facebook.

Esteban's daily ritual did not alarm those around him—"It's just that we all live like this," someone later explained. Someone asked if he had been depressed leading up to the incident. A man who was circling the bedroom with a red Solo cup collecting donations for the funeral said, "Esteban was always serious. He was always to himself. He didn't spend much time with others. But he'd been this way since we were younger." Presumably a hometown friend of Esteban's, this man suggested that Esteban's "problem" was that he did not go to church—surely a placeholder for any neighborhood organization—which caused his isolation. Perhaps Esteban had a timid personality and quiet demeanor, or maybe he had been socialized to emotional restraint and toughness. Or perhaps the trauma from exposure to persistent material suffering and lack of meaningful social and emotional support caused him to become withdrawn and avoidant. This unresolved trauma and grief might have prompted his suicidal ideation and his ultimate death by suicide.

During the vigil, attendees spoke stoically, as if suffering and death were normalized among them. Again, I heard them say that life in the United States was not what young people had envisioned for themselves, and while some had developed the social ties to cope with disillusionment and to unburden about their loneliness and angst, others, like Esteban, had not. One of Esteban's cousins said, "It's good that we're all here. We have twenty-three cousins here, and being here helps us not to feel alone." The gathering, he suggested, was a reminder of how good it feels to be supported by others.

That night, I contemplated what it meant for a room full of people to be simultaneously present and absent from each other's lives and the financial, legal, and social precarity that made this contradiction exist.[29] I also mourned the fact that Esteban's bedroom window faced a community garden where other Indigenous Maya youth spent their Sunday evenings *"cultivando"* (cultivating) plots of land to soothe their emotional distress through reconnecting with the land, as they did in their rural hometowns. I wondered if Esteban had ever seen the youth in the garden. I wondered if that would have made a difference.

Teetering on the Edge between *Perdición* and *Adaptación*

The pathways to *perdición* are not linear, nor is the outcome assured. Without meaningful social ties, youth can be stuck in long-term *perdición,* but the presence of significant others who provide orientation (and the space for unburdening) is a protective buffer against *perdición.* I observed this and just how fine the line is between *perdición* and *adaptación* in Moisés's case.

Most of the participants I spoke to were in the later stages of their settlement in the United States and could reflect on the early years following their arrival, including how the lack of orientation contributed to their delayed or denied adaptation. Seventeen-year-old Moisés, whom I met in 2015, had arrived in Los Angeles from Quetzaltenango, Guatemala, just three months before. Moisés spoke only K'iche' and stammered when he spoke, but said he understood Spanish. As a child, he had suffered significant abuse at the hands of his alcohol-addicted father, which contributed to his feeling *timidez* (timidity) when speaking to others and *miedo* (fear) when speaking in public. I never conversed with Moisés without one of his friends there as a translator. I tried to do so two or three times but noticed his discomfort. He would not make eye contact, and his body squirmed away from mine. I spared him the physical and emotional discomfort of conversation after that. It was not long before he did not show up to meetings anymore. In the months that followed, Moisés entered a pathway to *perdición,* but he was embedded just enough in a social network that he was able to find an alternative.

In July 2015, I joined nine Guatemalan Maya youth hanging out at a Pico-Union community garden. Around that time, I had made it a habit to drop by on Saturday afternoons as the Los Angeles weather warmed. Youth were scattered across the garden on picnic tables and the ground, playing with their phones, listening to music, and reading books. Caleb was among those present. He noticed me sitting at a picnic table at the garden's center and came over to talk. We joked for a few minutes before other *jóvenes* soon joined us at the table and began their own conversation.

The group talked about their interactions with Moisés the previous week: "*Lo vi afuera de su trabajo el martes, pero el siguiente día no regreso* [I saw him outside of his job on Tuesday, but he didn't return the next day]," one young man shared. "*Lo vi en la parada del bus* [I saw him at the bus stop]," said another. While they sought to determine Moisés's whereabouts by triangulating their sightings of him, Wilfredo, the Voces de Esperanza leader introduced in chapter 3, arrived at the garden. With his usual green canvas messenger bag slung across his chest, he placed one arm above his head on a nearby tree and only listened as the others speculated.

Wilfredo intervened after several minutes. "We've spent a lot of time today talking about Moisés," Wilfredo said as he prepared to set the record straight. "Well, it seems like ten days ago, Moisés didn't have *suficiente dinero para la renta* [enough money for rent]." Moisés, who was living with an older uncle and a male cousin, was sent out to pick up a money order of "$750 or $800, and he didn't have his 200." Moisés was responsible for his own share of the rent and tried to get help in putting the $200 together. He was unsuccessful. He took the money his uncle and cousin had e*ncargado* (made him responsible for) plus the little bit of money he did have—which some suggested was less than $100 based on their conversations with Moisés about how much he earned per week—and purchased alcohol. Too ashamed to return home, Moisés had spent a total of ten days on the street. He was intoxicated most of the time, Wilfredo explained.

Héctor interjected that he had seen Moisés "on Union and Eighth" and that "*se veía negrito*" (he looked black) from being covered in dirt. Moisés noticed him from across the street and yelled out to him, "Héctor!"—which Héctor reenacted with his arm raised and hand waving in the air—"Do you know where Flaco is?" Héctor explained that he had called Flaco (a nickname one of the friends was given for being tall and thin), and Elías, too, as if to convince the group that he had tried to help Moisés. "They didn't answer my call," Héctor confessed. Héctor had then called Caleb, who was out celebrating Jorge's birthday with Wilfredo at a nearby restaurant. Caleb, Jorge, and Wilfredo had planned to meet Héctor and Moisés but would need to finish their lunch first.

Wilfredo took over the story from there, detailing that "one hour [had] passed" between the time of the call and the time the guys finally showed up to talk to Moisés. Wilfredo had asked him what was wrong. Moisés, visibly distressed and tearful, had explained in K'iche' that he did not have his rent money. Caleb had translated for Wilfredo and Jorge. Wilfredo admitted, "My heart broke," because Moisés never gave the impression that something was wrong. In essence, Moisés had not unburdened. Bianca, a Salvadoran woman who worked as a live-in domestic worker in west Los Angeles and was accustomed to catching up with friends only on the weekends, interrupted Wilfredo to ask if Moisés had family in Los Angeles. Wilfredo said he did. He turned to Flaco to tell this part of the story. "Moisés's uncle told him that he needed to leave the house, and they did not care if he died in the street," Flaco said in a monotone, as if unsurprised by the callousness, if not outright violence, of this comment. Flaco seemed to want to make sense of his friend's behavior and began speculating about how emotional disorientation might push young people toward maladaptive strategies that offer immediate relief for their pain. "I think his uncle's rejection caused him a lot of pain," Flaco continued, "and he has been drinking since."

The group was dejected. There was nowhere to go from there. Wilfredo reminded the distraught group huddled around a picnic table in the Pico-Union community garden that this was an opportunity for the *jóvenes* to begin to focus on themselves. He urged them to be honest with themselves about what they were facing, to be honest with others, and to ask for help.

The following Friday evening, the *jóvenes* who had been at the garden the previous Saturday were joined by a few others at a Pico-Union community center to reflect on their week in a Voces de Esperanza gathering. A few had seen Moisés the night before (Thursday) and talked about how seeing him affected them. Andrés was motivated to try harder in school and learn new things to help others when they struggle. Héctor admitted that he was afraid to see Moisés and to come face-to-face with the reality of how easily one could slip from stability to instability and from having housing to being unhoused. Caleb reflected on when he and Moisés worked in the same building and had lunch together. He recalled a conversation about income and Moisés's reassurance that he made "good money," only to learn through a mutual friend that Moisés made only about $100 per week despite working twelve hours a day, five days a week and half days on the weekends. At most, he was making $2.35 per hour, Caleb speculated. On his income, Moisés was paying back his migration debt ($9,000), remitting some money to his mother and four siblings, and paying rent of $200 per month. Others shook their heads as they listened to Caleb; they understood this financial burden all too well.

Flaco had "never felt this sad to see someone on the street before." He was "very affected" by seeing his close friend in this condition, saying, "Moisés is like my brother. We spent a lot of time together." Flaco confessed that he knew a bit about Moisés's problems but was unaware that Moisés could not meet his responsibilities. He asked the group, "Was there something I could have done to make things better or help Moisés find a solution?"

Wilfredo pondered the same question, sharing that he often found Moisés sitting alone at a nearby church, playing with his phone. Wilfredo would talk to Moisés and invite him to share a meal. But because Moisés was "80 percent K'iche'," it was difficult for them to communicate. Still, there was warmth between the two. Moisés hugged Wilfredo tightly each time they crossed paths. "He said I was like his father," Wilfredo reflected, which evoked sadness because he could feel a "longing for a parent's affection in Moisés." Several months later, as Adán explained the pains of *soledad y agonía* to me in an East Los Angeles Starbucks, I thought of Moisés and his peers' concerns about his fate.

At the time of this Voces de Esperanza meeting, I was unaware that a handful of the group's participants had gathered the night before to take Moisés to an Alcoholics Anonymous (AA) shelter in South Los Angeles for a few days. Wilfredo shared with the group that he planned to take Moisés to another shelter that could help him for up to two years, providing food, clothing, housing, language classes, and job placement. Usher sat quietly as others shared. I thought that perhaps he had not taken part in the events involving Moisés and, like me, was only catching up the next day. To my surprise, Usher confessed that Moisés had tried to hug him the night before to say goodbye as the group dropped him off at the AA shelter. But Usher stepped back to dodge the hug, explaining that Moisés was "so dirty," and Usher, who cared very much about his appearance, did not want his white T-shirt to be soiled. It seemed that Usher made this confession to get it off his chest, to *desahogar* from the guilt he felt. Usher continued to say that others hugged Moisés and felt sympathy for him. Caleb spoke up, in response to either Usher's regret-filled confession or Moisés's experience: "I am realizing that we can be our own worst enemy."

Migrant teens understand that unexpected moments of material hardship, social isolation, and overwhelming emotions, like unforeseen moments of material and emotional support, can be the difference between *adaptación* and *perdición*. Social and emotional support is important in diverting youth from *perdición* and toward *adaptación*. This certainly resonates throughout Wilfredo's appearances across chapters, but here, it shows up in how other young men discussed Moisés and their desire to help him. Over time, and in the transition to adulthood in the United States, participants became oriented to their capacity to support their peers' *adaptación*, sometimes even standing alongside the significant adult figure in their own lives to become supportive figures for younger unaccompanied migrant teens. The ability to support others builds youth's positive self-concept in their transition to adulthood and becomes a marker of their orientation, adaptation, and incorporation.

Conclusion

Attending to the simultaneous processes by which these young people adjust to their lives as immigrants in the United States and the transition to adulthood sheds light on the intensity of feelings of loneliness and angst that unaccompanied migrant teens navigate daily. It also reveals that incorporation is about socioemotions just as much as it is about socioeconomics. Lacking meaningful social ties meant being locked out of relationships through which information about jobs, housing, and opportunities for community participation is shared, as previous research suggests, but it also meant lacking the social and emotional space to unburden from anxiety, fear, stress, and isolation. This is essential for all people, but especially those in the critical life stage between adolescence and young adulthood. Young people coped with their emotional distress by adopting socially acceptable practices that offered immediate relief through numbing and companionship or escape from the indefinite nature of emotional distress through self-harm. These practices reproduced harm by worsening material insecurity and social isolation. This is the feedback loop that moves the process of *perdición* forward.

Traditional immigrant incorporation theories might consider *perdición* and practices youth adopt in *perdición* as evidence of a downward incorporation outcome marked by deviance and risky behaviors. However, by understanding it as a process in which emotional disorientation destabilizes one's already precarious material position, exacerbating emotional distress, we can turn our eyes to the systems and structures that originally cause the disorientation itself. Most noteworthy is the US immigration policies that displace child migrants, block family migration, disempower immigrant families across generations, and weaken receiving households' ability to provide a materially and emotionally supportive welcome upon arrival, ultimately isolating youth in their *soledad y agonía*.

As a process, there is no singular intervention point to *perdición*, but the possibilities of intervening by introducing meaningful social ties to adult figures and peers who act as witnesses and motivators and offer a sense of accompaniment and belonging are ongoing. I return to the implications of these takeaways in the book's conclusion. For now, I turn to how the migration and coming-of-age experiences cataloged across this book, including those of orientation and adaptation and disorientation and perdition, shape how young people make sense of the meaning of success in young adulthood.

6   *Success*

The United States was in its second year of persistently high rates of unaccompanied child apprehensions at the southern border when I was finalizing interviews for this project in the fall of 2016. Donald Trump's presidential campaign was in full swing, and his vitriol against Latinos, including unaccompanied Central American and Mexican children, was constant and increasingly feverish.[1] In several speeches, he referred to Mexicans as "bad *hombres*" and Central Americans as criminal threats to American families. He ignited his base with promises to build an "impenetrable, physical, tall, powerful, beautiful southern border wall" and to militarize the border against a hyperbolic enemy invasion spearheaded by caravans of unsavory Central Americans.[2] Once in office, the Trump administration immediately began dismantling DACA, doing away with the asylum system, and rolling back protections for unaccompanied children. Family separation was used as a deterrence tactic, and Trump's attorney general, Jeff Sessions, referred to unaccompanied children as "gang members who come to this country as 'wolves in sheep's clothing.'"[3] Throughout his presidency, Trump enacted 472 administrative changes to the immigration system.[4]

While my field sites buzzed with conversations about the more recently arrived children and their fates, many people expressed that they were baffled by the hostility toward migrant children. Participants related to the children at the border. They knew well the desperate conditions, both material and emotional, that prompted children's migration. Growing up in Los Angeles as unaccompanied teens who did all in their power to ensure their survival—and in many cases that of their left-behind families—people in my field sites were also dismayed by the portrayal of unaccompanied migrant children as deviant criminals. These young people had left their countries of origin with distinct *metas* for their personal and family's imagined futures. And despite their hopefulness about life in the US, they experienced intense material and emotional disorientation upon arrival and in the initial years following migration. Over time, and alongside adult figures and peers, some youth came to know ongoing orientations and adaptations to their social roles and responsibilities, the norms and values of US society, and their agency, all of which expanded their social worlds. *Perdición* occurred for those bereft of meaningful social ties, but *perdición* is never what youth aspired to. Those who experienced it and made their way out celebrated their escape; those caught in the throes of *perdición* felt immense shame. To the best of their ability, they engaged in the incorporation process through orientation and adaptation in the transition to adulthood. In several communities I observed, study participants urged me to look around: they and their peers were simply not who the public assumed they were, nor were they the criminal actors politicians warned that today's children would inevitably become.

During interviews, many agreed that their lives directly contradicted the messaging the American public was receiving about the potential threat of unaccompanied child migrants following the humanitarian crisis in 2014. Patrick was adamant about this. "Many people talk about how we are," he asserted. "Many people say that we don't work or that we come here to make trouble, but that's not us."

I nodded and leaned forward, placing my right elbow on the table in front of me and my chin in the palm of my hand. "Why do you think that happens?" I asked him with genuine concern. Patrick continued:

> Sometimes people see one person [doing something bad], and they think that that's everyone. But we invest our time in positive things, not, well, not in things that bring negative consequences. A lot of us do many different things to be able to help other people. We are trying to help our families. We are trying to support one another. We also try to teach others that we are not here to do bad things.

In the US, a neoliberal capitalist society, where the promise of legal protection and social inclusion is conferred on immigrants who reach the narrow and static socioeconomic markers of incorporation (e.g., high educational attainment, occupational mobility, and wealth accumulation), unaccompanied, undocumented youth workers are left in the margins. Social scientists who rely on similar indicators of successful incorporation and transitions to adulthood might cast these young people off as destined for the "underclass." But when you talk to young people like Patrick, they articulate a different image of success, one that reflects the notion that incorporation is an ongoing process of orientation and adaptation and that, as a process, achieving incorporation in the transition to adulthood is subjectively defined by individual and social responsibility.

In Patrick's view, he worked to support himself, which refuted the false assumption that he and immigrants like him were lazy or unproductive, but he also gave back. He gave back to the family he had left behind, he gave back to his local community, and he sought to influence the social world around him positively. To Patrick and other unaccompanied and undocumented low-wage youth workers portrayed in this book, they could give back precisely because they had achieved status mobility. However meager this mobility looked from the outside, it stood in opposition to unaccompanied migrant youth's portrayal as threatening in the media.

Research shows that marginalized groups resist notions of inferiority by constructing alternative identity narratives.[5] Among these narratives is the giving-back frame, which allows immigrants and people of poor and working-class backgrounds to refute claims about their immobility and exclusion and instead imbue their everyday lives with meanings of hard work, personal growth, and moral self-sacrifice.[6] Giving back is a sort of currency, evidence of marginalized groups' and individuals' productivity and positive contributions to local and transnational societies within a moral economy of deservingness, defined as "a site in which social actors demonstrate a particular kind of behavior and/or adhere to a particular set of values and ideals in exchange for rights, resources, and or/recognition."[7] As they were growing up, my study participants were working to understand themselves as deserving of material stability and emotional well-being despite not having formal legal status, high levels of educational attainment and degrees, or other forms of socioeconomic recognition, and in the shadow of the xenophobic rhetoric launched against them.

The remainder of this chapter details how notions of individual and social responsibility, especially within the giving-back frame, were leveraged to articulate unaccompanied youth workers' successful incorporation while coming of age. Giving back signified ascension into an achieved status of material stability and emotional maturation through orientation and adaptation. I analyze how young adults embodied success through local giving-back practices in the first section, then turn to examining giving back across transnational societies in the second. I show that locally, giving-back practices and beliefs reflected the reframing of migration *metas* within the limited structure of opportunities available to unaccompanied and undocumented teens in Los Angeles society. To highlight their increased material stability in young adulthood, participants pointed to new skills learned over time, the products of their everyday labor, and the establishment of entrepreneurial goals for the future as subjective markers of success. Meanwhile, community service with neighborhood organizations and increased capacity to mentor and guide their unaccompanied peers and other compatriots served as evidence of emotional maturation through orientation and adaptation. Giving back locally showed that teens and young adults had progressed from (dis)orientation to adaptation, away from *perdición* and toward making meaningful contributions to their communities through the guidance and social support of newcomers and long-settled coethnics.

Giving back to transnational communities, just as in the local community, positively informed participants' construction of moral identities as successful immigrant young adults. Because mastering individual responsibility in Los Angeles took such great effort, given youth's low wages, the high cost of living, and the everyday material and emotional hardships of growing up as unaccompanied and undocumented low-wage teen workers, the ability to maintain material and emotional transnational ties proved to migrant youth and their families that they were moral, responsible, and committed members of the transnational family unit. This was especially the case when older siblings had tried and failed to better a family's economic and social position before my study participants' migration. To many, these young people had achieved the impossible.

Teen and young adult workers in Los Angeles indicated that their transnational success was hard won, as it often came at the cost of personal mobility goals in the US. Participants relied on the giving-back frame to dignify the potential setbacks or deterrence they negotiated in attaining individual *metas*. Children's sacrifices evoked joy and pride in their parents, who could not watch them grow to become materially stable and emotionally mature young adults. Parents deemed their unaccompanied migrant children successful in fulfilling promises to their left-behind families, which mattered to participants' sense of achieved status. But the story doesn't end there. Demonstrating the persistence of futurity of migration and coming of age in young adulthood, the young people with transnational ties often detailed new imagined futures wherein their transnational material and emotional attachments would change and in which their subjective markers of success would eventually evolve. Still, what this chapter will show is that, in both local and transnational contexts, giving back demonstrated the successful assumption of the caregiver role in the transition to adulthood, which allowed participants to claim a moral identity that directly resisted any portrayals of unaccompanied youth as dependent, unproductive, and deviant. I turn to these narratives next.

Embodying Success through Local Giving-Back Practices

Unaccompanied youth workers pointed to the economic and social contributions they made to American society generally and the neighborhoods and communities that they participated in across Los Angeles specifically to mark their success in the US context. Their economic contributions included the construction of buildings, the sewing of garments, and their plans to establish businesses to employ coethnics under better conditions in the future. Their social contributions included becoming mentors and guides for newcomer immigrants, including unaccompanied teens, which they had longed for upon their arrival. Giving back to their local society—economy, neighborhoods, and communities—was evidence that young adults had successfully navigated processes of orientation and adaptation.

Everyday Contributions through Work

The passage of time allowed youth workers to make material contributions to the Los Angeles economy and community in their transition to adulthood. These contributions informed their claims making about social and emotional embeddedness in Los Angeles life. This was evident in Wilmer's framing of his belonging in US society as based on his accomplishments as a construction worker. Wilmer arrived in Los Angeles from Honduras at the age of sixteen; he was nineteen when we met. He asserted that his labor as a construction worker and his direct involvement in producing commercial buildings across Los Angeles were tangible evidence of his contributions to Los Angeles and his utility within the economy and society. "I am contributing to this country when I work in different places, like constructing buildings," Wilmer said. "Immigrants are building the infrastructure of this country. They are making the country grow. Making the country grow is what makes someone part of the country." Although Wilmer needed to work to survive—and was only barely surviving on his meager earnings—the completed products symbolized his success.

Most young adults in the study could not cite grand symbols of their contributions, like Wilmer, who could point to specific commercial building projects he worked on in neighborhoods surrounding Pico-Union, where he lived. Instead, they spoke of their quotidian but consistent contributions to the local society and the commitment and skill required to make such contributions. Samuel, who had spent seven years in *perdición* due to alcohol addiction, had very little in terms of material accomplishments to call on but exemplified how young adults can leverage the products of their everyday work as evidence of their giving back within their local community and, ultimately, as indicators of success. Samuel remembered that when he "got here," he "didn't know anything about garment manufacturing." Since Samuel's older brother already worked in the same factory, the floor manager "gave [him] one week to learn. And after that week, I started working. My first paycheck was $90 [for a week's work], but I liked it." As Samuel learned, he enjoyed it so much that he began to see himself as an artist. He spoke with pride about the "art" (garments) he made that required technical skill to operate machinery but also "*un ojo*" (an eye) for design and measurements.

To make sense of how one could enjoy a job that required sixty hours of labor for an end-of-week paycheck of $90, I asked Samuel what he liked about the work. Samuel replied by talking about garment making with an air of romance. He enjoyed "the art of constructing a garment," he said:

> It's all cut into pieces, and there is nothing there. It's an art to put it all together. It's a sort of puzzle, and I like putting all the pieces together each day. I enjoy it, and that's why I've stayed. It has motivated me to learn English. I want to learn what I need to become a designer. I have that goal now because I like it. I like clothes.

Samuel converted his everyday tasks into training sessions through which he gained designing skills and knowledge to implement as a garment factory owner one day. Although research shows that altruistic business start-up motives do not always result in greater ethnic solidarity, Samuel planned to employ coethnics in his future factory to provide better work conditions, hours, and wages.[8]

Samuel and others also talked about how their work contributed something real to everyday life in Los Angeles. From award-show red carpets to the clothes on their backs, young adults saw their work throughout the city, affirming that they contributed a vital function and resource to the people and culture of Los Angeles.

Unaccompanied immigrant youth working in the garment industry resisted claims of being uneducated and unskilled by detailing the tenacity and artistry necessary to sew a straight seam, embroider tops, or bead satin gowns. This work, many youth sought to emphasize, was brutal and exploitative, but their continuous labor displayed their dedication to contributing to US society.

The ability to give back to local communities put young adults' strides in material stability and emotional maturation on display. This was success embodied in and of itself, but the practice of giving back, of "serving that place where you live," also informed young adults' positive self-concept and directly contradicted the negative discourse about immigrant youth arrivals as deviant criminals, un-American, and nonbelonging.

For Samuel, this took the form of being involved in a church youth group that volunteered at local community centers for socially marginalized groups. "Aside from being part of the group of *jóvenes*," Samuel explained, "I go to help special needs kids." He elaborated:

> We go to teach them and help them study [at church]. In the evenings, we visit the nursing homes to visit older adults. It's such an experience; sometimes it's happy, sometimes it's sad. It gets sad because you see so many people abandoned there, but they are so excited to see us there, too, to be with them. It's such a nice experience. Sometimes, we do fundraisers to help people who need to go to the hospital, so they are not alone in that, and we help them.

I was intrigued by Samuel's commitment to serving his local community and compatriots after spending seven years in *perdición* marked by social isolation, substance abuse, and financial precarity. He seemingly jump-started his adaptation through community service guided by a church youth group program. When I asked Samuel about his motivation for this volunteer work, he responded, "It helps me personally, too. It helps me mature in areas where I have struggled." Samuel was attuned to how giving back returned to him as motivation for continued material and emotional well-being. "I like being in this city. I like where I live," he said in a commonsense way, implying that giving back was his way to show his affection toward and appreciation for the place he lived.

Young adults came to see a dual-sided relationship between themselves and the city. They contributed to Los Angeles, but the city and time in the city also contributed to youth's coming of age and maturation of self and identity. Samuel explained:

> You become a part of a place when you dedicate yourself to serving that place where you live. That's what makes you part of it. That's what makes me part of America and the United States. Where you live also becomes a part of you, too. I've lived half of my life here. I have been here for half of my life. I feel a part of this place because I know so much about it. I have learned the traditions. I have had experiences here, and those will stay with me. Your [life] experiences make you who you are, and my experiences in America make me American.

Wilmer's and Samuel's experiences show that as unaccompanied, undocumented youth labor in the moral economy of deservingness, they are also engaged in a process of what Pierrette Hondagneu-Sotelo and colleagues refer to as "homemaking" and what Jennifer Bickham Mendez and Natalia Deeb-Sossa call "place-making," both of which enhance feelings of belonging through attachment to place.[9] This research shows that engagement in "public activities" gives low-income immigrants "attachments to place and constructed feelings of 'being at home,'" which counter potential earlier feelings of disorientation and indicate success.[10]

Embodying Success through Role Modeling

The embodiment of successful incorporation in the transition to adulthood was made especially real when young adults used their experiences of (dis)orientation and adaptation or recovery from *perdición* to role model and give social and emotional support to newly arrived and long-settled compatriots. As we dug deeper into Samuel's giving-back beliefs and practices, he elaborated on how his experiences in *perdición* motivated his efforts to give back. Using his past experiences and hope for the future to frame his motivation, he said:

> I am against delinquency, and I don't want kids and teenagers in the future to get caught up in alcoholism and all of that because I have that experience of drug addiction and alcoholism. That's what leads to violence. So, I want to help the community be safer. I want it to be a place where people could go for a walk at two in the morning if they wanted to. To go for a walk and not be afraid. Maybe it's just a tiny grain [of sand] that I am contributing, but I am doing something.

Role modeling was an important giving-back practice that marked successful incorporation, as it indicated to young adults their mastery of orientation and adaptation and ultimately enhanced their feelings of belonging. Whereas women noted the importance of youth guiding one another, such as when Serafina referred to young people in her community working "like little ants" to support each other, men often took on leadership roles in the Pico-Union community. The reading groups and book clubs that Zacarías and Aarón initiated in 2014 and 2015 serve as examples. These were educational groups, but young men also started recreational groups like soccer, running, or hiking clubs. Indeed, Nicolás and Patrick joined forces and used their experiences participating in various groups across Los Angeles to dream up a new kind of community. Patrick shared:

> [When I was in the] karate classes, I formed a family. I also had friends there and met many kids I taught in my classes. I liked to teach them, but I also had a problem there because the owner was Korean, so a lot of the kids there were also Korean, and they spoke English, and I couldn't speak with them. I couldn't explain what they needed to do. So [the owner] told me, "Come back when you can explain things well." I started attending church [after that] and formed another family in that group. It's a family and friendship that I like because we try to help one another. When we come from another country, most suffer because no one helps us. We need to distract ourselves a little, and that's what we do in that group. When we are facing problems, when we are sick, they support us. And, well, because of that, I like to be in that group.

In a separate interview, Nicolás explained:

> It's important to grow spiritually and get that education, but there is a different reality outside of the church. So many people suffer here. Like I told you, people suffer from loneliness, and no one helps us. People suffer because they don't feel loved, so they go to drugs. They go to alcohol. The people who earn just a small amount don't have enough for their expenses. People get mistreated, like I have been mistreated. They get sad, so two or three friends will all invite each other to drink beer, and they throw themselves into addiction. So, I started thinking, we sacrifice so much; we leave our dad, mom, and brothers. Some people leave their lives and kids. They get here, get into debt, and then end up with addictions. So, this is why I'm telling you that I think about the reality of what's happening around me. It's very complicated because there are really so many people suffering.

So, what we do—you know, the character I've built—is trying to help other *jóvenes*.

For example, in the garment industry, you earn more money if you can work faster. How do you work faster? You must be able to do many things with your hands and your feet. You must move quickly. In construction? It's the same. "Hand me that," [mimicking hammer sound], "Pam! Pam! Pam!" When you are fast, when you are strong, you can do it. That's what I invite *jóvenes* to do.

Nicolás and Patrick thoughtfully shared how their experiences in community spaces across Los Angeles revealed their and other immigrants' longing for social embeddedness and belonging and their care for the individual and collective futures of the people involved. Patrick expounded on this care:

Doing these [positive] things will be useful for us in the future because we are doing exercise. We stay healthy, and it helps us with other things. When we started the group, there were maybe five of us, and then four months later, there were fifteen people. Now it's like thirty people. It's thirty *jóvenes*.

Surprised by the size of the group, I asked, "Wow, thirty people every week?" Patrick smiled, nodded vigorously, and said, "Yes, every week. *Jóvenes* and women, too. There are even older men with us who like what we are doing. We ask them why they spend their time with us, and they say, 'I feel good being with you because you are doing something good here.'" Patrick and Nicolás had captured the attention of community elders and felt pride in fostering a community of solidarity and reciprocity. After I congratulated him on this accomplishment, Patrick continued, "Yes, this is why these groups get together. In church, it's the same thing. In church, they talk about God because, well, that sort of thing is important for us. The group gets together on Sunday mornings every week, welcoming everyone that hopes to join the group for a distraction."

Young people like Nicolás, Patrick, and various others thought their role modeling could save newcomer unaccompanied children and youth and others, perhaps young adult or adult immigrants, against disorientation and *perdición*. For young men, especially, disorientation and *perdición* included addictions that stole years of their lives, depleted their resources, damaged their health, and deterred the achievement of their migration goals. For example, twenty-eight-year-old Jayson stated that after fourteen years in Los Angeles, he regretted that he had "fallen" into addiction. Motivated by his desire to compensate for lost time and opportunities, he celebrated overcoming his addictions by giving back in the form of supporting his family and mentoring newcomer youth. Jayson's acts of giving back reflected his future aspirations and served as determinants of his successful incorporation. "My responsibility now is to take care of my family, to give them a better life," he said of his desire to give back to his family, as initially intended. He added, "Well, apart from that, my responsibility now that I've come out of my addictions is to talk to other kids that are here because there are still so many [struggling with addiction]." Hoping to use his experience as inspiration, he felt compelled to guide young people, steering them away from *perdición* by practicing *desahogo*. "I want to talk to them to help them so they don't fall like I did. I think that's my responsibility." Social responsibility was the marker by which Jayson measured his success.

The undocumented young adult workers in this study were not attaining academic degrees or accumulating wealth in their transition to adulthood in the United States. But giving back to their local economies, neighborhoods, communities, and left-behind families indicated that they had achieved some material stability and emotional maturation that could be shared with others. This is the feedback loop between orientation and adaptation at work, and beyond being an individual benefit, youth's incorporation—as orientation and adaptation—supported the collective.

Giving Back Transnationally and the Promise of Collective Success

Transnational giving-back practices contributed to narratives of successful incorporation in the transition to adulthood for young people who left their origin countries with collective *metas* and imagined familial futures. The abilities to sustain consistent remittance practices and to reengage in economic remittances after seizing support to gain financial stability, while becoming oriented and adapted to financial independence, hypercommodified markets, and work primacy in their transition to adulthood, were key markers of successful incorporation. Giving back transnationally involved more than simple economic remittances. Young adults also transmitted stories of overcoming that reassured left-behind families of the competence and maturity that the young people had achieved and evoked left-behind parents' pride.

Securing Transnational Families' Material Futures

For some young adults, giving back meant completing a construction project, like building a new house, in their origin country. Although it was often the case that young people reported only starting a house, which typically meant a cement foundation with nothing yet on top of it, at least a dozen participants described their satisfaction and pride in having constructed a home for themselves and their families. For these young people, the memory of not having food to eat, not having a weatherproof home, or both planted the seed of migration and informed the tangible migration *metas* that teens set before departure.

Ander was among those who left his family behind with a promise to build a house. "When I left Guatemala, I dreamed that I would one day build my house, buy land, have water, and have everything I needed. And well, now I have that. I worked hard, and I have that," Ander shared. At twenty-four years old, he was a homeowner. Although he did not live in that home in Guatemala but rented a room in Los Angeles, he had achieved his migration goal and deemed himself successful. Some left-behind families moved in and enjoyed the comforts of new appliances in multistory houses. Other families said they would wait for the young migrant to return home so that they could be the first to break in a house. Of course, this could be bittersweet, as some young adults funded the construction of houses as teenagers that they knew they might never see as adults. In congruence with similar studies, the young adults in this research reported having only seen their newly constructed houses in photos.[11]

In the years following the 2014 humanitarian crisis, success became increasingly rooted in how left-behind families—especially younger siblings—were faring. Young adults emphasized the need to invest consistently in the home life and education of left-behind family members—either by creating safer home and community spaces, securing children's school going rather than work lives for children, or giving family members a sense of purpose and hope for the future. The young workers in Los Angeles wanted to ensure that their left-behind siblings achieved their *metas*.

As a child, Patrick wanted to attend school in Guatemala but could not because of family poverty. When he migrated, he committed to putting his siblings through school—in a sense, sharing the parenting responsibility with his mother. He recounted, "They [my siblings] were studying and [doing] well. My mom would say, 'No, they are not going to school anymore because I do not have money to buy them their notebooks [and] uniforms.' So, I said I would work to send them a bit of money so that they could continue to study." He reassured his mother that he could help her with various things. "That's why I came [to Los Angeles]. And now my siblings are studying."

> STEPHANIE: Why are you helping them to study?
> PATRICK: I am helping them because . . . I am responsible for
> them. I don't want them to live a life where it is difficult to find
> a job or that they . . . well, I don't want them to come to this
> country. I know that if someone helps you when you're here,
> yes, it can be good. But I do not want them to live what I did.
> I do not want them to have to walk here because you really don't
> know if you will make it or not. I don't want my siblings to suffer
> what I did.

Patrick considered himself successful because he gave back to the local community through his recreational group, but also because he could right the wrongs that resulted in his dislocation from his *metas* in his origin country, that prompted his migration. Righting such wrongs enabled young men to mature into manhood, signaling their successful transition to financial providers and protectors.

This was the case for Danilo, who promised his mother he would financially support her and his younger siblings through remittances when he migrated at fifteen. When I met Danilo, he was twenty-five and still supported his family through remittances. For his siblings in El Salvador, attending school meant evading gangs that target adolescent boys. Danilo explained what his family did with his remittances:

> Well, I know my mom is helping herself to keep my little brothers
> in school. I'm trying to help my little brothers. That's pretty much
> what I care about the most. I care about my mom but think about my
> brothers most. I try to keep them in school because the crime rate in
> El Salvador is sky-high right now with the gangs.

Danilo also sought to protect his siblings by trying to "keep them busy" indoors: "I bought all of them PlayStations [and] computers so that I could keep them home, not outside."[12] Because Danilo's migration *metas* were rooted in transnational family life, his incorporation into American society was measured by whether he successfully kept his siblings out of gangs and trouble and in school. At the time of our interview, he was succeeding. This illustrated that sacrificing one's economic mobility could provide a sense of emotional stability.

Self-Sacrifice in the Achievement of Transnational Success

Teens' sacrifices during their transition to adulthood often came at the cost of their mobility, prompting participants to rely not only on interrelational material mobility but also on social and emotional markers of success. Gael was clear: "I came to Los Angeles for economic reasons. We didn't have money. We were poor. I heard over there that 'You are going to pick up money here, woah!' You hear that there is money to get in Los Angeles; that the American Dream is in Los Angeles." Gael thought he would find work in Los Angeles that would allow him to "make my house and to help my family." He quickly learned that this would be no easy task:

> I just don't think the American Dream exists anymore because this country is now in [political and economic] crisis. Sure, this is a country of education opportunities. We can take advantage of the few opportunities that this country gives us. But I came here because we just didn't have money. I came here to help my family. To get them out of poverty and move my siblings forward. I came here so they could be educated, praise God, and to help my mom.

Gael subjectively measured his success according to his ability to achieve his migration *meta* of helping his family. He thanked God that he had reached his goal of sending remittances to his mother for his siblings' education and broader family support. "I still have four brothers and one sister over there," he said, "and I am helping them to keep studying. Well, my brother is in his last year of schooling this year. He is going to become a teacher. Well, I think that I have already spent a lot of money, and I am working really hard for him." While Gael recognized that others might not see the fruits of his labor or might admonish him for having wasted time and resources in the United States because of his social position, he asserted:

> I know a lot of people say that I don't have a house, I don't have my education. I have been here for five years, and I have accomplished nothing. But you know what? I always think about what I am doing for my family. It has always been my goal to get here. This is the mentality I have: there is a positive, and there is a negative. I had to experience that negative so that I can now be positive.

Gael remained committed to what he had imagined for himself: "I haven't built my house yet, but I will in the future." I asked him if his first two goals—facilitating his siblings' education and supporting his mother—got in the way of his goal of building a house to which he could one day return. He responded:

> Well, what gets in the way of me building my house now is that I am still helping my siblings. My brothers and my sister, I am helping them all in school. One of my brothers is studying right now, and it costs a lot of money, about $150 to $200 a week. Over there, you pay for school, and you don't get help with that.

The unique emergent frame of reference that allowed young adult immigrants to compare circumstances in their origin country to those in the destination country motivated them to continue giving back despite the resultant delays in their mobility strides. When considering his siblings' opportunities for mobility, Gael reflected on the structural barriers to accessing education in Guatemala:

> Unlike here [the United States], it's rare to get help to go to school [in Guatemala]. You can apply for financial aid if you have a Social Security number. It's very different over there. Everyone is on their own, and you pay for everything. One sheet of paper is one quetzal, which comes out to about one quarter [25 cents].

I asked Gael if he felt a sense of responsibility to provide the resources that he thought his siblings lacked but required:

> The responsibility I have is to send money every week. I don't think it's an obligation from God [meaning that no one mandates it], but the desire is inside me. It's a responsibility I have taken upon myself because I know how they live over there. Someone can tell me, "Well, it's not the same. These are not your children; they are nothing to you. You'd have to give them money if they were your children." But I see it differently because it is my responsibility. I've taken it myself because, like I said a while ago, I want to study. It costs a lot of money to have a family. And I have to give them what I can.

But what did Gael's family think about his living in Los Angeles for an extended period and how he was faring in the city? Gael's response confirmed the interconnectedness of young adults' material and emotional conditions and of immigrants' lives in Los Angeles with those of their left-behind families, as well as the value of being witnessed by others throughout processes of orientation and adaptation. He said, "They are happy. My mom is happy. Everyone is [happy]. They admire how much I've overcome and how much I've advanced. She's [his mother is] very happy because of how much change I have inspired over there." Gael and his mother affirmed his achieved autonomy and authority in the family—a display of masculine manhood despite the distance. What's more, Gael felt proud of himself that his mother attributed improved family relationships and community ties to his social and emotional remittances.

Gael's proven economic stability and emotional maturity earned him respect and increased his status in his transnational household. He wielded his status to influence transnational family life. Gael invested further efforts in the emotional and spiritual support of his family, inspired by his attendance at church youth groups in Los Angeles. He encouraged his mother and siblings to attend a Catholic church in their community. Respecting his *consejos* (advice), they joined the church and were subsequently baptized into Catholicism.

In an act that can be interpreted as reversed parenting, Gael also began mentoring his mother on how to relate to her younger children, specifically to hug them more often and to recognize and celebrate their birthdays. He sent extra money on holidays to buy cakes or gifts. He reasoned that these efforts would keep the family embedded in the community and his siblings embedded in the family; his family's socioeconomic and socioemotional achievements would deter their future migration. As for Gael's mother's views of his life in Los Angeles, he beamed while explaining that she was "very happy with me because I don't have any addictions, I don't drink, and I am healthy." Young adult children feel pride in sharing stories of stability and competence and consider these markers of success with their parents.

I wondered how long Gael planned to send financial, social, and emotional remittances to his left-behind family and prodded him about any goals he'd set during his transition to adulthood that were distinct from the interconnected future of his family unit. Unsurprisingly, Gael had a plan. Recognizing the structural barriers that he faced in his education and perhaps his institutional age and the age appropriateness of schooling for his younger brother, Gael's goal was to support his younger sibling until he completed formal schooling in Guatemala and successfully transitioned into the labor market. He anticipated that day coming soon:

> I plan to stop sending money there this year because I want to save money to go to school, too. My goal is to attend college, but I must keep helping [my family] until my brother finishes school. I have always told him, "If you graduate, you must work to find a good job." That's my goal.

Gael would consider himself successful in reaching his goal if his sibling graduated, found a job in Guatemala, and did not migrate to the United States. Demonstrating the futurity of the transition to adulthood, Gael had already set his next goal: to see himself through his education and the attainment of his career in Los Angeles. I asked Gael what he wanted to use a college degree for, having worked in the garment industry, in hospitality as a dishwasher, as a line cook, and then as a florist. He replied, "*Pues, quiero ser un chef profesional*" (I want to be a professional chef). Gael's vision of success for the future was still evolving.

The salience of making parents proud in the meanings young adults applied to achieved success also came through in Camelia's coming of age. She detailed that caring for left-behind parents and siblings came at the cost of being able to one day form and care for her own family. This reflects how young people contend with the gendered social expectations at different stages of their lives. Young men's delayed personal *metas* in Los Angeles did not affect their sense of manhood and masculinity, which are traditionally built on men's ability to provide material and financial support and establish autonomy. Young women's long-term financial support of left-behind families—especially when older siblings married and abandoned their transnational economic ties, applying greater pressure on younger siblings to prove moral commitment to family—could delay women's progression toward marriage and motherhood, important markers of women's maturation in patriarchal societies.[13]

Camelia framed her success within the structure of opportunities available to her in the present and in hopes of an imagined future. Recall that she migrated to the United States because her two older siblings, who had migrated before her, stopped remitting after marrying and starting families in Los Angeles. Camelia thus measured her successful incorporation primarily by the maintenance of her migration *meta* of supporting her family, framed as a responsibility: "My responsibility here is to not forget about my parents because as time passes, they are getting older and because of their age, I feel a greater sense of responsibility to always take care of them. Above all, I need to send them money."

"What does your family say about your life here?" I asked Camelia as I did with Gael. "They feel very proud of me," she replied, "because they have seen what I have really wanted to do, and they are very thankful that I have not forgotten about them." Camelia worked to ensure her survival in Los Angeles and to remit $300 per month to her family for several years. In this case, remembering one's family and making sacrifices for them serve as currency in a moral economy. "They are happy because, at the same time, I have not gotten married," she continued. Camelia's reframing of the nonattainment of marriage and motherhood as an act of morality and deference to her parents led her to consider herself successful. This was her view of women who chose differently: "You know, a lot of women come here, and within a few years, they are married, and they forget about their families." Camelia recognized the disadvantage this created for families but expressed that this was "normal." In that moment, Camelia prided herself in her resistance to the norm.

In one breath, Camelia defined success as the ability to support her family, made possible by her delaying marriage and motherhood, but in the next, she spoke of success being differently defined in the future as she was adamant that "one day, I will have my family." This could, however, come at a new cost. "I won't be able to send [money] to my parents because I am going to have to look after my own kids," Camelia said, but she was orienting and adapting to her new goal with a plan.

After several years of shouldering the burden of providing for her left-behind family, Camelia had devised a system in which the three siblings would take turns sending their mother $300 per month. In this way, she could gain a sense of financial control and make room for financial planning for the future. Camelia felt proud of herself for starting to implement a system that could move her toward her personal goals, but more importantly, that would allow her to keep her promise. Her family's happiness, which was based on honoring her promise to support them—especially after her two older siblings had lost touch—was the foundation on which she built her self-concept of being successful. Still, as Camelia transitioned to young adulthood, her idea of family was being reoriented from the family of origin to the family she could form in the future. Through this, she would perhaps measure her success relative to her identity as a partner and parent rather than a daughter. Here, we see glimpses into the phases of the incorporation process again, and we are reminded that success, too, is a process.

Conclusion

The typical socioeconomic markers of incorporation and coming of age, such as high levels of educational attainment, occupational mobility, and wealth accumulation, are unavailable to young, unaccompanied, and undocumented workers who experience marginalization and subordination across various social spheres simultaneously. Emphasizing these markers as the standard by which US society measures "good" and "deserving" immigrants can reinforce the narrative that unaccompanied, undocumented immigrant youth threaten US society. Centering young people's subjective markers of success along the incorporation process reveals that success is also a dynamic and ongoing process. People define success from their social position within their social roles that are bound within nested social contexts and across societies. For all study participants, success was experienced locally. But for young adults who grew up with transnational ties, subjective meanings of success were also made across societies.

Recalling their *metas* for migration and disorientation as their starting point of incorporation, giving back signaled to young adults that they had reached a state of material stability and emotional maturation in their incorporation, which allowed them to take on the role of caregiver more successfully in the transition to adulthood. Giving-back frames empowered young adults to claim individually and socially responsible moral character, garnering feelings of dignity and pride even though their communities were cast as extractive and dangerous. In all, giving back allowed young adults to resist notions of failure and exclusion and instead build identities around narratives of success and belonging in local and transnational societies.

The stories shared in this chapter are not meant to romanticize experiences of marginalization, exploitation, or poverty within a neoliberal and racist society—on the contrary. While narratives of giving back bolster a strong sense of material mobility and social and emotional inclusion for those who rely on them, these narratives also reinforce existing social hierarchies and dominant scripts about the "good" immigrant and the "competent" teen. Interwoven into each narrative of material mobility and emotional maturation are depictions of failure. A giving-back frame can establish a new hierarchy among this population that reifies intragroup stratification organized by the logic that those who engage in processes of orientation and adaptation represent the ideal immigrant, while those caught in disorientation and *perdición* do not. I discuss the implications of undocumented immigrant teens' and young adults' subjective meanings of success in the conclusion.

Conclusion

It has been a decade since the US collective awakening to the crisis of unaccompanied child migration in 2014. As this book moves into press, high rates of child migration persist. An estimated 152,057 children were apprehended at the southern border in 2022; another 137,275 were apprehended in 2023.[1] Each year, thousands more enter clandestinely and will continue to do so. By 2023, the media was buzzing with news of the pervasiveness of the unauthorized employment of unaccompanied migrant children in hazardous low-wage labor occupations and exposure to exploitative labor practices, illness, injury, and, in the most egregious cases, the loss of workers' limbs or lives. Debates about how the United States should respond to these trends are ongoing.

On one hand, there is public concern that children are migrating in astounding numbers, and resistance to providing legal and social protections for them and their (typically undocumented) immigrant families, invariably pushing children into work. On the other, there is a widespread outcry that migrant children are growing up as exploited, low-wage workers under conditions that are far distant from the "priceless" childhood that Americans hold so dear.[2] Scholars, policymakers, and the public have much to reconcile if we are to develop an immigrant-youth incorporation agenda thoughtfully. I hope this book offers insight into developing a humane way forward.

The research that informs this book shows that incorporation is a process that is undergirded by the interactions between structure and agency spanning institutions like family, school, and work, within and across societies over time. Findings show that an immigrant's destination country incorporation prospects are shaped by their circumstances and social position in the origin country, before and at the point of departure. Central American and Mexican children are displaced from their origin countries without their parents by structural and interpersonal violence that denies them safety, security, and well-being and dislocates them from culturally specific transitions to adulthood. Despite the US role in creating the conditions of displacement and constructing the illusion of the American Dream, this country does not provide a reprieve for most. Growing inequality affects all Americans and complicates all adolescents' transitions to adulthood, irrespective of immigration status. Yet, transitions to adulthood are ever more complicated when they overlap with immigration processes, as US immigration policies disallow family migration and criminalize children and their families who flee life-threatening conditions. Once in the United States, unaccompanied migrant youth contend with the consequences of the derailed incorporation pathways of migrants who were displaced before them—another example of "multigenerational punishment."[3]

The intertwining of immigration and criminal law produces legal and economic precarity within and across immigrant families and communities. Most study participants' precariously situated, long-settled relatives could not afford to support the newcomer youth without risking destabilizing their homes and families. Immigration policies render families vulnerable to extreme poverty through labor exploitation and separation through deportation, the fears of which make familial ties tenuous, with material and emotional consequences for newcomer youth. Without access to family-led households, youth are denied their roles as children and the normative childhood experience in families and, subsequently, in schools—two key socializing institutions considered harbingers of positive incorporation and coming of age. As a result, these unaccompanied migrant youth become low-wage workers.

Further, without immediate access to supportive and meaningful social ties, youth experience social and emotional isolation. Many unaccompanied migrant teens begin their lives in the United States in a state of material and social poverty and emotional disorientation—this while their identities and sense of self are developing in the transition to adulthood in relation to others and within institutions. By all traditional metrics, these migrant youth would not experience successful incorporation but would be subject to downward mobility and exclusion in an "underclass." The Central American and Mexican young adult participants in this research offer a different perspective.

I have argued that immigrant incorporation is less an achieved static endpoint than a set of dynamic processes that co-occur across major social institutions in the origin and destination countries. The experiences of unaccompanied, undocumented Central American and Mexican teens demonstrate that incorporation, when positively experienced, constitutes ongoing stages of material and emotional orientation and adaptation. When incorporation is negatively experienced, prolonged periods of disorientation result in a state of material and emotional perdition. Reconceived in this way, success is not a static outcome; it is also dynamic and ongoing. As migrant youth evolve from newcomers to long-settled migrants during their transition to adulthood, they define their success subjectively, according to their *metas* for migration, their experiences in adaptation to or perdition in a new *sistema*, and their ever-expanding understanding of self and community. In what follows, I discuss the implications of these conclusions for our theorization of immigrant incorporation and how the findings of this work might apply to other populations and in different localities. I end with suggestions for how to address the salient issues presented throughout the book.

Theorizing Immigrant Incorporation in the Transition to Adulthood

Western societies classify children as a protected class, transitioning to adulthood with the guidance and supervision of parents in the home and invested in by extended family and community.[4] Societies assume children participate in the public sphere through K–12 schools, which are intended as protective spaces. At school, children are deemed receptacles of care and socialization by teachers, counselors, and peers until they age into the majority and the workforce. Within this frame, scholars, policymakers, and the public consider successful transitions to adulthood as marked by completing school; leaving the parental home; entering full-time work; and engaging in gainful employment, marriage, and eventual parenthood.[5] Likewise, successful immigrant incorporation is socioeconomically marked by educational completion, occupational mobility, wealth accumulation, and adoption of the society's dominant cultural practices, like English-language dominance.

Advancing previous research suggesting that incorporation is a dynamic process within a singular institution, my ethnographic observations and in-depth interviews conducted over six years revealed that incorporation is a process that also unfolds across an array of institutions with meaning across multiple societies.[6] Relying on youth's own words, I introduced (dis)orientation, adaptation, and perdition as phases in the incorporation process. I analyzed these phases' material and emotional components as jointly (re)producing one another throughout and as informing how young people measure their success as immigrants and young adults. This definitional expansion acknowledges that incorporation can occur across the life course and makes room for us to account for the reality that in US society immigrant youth are coming of age during a time of increasing inaccessibility of the normative markers of success. Meanwhile, neoliberalism superimposes notions of meritocracy on an unequal society that stratifies access to opportunity and (re)produces social inequities.[7]

This theoretical intervention urges a consideration of the multidimensionality of human life in our understanding of immigrants' everyday patterns of participation in society, the meanings they make of success, and the claims they make to incorporation. Immigrant children, for example, do not solely attend school while their adult counterparts work. Some immigrant children, those from the poorest and most vulnerable backgrounds and with few options to do otherwise, grow up as workers. However, immigrant youth workers, like all other workers, do not solely participate in workplaces or act as laborers. They participate in family, community, and, for teens and young adults, in schools and nontraditional learning spaces. Immigrants' work lives shape their participation in nonworkspaces, just as their nonwork lives shape their participation in work. Immigrants' understandings of their social roles, responsibilities, and identities are formed through these interactions across various institutions. The data also reveal that structural forces—material constraints and socioemotional barriers—can supersede immigrant youth's desire to achieve mobility and live well. It is not enough to set goals and work hard to achieve them. Systems of power and opportunity structures must be aligned in one's favor. The youth at the center of this book endured misalignments throughout their migration and coming of age. As they navigated these, young people made new meanings of success.

To demonstrate this, this book began by showing how departure and arrival contexts propel youth toward or move them away from the lives they imagined in Los Angeles and set the stage for achieving their *metas*. Until now, the arrival or reception context has been regarded as a national-origin group's political, social, and economic position at national and state levels. [8] Local institutions and coethnic communities act as mediators in potential hostility and as bridges to mobility.[9] I conceptualize a still more specific arrival context: the household, to advance research that shows family characteristics matter in determining children's mobility and incorporation across the life course. The household context of arrival also calls into question the assumption that children migrate alongside parents or other adult caregivers or eventually become reunited with them.

Household arrival contexts, ranging from complete to partial material or emotional support to no support, were important mechanisms shaping immigrant youth's divergent on-ramps to the incorporation process. Once in Los Angeles, some youth relied on relatives already living there. These young people experienced an orientation to normative adolescence wherein they were alleviated from having to enter work to secure their survival. Instead, they began their schooling and eventually followed the incorporation pathways of other undocumented youth, as explained in existing work.[10] They also experienced *desahogo*, an emotional unburdening from premigration stressors and fears, accompaniment, and material and emotional support in planning for the future.

Yet most study participants could not rely on long-settled relatives with stable financial and domestic situations. In the case of Latin American–origin families, this finding challenges generalizations of *familismo* to shed light on how immigration policies that allow for labor exploitation and familial poverty, threaten deportation and family separation, and make everyday life precarious result in selective receptivity to recently arrived children. Evidence of relatives' reliance on individual characteristics like gender and age expectations to justify the difficult decision to deny support should not detract from the culpability of macro-legal, economic, and social structures that force them to make these difficult micro-level decisions but apply more pressure to reform these unequal structures. If this is the case among altruistic families in a sanctuary city nested within a sanctuary state, there is reason to be alarmed for the fates of children who arrive in less-welcoming cities and states across the United States and whose long-settled families face even more constraints to stability and well-being.[11] Indeed, the immigrant household and family must be central to any effort to support unaccompanied migrant children moving forward.

I introduced orientation to explain confrontation with and sense making of youth's entry into US society. It is distinct from long-standing concepts like acculturation or socialization that are suggested as passively occurring over time and, among children, assume that social learning is age appropriate for their roles and responsibilities within a normative childhood frame. Orientation acknowledges that youth's departures and arrivals are often unplanned and unpredictable and that their institutional and interpersonal starting points for incorporation are diverse and contextually defined. Some youth were oriented to normative childhood and student roles. Others were oriented to independence. Migrant teen workers first had to learn how to survive by learning their unique expected roles and responsibilities, what institutions they were required to participate in, and their social position within them. They also had to learn the norms and values that shape interactions within the institutions they participated in and in the broader society.

Throughout these processes, youth developed an understanding of how their social positions and everyday lived experiences compared to those of their origin countries and their peers in the destination society through an emergent frame of reference. Women and Indigenous teens were oriented, too, to their subordinate position within gender and ethnoracial hierarchies that constrained even further their limited structure of opportunities as unaccompanied, undocumented, low-wage workers. As they came of age, youth were oriented to their need to socialize with peers and compatriots, and their time in the United States exposed them to organizations and groups in which they could achieve that. Some social ties offered significant material and emotional support, especially when young people developed meaningful relationships with adult figures and peers. Others exacerbated teens' material and emotional disorientation.

Once oriented to the contours of their independence, young people began to adapt to and around their roles and resources as low-wage workers. The dual pressures of securing their survival in Los Angeles and providing for left-behind families in the origin country for those with transnational family ties were compounded by low wages, financial insecurity, and limited time and energy to produce work primacy. Young people's roles as workers within low-wage, exploitative occupations determined not only the nature of their work lives but also the contours of their educational opportunities, community participation, and family relationships—any decisions youth made to participate in nonworkspaces required negotiations of finances, time, and energy and a cost-benefit determination.

Migrant youth adapted to work primacy by prioritizing participation in spaces that bolstered their productivity at work and promised mobility. Educational pursuits, for example, were sidelined by the pressures to repay migration debts, send remittances to left-behind families, and survive in one of the most expensive cities in the United States. Due to work primacy, educational pursuits tended to be focused on the pragmatics: learning enough English to get by and get ahead. As such, immigrant youth's frequent absence from K–12 schools should not be understood as a deficit for youth who grew up as workers but as evidence of their adaptation to what was required to survive. Participants' creation of alternative learning spaces high-

lights immigrant youth's reverence for education and their ingenuity and agentic adaptability in developing adaptive strategies to
achieve pragmatic mobility. Indigenous young people's efforts to
learn Spanish and English to navigate nested linguistic contexts further prove this.

Chapters 3 and 4 illustrated how orientation and adaptation were
ongoing in tandem. Orientation to one institutional context or routine increased material, cultural, and emotional capital to achieve
adaptation to that institution or routine and created inroads to participating in another institution that again required orientation, and
so on. We saw this in several cases where youth once strictly confined
to workspaces gained access to community spaces like churches or a
running club, experienced orientation there, and gained confidence
and peer motivation to participate in another space, like English-
language classes. English-language proficiency might support job
jumping or greater community participation, both of which offered
material and emotional mobility resources. Orientation alongside
guiding adult figures cultivated planful competence—an understanding of the structure of opportunities, the establishment of new
metas within that structure, and confidence in their decisions to
reach those *metas*.

It is possible to experience material orientation to independence
and hypercommodified markets and adaptation to work primacy
as a matter of survival, but without orientation to meaningful organizational and interpersonal ties, immigrants can remain socially
isolated and emotionally disoriented. Young people in this study
entered a pathway of *perdición*, in which strategies deployed to cope
with emotional instability—what youth identified as loneliness and
angst—weakened material stability, which exacerbated emotional
distress. Disorientation and *perdición* also worked in tandem and
were ongoing. I discussed in chapter 5 how gender, social life participation patterns, and emotional expression processes critically

shaped pathways into and experiences of *perdición* such as substance (ab)use, romantic relationships, and suicidal ideation and self-harm. Perdition, as a process rather than an endpoint, can be reoriented to adaptation by establishing meaningful social ties.

Youth who developed meaningful social ties as they came of age made significant inroads into emotional stability in everyday life. I observed the impact of *desahogo* (unburdening) in enabling the progression through phases of orientation and adaptation. Youth who could not unburden in welcoming household contexts might have been oriented to unburdening later in community spaces alongside significant adult figures and peers. Their ongoing unburdening from past traumas, fear in the present, and uncertainty about the future with trusted individuals provided a cultural and emotional orientation that worked in tandem with material stability to counter interpersonal isolation and organizational marginalization. Unburdening strengthened interpersonal relationships that offered the witnessing and motivation that teens and young adults in *perdición* identified as missing from their lives. Their unburdening also prompted curiosity and confidence to pursue new—perhaps better-paying—work opportunities, new forms of community engagement, imagined futures, and positive incorporation. This draws attention to the importance of immigrant-serving organizations in the regions where youth arrive. Without access to supportive communities, independent undocumented teens have limited options for *desahogo* alongside trusting adult figures and peers. They might be more likely to experience *perdición* as they attempt to cope with their *soledad y agonía*.

The concept of unburdening illuminates what has largely been left unsaid in immigration and immigrant incorporation scholarship, which tends to ignore the socioemotional dynamics: the migration trauma and immigrants' handling of trauma as they move through the settlement and coming-of-age processes determine patterns of participation in the public spheres of life that are necessary to achieve mobility, embeddedness, and belonging. Valentina and Marvin were examples of how growing up in adult-led households can offer this taken-for-granted emotional support. Immigrant and nonimmigrant adolescents coming of age alongside their caregivers might experience unburdening in intimate household attachments. However, not all households are emotionally safe, even those led by parents. Still, migration scholarship tends to assume that they are and that relationships with teachers, peers, and other significant adult figures can similarly offer unburdening for schoolgoing adolescents and teens. This reinforces the value of examining household arrivals as immigrant teens' immediate reception context.

Together, orientation, adaptation, and unburdening are organizing concepts that exemplify the agentic practices that move young people from marginalization and exclusion to material and emotional stability within and across societies during the transition to adulthood. These concepts reveal the various forms of labor that youth engage in as they come of age *sin padres, ni papeles*—without parents nor papers. As others have convincingly argued, social ties and their capital matter for all immigrants, especially adolescents in critical developmental stages of their lives.[12] Patchworking social ties and capital is necessary throughout. Researchers acknowledge that immigrant incorporation requires financial, cultural, and emotional labor. Previous incorporation models are adult centric, framing adults as paving the way for children and youth. This research shows that coming of age as unaccompanied and undocumented immigrant young people required not only remunerative labor, but cultural and emotional labor enacted across social spaces and ties—and they labored in both spheres independently.

This research also revealed that immigrant youth's incorporation was structural and subjective. Although participants could not call on normative markers of success, they made meaning of their success with consideration for their departures, arrivals, and intertwined migration and coming-of-age experiences. While young adults had reached stable individual responsibility, the reciprocal process of giving back—as evidence of fulfilled social responsibility—became an important indicator of financial mobility and emotional maturation. Success, subjectively defined within a giving-back frame, was achieved in the local society for young adults whose ties to origin families and communities were fragmented in adolescence. Success was local and transnational among young adults who maintained their ties to left-behind families. Moving forward, scholars of immigrant incorporation, youth life course, and work and mobility might consider how the incorporation starting points and experiences through incorporation's phases shape the meaning that immigrants make of success.

While building an incorporation process theory based on the experiences of unaccompanied migrant youth in the United States, it is my hope that readers might find parallels between study participants' experiences of (dis)orientation, adaptation, and perdition, and subjective meanings of success, and other immigrant groups. What's more, I hope readers find parallels with their own lives. Indeed, we have all, at some point, been newcomers to a social community or a routine organization and/or have stepped into a role that felt disorienting at first but to which we oriented and adapted over time and have assigned meanings of stability and mobility from within. Whether native or foreign born, no one enters a society as an all-knowing actor. Instead, we learn, from either birth or time of arrival, what our host society's structures of opportunities are; the hierarchies of power and systems of disempowerment that determine our life chances; and the norms, beliefs, and values that guide our everyday behaviors and interactions.

Ultimately, incorporation is not *just* an immigrant issue. We experience incorporation processes every day, across our life courses, regardless of the society we are in and our social location within it.

As such, we know that there are some opportunities that are simply not available to us based on our identities and backgrounds. We know there are some traditional markers of success that have been or continue to be harder to reach than others. If we understand this for ourselves, can we also understand it for others? If we have empathy for the native born locked out of opportunities for mobility, can we also have empathy for the foreign born? What's more, can we implement policies and programs and adopt practices that reflect this understanding and empathy? Can we apply pressure to systems and structures that produce inequality and cause deep material and emotional suffering rather than blaming those who suffer? Can we create new systems centered on equity in opportunities to achieve material and emotional incorporation and to live well? I think we can.

Where Do We Go from Here?

The experiences and perspectives of unaccompanied, undocumented young people shared in this book offer insight into how disconnected youth can be reached and the types of policies and programs that might be critical for their survival and well-being as they come of age. The experiences of disconnected youth also shed light on how we can better conceive of the types of child and family services that would better support children who are within the purview of the state. As unaccompanied child migration rates continue to rise globally, this book's findings suggest several policy goals to safeguard children's rights. I lay these out below.

The Right to Stay

Academic and policy research demonstrates that foreign intervention through colonialism and imperialism and US-backed armed conflict have disrupted Central America's and Mexico's political, economic, and social infrastructure for decades, resulting in domestic and international displacement of working-aged people.[13] The prioritization of US market interests by foreign governments (mis)guided by the promise of economic integration and growth comes at the expense of those nations' citizens. Defunded or underfunded education systems in origin countries render children unable to enter or complete their education in their origin countries. Therefore, they cannot become integrated into the labor market segment that offers mobility opportunities as they age. Meanwhile, the US economy, particularly the secondary labor market, relies on the labor of immigrants at all skill and education levels. Latin American immigrant workers, including adolescents and young adults, enter the workforce to fill that need.[14] Participants were often pained by their need to migrate, but their pain was outweighed by the visible pain of their family and community members, who experienced unemployment, hunger, illness, extreme poverty, and hopelessness about the future. Consequently, youth departed from their origin countries, often with plans to return that remain unfulfilled well into adulthood.

Like other social scientists, I suggest that the first policy response must be to secure young people's right to not migrate.[15] US-based efforts to alleviate these social problems should include strong support of the social, political, and economic vitality of these young people's origin countries—not through development projects and securitization programs but through direct investments in community and youth-led organizations in origin regions. Chapter 1 demonstrates that institutional displacement and emotional dislocation are localized experiences and that young people negotiate how best to respond to their present-day needs and aspirations. The right to not migrate includes the right to materialize youth's imagined futures within their origin countries, alongside family and community.[16] Strategies to mitigate displacement and dislocation must be localized and center youth's voices and experiences. Policymakers should turn to activists, advocates, and community leaders to understand when and why migration is deployed as a response to historical and present-day violence and poverty, and they must turn to children to understand the alternatives they envision for their communities, their families, and themselves.

Addressing the historical and present-day causes of migration in origin countries is an important first step in meaningful intervention in child migration. The United States must recognize its role in creating the social, political, economic, and environmental conditions in Central American countries and Mexico that lead children to its border. Without this piece of the puzzle, efforts to address the root causes of migration from within child migrants' origin countries are futile and risk empowering the very systems of displacement and oppression that prompt migration.

Additionally, awakening to culpability should motivate the above-mentioned investments in localized efforts to meet children's needs for safety, mobility, and well-being in their origin communities and encourage the recognition of child migrants as refugees and a sense of obligation to provide safety, security, and mobility denied to them in origin countries. Children migrate because their lives and futures have been threatened by present-day iterations of violence and poverty that reflect histories of political repression, economic privatization and resource extraction, racism, sexism, and other forms of discrimination that marginalize entire communities and groups within them. While the United States has developed programs—like the Central American Minors Program—to allow for in-country applications for refugee status, the application and approval processes do not reflect the haste with which decisions are made and the urgency of departure.

Without swift and secure child migration systems in place, the United States must end the dangerous practice of criminalizing refugees and blocking asylum. In recent years, migration deterrence through policies like Zero-Tolerance in 2018, Remain in Mexico in 2019, Title 42 in 2020, and the more recent reincarnation of these through the asylum transit ban implemented by the Biden administration in 2023 have penalized asylum seekers and put them in danger of violence ranging from hunger and housing insecurity, to kidnapping and extortion, to expedited removal without due process. Deterrence policies such as those listed here, along with the militarization of the border and the recruitment of Mexico as a militarized vertical border, can propel more and more people into clandestine migration efforts. The luckier ones face increasing migration costs and often-crippling migration debt; the less fortunate face injury or death during transit.[17] Channels for authorized migration and possibilities to make asylum claims, regardless of age and mode of entry, are essential for the survival and well-being of children and their families. Scholars of unaccompanied minors' legal incorporation and socialization argue for greater inclusion of asylum officers who are knowledgeable about refugee law, country conditions, and trauma-informed interview methods in deciding asylum claims, an effort that is written into the Biden administration's asylum processing rule.[18]

The Right to Safety and Well-Being

Research-driven origin country investment and migration policy could decrease the number of displaced children and support the children who are yet to migrate. For those already living in the United States, a comprehensive policy response should reflect the nested organizational and interpersonal ecologies in which migrant children come of age and work to bolster the strength and vitality of those ecologies—starting with immigrant families.

The greatest US impact would be investment in the resilience of immigrant households and communities where children arrive. This could be accomplished by implementing a legalization program for the 10.5 million undocumented immigrants currently living in the United States.[19] This book strongly argues that upon arrival, children endure hardships tied to independent orientation and adaptation, or prolonged disorientation and *perdición*, because their arrival households cannot offer complete material and emotional support. Long-settled relatives, however well-intentioned, are constrained in their ability to offer a supportive welcome by their positionality in political, economic, and legal hierarchies. Rising economic inequality and poverty in US society foreclose opportunities for full social incorporation for many, and working-class individuals in the United States, regardless of immigrant or legal status, share profound financial insecurity.[20]

Precarity is exacerbated for immigrants who are denied legal and social membership in the United States. Without legal status, immigrants are inevitably subject to the structural violence of labor exploitation and housing insecurity, which produce material poverty within immigrant communities across generations.[21] Furthermore, the expanding reach of the enforcement arm increases the likelihood of social isolation, which decreases information and resource sharing and (re)produces social poverty.[22] Recently arrived migrant children face these barriers independently—as shown in chapters 3 through 5—largely because their long-settled relatives were immobilized by them well before the children's arrival. If policymakers cannot be motivated to protect recently arrived children, they should at the very least provide pathways for legal integration for long-settled immigrants.

The last large-scale legalization program was implemented in 1986 and resulted in significant socioeconomic mobility and coethnic community strengthening for those who benefited from it and their descendants.[23] We should prioritize such reform today. Among the undocumented population, 66 percent are of Mexican and

Central American origin, 80 percent are over the age of twenty-five, and 62 percent have been in the United States for over ten years.[24] At the time of my research, that included many of the study participants' long-settled relatives. As of 2024, this number includes this study's participants themselves.

Ultimately, a legalization program would benefit the long-settled, working-age relatives of present-day unaccompanied minors. A legalization program that reaches this population would make room for family petitions for child migration and create a buffer for children's direct entry into the labor force by boosting legalized, long-settled relatives' economic and housing security, providing access to social services like a food assistance program for which they would become eligible, and eliminating the fear of family separation through detention and deportation. A legalization program must include efforts to educate eligible populations about their legal pathways and secure access to legal representation in immigration courts for poorly resourced families and communities. The federal government can collaborate with states to identify immigrant-serving regional and neighborhood organizations that have established trusting relationships with undocumented communities to ensure that information and services about a legal reform program are delivered in trauma-informed and culturally responsive ways.

Legalization will also empower immigrant workers—both long settled and newly arrived—to report labor rights violations and workplace noncompliance that keep them in poverty. The work experiences of unaccompanied migrant teens detailed here add to decades-long scholarship demonstrating that workers in the secondary labor market have their rights violated daily regardless of legal status. Violations are more egregious when employers can threaten workers with decreased wages, dismissal, or even deportation when discontent is communicated.[25] Lifting the threat of deportability through legalization would instill in immigrant-origin individuals the confidence that labor-violation reports will not be retaliated against. In the case of undocumented immigrant workers, state labor oversight committees and labor-rights advocates should continue to educate workers about their rights in accordance with the National Labor Relations Act and the right to deferred action for workers in labor disputes when a worker's current or former employer is under investigation for labor violations.

This research has shown that individuals often leverage their increased orientation and adaptation within and across institutions to support coethnics and peers. Hence, empowering (young) adults to take action to secure labor rights and report labor violations can inevitably result in support for children of immigrant and nonimmigrant backgrounds in securing their rights. However, the onus of righting the wrongs of labor noncompliance and violation of worker rights should not fall on individuals. Corporations and employers should be held to account for sustaining safe workplaces, paying fair and consistent wages, and providing appropriate safety training and equipment. This will ensure that the adult workers in the households where children arrive are financially stable and physically well enough to receive newly arrived children.

Enforcing labor standards matters directly for unaccompanied migrant children, but its impact will scale much more broadly than the scope of the study sample. According to the US Department of Labor, child labor violations have nearly quadrupled since 2015, while the unauthorized employment of minors, including immigrant children, has increased by 69 percent since 2018.[26] However, this is not just an immigrant problem. By spring 2023, legislators in ten states, including Iowa, Missouri, Ohio, and Arkansas, had passed, or were urging the passage of laws that allow for industry- and age-specific subminimum wages that permit companies to hire children without work permits and allow children to work longer hours.[27] This puts more children—immigrant and US-born alike—at risk.

While all child workers are at risk of labor violations, workplace injury, and even death, not all children are at risk of being low-wage workers. Child labor is motivated by the urgency of individual and familial survival; thus, poor and working-class children, who are disproportionately Black and Latina/o, are under threat.[28] Power differentials in an age hierarchy intersect with race, class, gender, and citizenship hierarchies to make poor and working-class children, children of minoritized groups, young girls, and undocumented children especially unlikely to "tell on adults" who are imposing violence on them. Federal and state governments must proactively identify all labor violations, especially those against children. At the federal level, Congress should prioritize the funding of the Department of Labor's Wage and Hour Division to ensure the enforcement of labor law across the United States. Following this, corporations should be obligated to pay significant penalties for their labor violations. States can take actions like raising the minimum wage for workers and eliminating the subminimum wage allowances for younger workers and for workers in exempted industries, like agriculture.

State enforcement of national and state-level labor compliance could loosen the grip of work primacy on immigrant workers' lives and allow for increased mobility earlier in life by making room for immigrants' participation in other incorporation-promoting institutions. Specifically, when adapted to work, young people are drawn to engage in education because they are oriented to the importance of language in securing advancements in wage and occupational mobility and navigating multicultural Los Angeles (chapters 3 and 4).

Federal and state governments could invest in alternative and flexible education programs, like English-language schools, typically regarded as reserved for adults, but on which unaccompanied teen and young adult workers rely to learn English and build community. These alternative education programs might focus on pragmatic education, such as conversational language learning or entrepreneurial skill development, for young people with limited financial resources, time, and energy. Educational curricula and classroom engagement should also more thoughtfully teach to the range of lived experiences of students. Many teen and young adult workers arrive in classrooms after a full day of exhausting, exploitative work and with a mind full of worries about tomorrow. Classroom activities should be more student centered and culturally responsive. Within the K–12 system, the Oakland Unified School District Newcomer Program in California offers an example of such a curriculum, including extended classroom hours and specialized literacy development for working teens and mental and emotional wellness initiatives for newcomer teens experiencing trauma.[29]

These reforms would benefit teens and young adults in the United States of all legal statuses, as increasing inequality and poverty across the country contribute to changing household structures and dynamics and foreclose adolescents' and teens' ability to focus solely on school or to access K–12 classrooms full-time.[30] Additionally, educational reforms can support the labor reform agenda, as educational investments will inevitably support efforts to ensure workplace and worker safety by motivating claims making. A recent study found that education significantly impacts noncitizen workers', especially undocumented workers', claims making of their rights as workers.[31] Improving educational opportunities for undocumented immigrants, including unaccompanied minors, can improve their work conditions through advancements in language proficiency. It can also improve workplaces nationwide by encouraging workers to make claims to workplace rights regardless of legal status. Again, legalization would have the greatest impact on these processes.

Evident throughout my work is that neighborhoods and communities play an important role in immigrant youth incorporation and coming of age. Research emphasizes the importance of "really significant others" who promote the development, integration, and well-being of immigrant youth, especially undocumented immigrants.[32] These significant others have been identified in coethnic spaces but primarily in schools. Youth without parents or adult caregivers to liaise with organizations and other adults must make these interpersonal connections independently. Youth outside of schools rely on coethnic spaces to create social ties to make ends meet. Chapters 3 and 4 discussed how faith-based spaces are often the first stop for unaccompanied, undocumented Central American and Mexican immigrants. Beyond the legal motivations highlighted earlier, federal and state governments should partner with immigrant-serving organizations to center children's social incorporation and emotional development.

Leaders within these communities should be made aware of young girls' and Indigenous youth's needs. Additionally, government and nongovernmental organizations offering support services should look beyond schools, after-school programs, and educational institutions, like libraries, to reach underserved immigrant teens in nontraditional youth spaces. Factories, car washes, restaurants, day labor centers, and other worksites common among undocumented immigrants offer viable public spaces in which immigrant teens are active and available to receive information about immigration and rights, material resources, and other forms of social and emotional support.

Organization leaders and staff reaching out to unaccompanied children must be trained in trauma-informed and culturally responsive approaches, wherein advocates and service providers understand unaccompanied migrant teens' motivations for migration and the material and emotional contexts of departure, arrival, and coming of age. Subjective understandings of displacement, disorientation, and the meaning of success inform everyday decisions and behaviors. Hence, imposing generalized, ahistorical, and decontextualized understandings of unaccompanied migrant children and their families, communities, and origin countries risks undermining these subjective experiences and misunderstanding teens' orientations to work, school, family, and community life. Organizations should honor youth's responsibilities and socioeconomic aspirations. Providing spaces for socioemotional development through unburdening, not only from their past experiences but also from their present-day disillusionments and aspirations for the future, will support the social and emotional incorporation of unaccompanied immigrant youth.

The Right to Imagine New Futures

The goal of these recommendations is not to bring children into the purview or custody of the state. Scholarly, policy, and media research and reporting tell us that the state's awareness of or custody over child migrants does not equate to care. There is exhaustive evidence of the abuse in federal and privately contracted facilities and that children are "lost" after placement with sponsors. Over the last decade, migrant children resettled with sponsoring families by the ORR have been found working in construction, food manufacturing and packaging factories, and other occupations across twenty states, including Florida, Georgia, South Dakota, and Virginia. They have been found in Nebraska slaughterhouses, Massachusetts fish-processing plants, house-roofing companies, greenhouses, restaurant kitchens, Alabama's Hyundai Motor manufacturing plants, and Wisconsin meatpacking plants.[33] Measures like deferred action and employment authorization have been taken to ensure that beneficiaries of and applicants for SIJ status have the right to work. However, these children can still be exploited at work. Further, not all children placed with sponsors are eligible for SIJ status, and unauthorized labor is still common. I am mindful that, in the most harrowing circumstances, children are being placed with sponsors intent on trafficking them for labor.

This book has shown that it is the US immigration and legal system itself that propels children into work. Short of recognition of children's refugee status and right to asylum and a full legalization program that grants immigrants the ability to harness the benefits of democracy, we are left patchworking the abovementioned options. Still, none of these options fully encompass the unique social position of undocumented teens and young adults who grow up as low-wage workers by virtue of their unaccompanied status. While I have started to describe that experience here, I have only scratched the surface. This leads me to my final recommendation: community-level support of a youth-led social movement.

For several years now, I have been commended for my research findings and analysis and have, in the years leading up to this book's completion, been asked to offer my recommendations for social change time and again. But this research would not have been possible without the study participants' articulation of their lived experiences. Much of the existing research, policy, and media attention focuses on migrant young people apprehended at the US-Mexico border and released to an adult sponsor. Yet the research at the core of this book expands this empirical frame and, in the process, has uncovered several key and incontrovertible truths: that unaccompanied, undocumented youth who enter the United States clandestinely possess an undeniable capacity to learn, navigate, and negotiate mobility within *el sistema Americano*; that the absence of being witnessed and motivated in the orientation and adaptation process leads to *perdición*; and that the ability to demonstrate social responsibility and give back to local and transnational communities through role modeling orientation and adaptation constitutes the valuation system by which young adults assess their success during their transition to adulthood. I encourage agencies serving and working alongside unaccompanied teens and young adults to create youth mentorship programs that allow young people to unburden, guide each other through orientation and adaptation, and build community from the bottom up based on their *metas*.

I have suggested several policy and program remedies but firmly believe that youth hold the wisdom to inform meaningful policy change best. The Dreamer movement and the passage of DACA in the face of failed immigration reform are evidence of the power of telling youth's stories.[34] DACA was drafted by undocumented youth and young adult organizers. Building a youth-led movement will take significant time and care to ensure that movement building and storytelling do not retraumatize migrant young people. Unlike the Dreamer youth, whose presentation to the public included framing around having little to no memory of the home country and the migration journey and their dependence on parents in their migration decision, the unaccompanied youth in this research (and those who have come after them) recalled the reasons for displacement and possessed a collective memory of the violence of displacement and migration. Any movement must be trauma informed and culturally responsive.

Doing this effectively requires that community organizations embrace the migrant child workers among them. This means contending with the contradiction of childhood and labor, working to honor the *metas* youth set for themselves. This might also require that social advocates align seemingly disparate agendas, with immigration, child welfare, and labor-rights organizations working together to harness the collective wisdom of those with shared experiences in their ranks. Since many of my suggestions include leveraging federal and state government resources to empower regions and community organizations, I urge governments to act in ways that support community helpers' material and emotional well-being, too. I also urge scholars who are critically examining the spillover effects of punitive immigration laws beyond immigrant children and families who are targets of these laws to ask how community helpers might also be harmed and to hold policies and policymakers to account.[35]

Concluding Thoughts

Through a critical examination of the simultaneous passages from newcomer to long-settled immigrant and from adolescence to young adulthood, we can understand how material and emotional conditions are intimately connected to the immigrant experience. But our recognition of these interconnections and youth's ability to remedy social dislocation and emotional alienation through their individual and collective labor should not absolve us from our collective responsibility to support them in this work. An approach focused on individual behaviors decontextualizes the historical and structural forces destabilizing youth's origin countries and, therefore, their lives. The culpability for trauma does not lie with the individual; seeing it as such makes trauma a personal rather than a systemic problem. We must attend to youth's emotional worlds, the meanings they make of their material experiences, how they interpret what these experiences mean about them, their value, and the decisions they have made and should make moving forward. However, the onus of healing trauma should be placed back on the systems of power and subordination that produce structural marginalization and social exclusion, unaccompanied child migration, and undocumented youth's precarious coming-of-age trajectories.

The changing dynamics of labor migration, transnational families, and the global refugee crises suggest that theoretical frames, research methods, policies, and programs intended to support immigrant youth's well-being and mobility must be reconsidered to include unaccompanied youth. Undocumented young adults who grew up as unaccompanied adolescents see their fates and assess their successes across the life course as intimately connected with their local and transnational communities. I hope this research inspires its readers to see our fate and successes as a nation as intimately connected with the treatment of newcomers, especially children and youth, among us.

APPENDIX A

Interview Participant Demographics

TABLE 1. Demographic Characteristics of All Participants (N = 75)

Characteristics	Total	Percentage
Country of origin		
Central America	*61*	*81*
Guatemala	49	65
El Salvador	10	13
Honduras	2	3
Mexico	*14*	*19*
Ethnorace		
Indigenous	37	49
Non-Indigenous	38	51
Gender		
Women	22	29
Men	53	71
Median age, migration	16	—
Median age, interview	23	
Occupational status		
Students, with financial support	5	7
Full-time workers	70	93

TABLE 2. Demographic Characteristics of Full-Time Youth Workers (N = 70)

Characteristics	Total	Percentage
Country of origin		
Central America	*59*	*84*
Guatemala	48	69
El Salvador	9	13
Honduras	2	3
Mexico	*11*	*16*
Ethnorace		
Indigenous	36	51
Non-Indigenous	34	49
Gender		
Women	19	27
Men	51	73
Median age, migration	16	—
Median age, interview	23	
School going (at time of interview)		
Adult English-language school	22	31
No school	48	69
Occupation (at time of interview)		
Manufacturing	*31*	*44*
Garment manufacturing	30	—
Food manufacturing	1	
Hospitality	*10*	*14*
Domestic and homemaking	*6*	*9*
Auto services	*5*	*7*
Carwashes	3	—
Auto repair	2	—
Maintenance	*4*	*6*
Janitorial	3	—
Landscaping services	1	—
Construction	*3*	*4*
Retail	*3*	*4*
Tailoring	*2*	*3*
Warehousing	*1*	*1*

TABLE 2 (*continued*)

Characteristics	Total	Percentage
Occupation (at time of interview)		
Day laborer	*1*	*1*
Entertainment	*1*	*1*
Personal care	*1*	*1*
Unemployed	*2*	*3*

Note: Percentages may not sum to whole due to rounding.

Methodological Reflections

Respect and Dignity in the Field

As a qualitative researcher, I am mindful of the effect of my presence and participation in the social spaces I observe and my relationship with study participants. For participant protection and harm minimization, I used institutional review board (IRB) regulations as a starting point, not an endpoint. I aimed to develop culturally appropriate and trauma-informed research tools.[1] I did this by listening to study participants' questions and concerns, remaining open to incorporating these into the research approach and implementing data storage and dissemination procedures that protect participants' privacy. All names are pseudonyms— individuals, community groups, and organizations. In some cases, participants requested specific pseudonyms; I assigned others randomly. I used participants' nicknames when asked. Finally, I used the name of the chain business Starbucks because of its prevalence across Los Angeles and to give ethnographic context to common meeting spaces.

My ethnographic research methods intended to capture the sociological processes and patterns at any field site while minimizing disruptions to an organization's or space's natural flow and mitigating any distractions my presence might cause. In this study, I did this by observing the customs and norms of my field sites so that I might participate respectfully while safeguarding the dignity and agency of my participants to the best of my ability.[2] For example, when I first attended the support group, the group's leader, Wilfredo, suggested that he introduce me to the group and that I use my turn in the share-out portion of the meeting to explain my student status, research interests, and intention with the group. When I began attending religious community meetings, my participation depended on the size of the group. In large weekend mass services or midweek *comunidad* meetings, I did not introduce myself to the gathering, as these were open to the public, and hundreds of people were often present. However, in smaller group settings, like youth groups, book clubs, or adult English-language schools, where participants were fewer and interactions more intimate, I introduced myself during announcement segments of the meetings.

Similarly, throughout my ethnographic observations I took cues from my surroundings to determine when and how to appropriately participate in each space over the longer term. Because of the precarity of the intersectional social locations of the population I work with, I allowed my research to be guided by invitations. This often meant leaning into waiting and letting time build intimacy.[3] Importantly, I also had to learn when and how it was appropriate to take field notes. In some cases I benefited from organizational dynamics. In others I benefited from shared youth and social media cultures. For example, during community group meetings, such as in a support group or church where others carried notepads, I also jotted down handwritten notes. I used the notes feature on my iPhone when cultural events prompted young people's photo taking or social media use.

In all instances, I prioritized jotting down participant quotes in their original language (Spanish or English, but typically the former) to maintain their situational meanings. In these cases, the ubiquity of mobile phones created opportunities for note-taking in youth-centered spaces.[4] When limited in my ability to take notes, I audio recorded observations in my car after leaving the field and later converted these to written field notes.[5] While these strategies might have posed a challenge in recalling the specificity of informal conversations or in later having access to direct quotes for analysis and writing, I believe these flexible data collection methods strengthened my relationships and rapport in the field.

I took cues from each research site to recruit interview participants as well. For example, I relied on informal conversations with attendees at large church gatherings. I introduced myself as a researcher, explained my study, and distributed a Spanish-language, IRB-approved flier with contact information for interview participants. At the adult English-language schools, I recruited participants by making classroom-by-classroom announcements about my research and distributing fliers to all students. In small-group settings, like Voces de Esperanza or church youth groups, I recruited interviewees by making occasional group announcements and following up with individuals who expressed interest in the study through one-on-one conversations. In each case, the voluntary nature of the study was reinforced during recruitment. I also posted fliers in community

organization waiting rooms; however, the people who contacted me upon seeing these fliers tended to be living with a parent or other adult caregiver. This
confirmed an essential finding that children who arrived in the United States as
unaccompanied minors but who became accompanied through family reunification had increased access to formal organizational spaces that provided material
and emotional support.

I encouraged potential participants to contact me, rather than the inverse, to
ensure their voluntary participation. I reintroduced myself when potential interviewees contacted me via phone, email, or Facebook. I then screened participants
to ensure that they met the qualifications for study participation (i.e., unaccompanied minor migration, Central American or Mexican origin, did not have a parent
in the United States, between the ages of eighteen and thirty-one, had spent at
least eighteen months in the United States) and arranged dates and times to con-
duct the interviews. Participants selected an interview location where they felt
most comfortable. At the start of each interview, the participant was reminded of
the purpose of the study, given an overview of topics that would be covered, and
told that any question could be skipped entirely or answered without using an
audio recorder. Each interview participant received a study information-form and
gave verbal consent for their participation. These methods were preapproved by
the University of Southern California University Park Institutional Review Board
(UP-15-00606).

Interview Approach and Data Analysis

My original interview guide was informed by my knowledge of existing migration research and experiences with organizing alongside undocumented college
students but expanded as fieldwork added breadth and depth to my understanding of unaccompanied young people's lives in Los Angeles. This research took
an "informant-as-expert" approach.[6] During my initial months of fieldwork, as I
heard the *jóvenes* of Voces de Esperanza discuss memories of life in Guatemala,
I expanded my interview guide to account more systematically for premigration
work, school, and family histories. As my community embeddedness increased
and my recruitment and snowball sampling strategies came to include non-
Indigenous youth, I began asking all participants to reflect on how their experiences with displacement, migration, settlement, and coming of age in the United
States might have been different should they have occupied a different social location, including ethnorace but also legal status, gender, language, and parental
presence in each interview segment. For example, when I asked participants to

detail their work experiences in Los Angeles, I asked, "Do you think your experiences would have been different if you were (non-)Indigenous? You had legal status? You spoke the English language fluently? Your parents had migrated with you?" These questions allowed me to understand participants' subjective interpretations and meanings about their lived experiences.

As my time in the field progressed and the study participants were transitioning to adulthood, I became more attuned to how time and aging shifted, how participants discussed their relationships with their left-behind families, their local communities, and the futures they imagined for themselves. I began asking questions about adulthood and future aspirations across formal and informal conversations. All this is to say that my interview guide was a living document that evolved throughout my time in the field, reflecting the qualitative method of "following up" on ethnographic and interview data.[7]

I independently conducted all ethnographic observations, interviews, and follow-up conversations and prioritized participant consent. Moreover, I conducted all interviews at the interviewee's preferred time and location and in their preferred language. All but one interviewee agreed to be audio recorded. At each interview, I introduced myself, explained the study, and asked the participant their name before the formal interview started. Each interview began with the question "¿Puedo empezar a grabar?" ("May I start recording?") to ensure that interviewees understood when the recording began and what information was or was not on the formal record.

I transcribed all audio-recorded interviews verbatim in the original language. The unrecorded interviewee explained, through laughs, that she disliked the sound of her voice and preferred that I not hear her recording played back. I complied. With her consent, I wrote detailed Spanish-language notes during our unrecorded interview and later converted these into written English-language field notes. At the start of each conversation, I reminded the participant of the voluntary nature of the interview. I gave them the option not to answer questions or to answer questions without being audio recorded when that was preferred, typically in conversations about family violence and romantic relationships or in tear-filled detailings of their mental- and emotional-health challenges. This allowed me to account for potential distress and confirm ongoing consent to the interview procedure.

I remained flexible in my data collection strategies throughout my fieldwork. For example, I carried a hard copy of my interview guide during my first handful of interviews but noticed that the multiple sheets of paper made participants restless. I purchased an iPad Mini for the sole purpose of having an electronic interview guide that might create more ease in the conversation. I studied my interview guide before each interview to remind myself of the order of themes and questions within each theme so that I could rely less on the guide as the conversation evolved. I made every effort to create a conversational space, including spending time before and after the interview chatting with each participant about their day leading up to our meeting or their plans for after our interview concluded. When sensitive issues like loss, abuse, or intense emotions arose, I worked to give participants the space to share as much or as little as they felt comfortable with, asking, "Would you like to say more about that?" rather than the pointed questions "Why?," "How?," or "When?" I often became emotional when participants did and chose to stay authentic in those moments, practicing what sociologist Leisy J. Abrego refers to as "accompaniment."[8]

At the end of each interview, the participant was given $20 cash inserted in a handwritten thank-you card. The practice of offering incentives to research participants is debated, as incentives might be deemed coercive in some cases or presumptive in others.[9] I chose to provide incentives to account for the time spent and the potential cost of commuting to and from the interview, as well as to show my appreciation that many of these conversations took place after work or on weekends, when participants could have (and probably should have) chosen to rest instead of speaking to me. Many interviewees expressed gratitude for my interest in them and their lives, saying that few people had. For some participants, the interview process was their opportunity at *desahogo*. For others, it was a moment of "witnessing" (chapter 5). The National Science Foundation (NSF), which funded participant honorariums, asked that signatures be collected to confirm receipt of the cash amounts. However, collecting signatures would not only have violated the IRB regulation not to collect identifiers for this study but also would have violated my commitment to protect participants' identities. I therefore opted to number the interview participants and asked that they sign an "X" next to their interview numbers and dates of interview. I then submitted this information to the University of Southern California (USC) Sociology Department administrative assistant, who oversaw my NSF grant.

As my community embeddedness grew, I adopted a snowball sampling recruitment strategy. I asked each interviewee if they would feel comfortable telling others with similar experiences about my project. If they agreed, I provided a handful of half-sheet fliers and asked that they share details about the study, the interview format, and how to reach me with their friends, coworkers, or neighbors who met the study criteria. To ensure the voluntary nature of the study, I did not request potential interviewees' names and contact information but included several forms of communicating with me on the flier, including phone number, email, and Facebook link. Upon my initial contact with the referred potential participant, I explained the study's focus, the content of the interviews, and my intention to publish public and academic work based on the experiences of undocumented young adults who grew up in the United States without their parents. I arranged a meeting day, time, and location if potential interviewees met the sampling criteria. I contacted the potential participant twenty-four hours before our scheduled meeting time to confirm our meeting.

To supplement recorded interview transcripts, I completed an interview memo after each interview, which included field notes and observations about existing or emerging themes. I transcribed interview audio files in their original language through the service Datagain. I coded English-language field notes and Spanish-language transcripts using a flexible coding approach in the qualitative data analysis software Dedoose.[10]

I began coding by indexing the main themes in the interview guide, such as pre-and postmigration experiences in work, school, family, and community. I drew on existing literature to include themes such as migration, civic engagement and activism, feelings of belonging, and aspirations for the future. I then reanalyzed data within indexed themes, guided by extant literature and informed by emergent themes from field notes and interview memos. I wrote analytical memos as I coded to draw out such patterns as the role of gender and sexuality in long-settled relatives' receptivity to newcomer youth; the differences in work and school entry; participation trajectories between youth with welcoming household contexts and those who remained unaccompanied; the centrality of work and work conditions in youth's everyday lives; and the social contexts in which youth made meaning of their hardship, sacrifices, and accomplishments and came to understand their incorporation.[11]

This analytical approach allowed me to center young people's voices and agency in meaning making. As I analyzed data for the code "incorporation as process," the terms *desahogo*, *orientación*, *adaptación*, and *perdición* emerged as commonly used among participants, even those who did not know one another. In my analysis, I adopted these terms as the emic categories of unburdening, orientation, adaptation, and perdition to center participants' experiences and perspectives. Throughout my fieldwork and interviews, I paid close attention to young people's emotions and how they expressed them verbally and through body language. Indeed, "emotions" was among my codebook's most populated parent codes. I have attempted to account for the complex emotional lives of unaccompanied, undocumented Central American and Mexican young people in Los

Angeles throughout my writing here and elsewhere. While there was much pain, there was also much joy. While there were many disillusionments, there was also much hope. I hope that by relying on emic categories to explain immigrant incorporation as an ongoing and dynamic process, I have achieved "closeness" to the field and "palpability" of the findings.[12]

Intersectional Positionality

My family background and social identity shaped my access to the spaces I joined and the groups I engaged with over six years. Throughout this research, I contended with my age, ethnorace, linguistic proficiency, and citizenship status in the field.[13] I collected the data presented here as a graduate student in my mid- to late twenties. My age often allowed me to blend into youth and young adult spaces and easily participate in many of the youth's activities. My status as a US-born Latina researcher was cause for trepidation, and justifiably so, given the history of extractive research methods within immigrant and other minoritized communities.[14] I adopted two practices to mitigate this. First, I openly acknowledged my position as an outsider unfamiliar with the norms and experiences of the young people I spent time with but noted that I was eager to learn about how our lives might be similar or different and why. Youth were the experts on their own lives, and I was clear in naming this. Second, I availed myself of each group's and its members' needs when participating. To this end, I set up and tore down events, swept and mopped when asked, picked up food before meetings, and dropped participants off at their homes afterward. Abigail Andrews writes of her work with undocumented Mexican migrants, "The more I stuck around, the more people could tell I cared."[15] This was true for me as well. And because of this, the longer I was in the field, the more invitations I received to participate in organizations' and friends' group events.

Language played an important part in shaping my work pace and the relationships I formed. Despite being a monolingual Spanish-language speaker until age five, I entered the field with limited Spanish fluency—much of which had been lost during my K–12 education. During fieldwork, I learned that many undocumented young workers, particularly Indigenous youth, also felt insecure about their language proficiency in both Spanish and English. My limited Spanish proficiency seemed to level the interviewer-interviewee playing field by reinforcing that I was no more an "expert" than the study participants and that I was eager to learn. In cases where we stumbled to find the words to express ourselves, we offered the term in the language we felt most confident in or described the object, place, or feeling and came to the term together—a collaborative meaning-making process that bolstered rapport. As the years of my fieldwork progressed, so did my spoken Spanish-language proficiency. Much to my family's amusement, I picked up a Guatemalan Spanish intonation.

Alongside finding a shared language and meanings, a sense of shared community knowledge also facilitated my participation in groups. Familiar with the Pico-Union and Westlake/MacArthur Park neighborhoods, I could discuss the local neighborhood and share the excitement and anticipation of upcoming community cultural events. This facilitated introductions and informal conversations. Over time, youth began inviting me to more community events, and I enthusiastically accepted any invitation I received. These invitations allowed me to develop a mobile ethnography wherein I was not confined to one sphere of youth's lives, like work or community, but could observe how participation in one sphere influenced another.[16]

The intersection of age and gender proved critical in my fieldwork as well. I made several attempts to recruit interview participants outside organized community spaces and at day-labor sites, including outside a Los Angeles Home Depot location and two labor centers in central and northern Los Angeles. These recruitment attempts were not only unproductive but at times unsafe. At each of these sites I was verbally harassed by older men who demonstrated an apparent lack of interest in hearing about my work and instead asked questions about my age, where I lived, if I had a romantic partner, and when I would be back. Feeling objectified and unsafe, I discontinued my attempts to recruit workers at public sites. Instead, I relied more heavily on organizational ties and referrals. I recognize the limitations of the data, given that I was limited to interviewees affiliated with organizations aimed at increasing community participation. This certainly affected my ability to tell the story of youth's *perdición*, as I could not access interviewees outside organizational or fictive kin networks. In hindsight, and with appropriate funding, I would have liked to hire a research assistant, preferably a self-identified Latino man with Spanish-language proficiency. This person could have interacted with individuals at these sites more safely; potential interviewees could have more easily related to this person, who could have gained information about experiences of those participants who were inaccessible to me.[17]

Beyond these interactions, being a young woman presented several challenges throughout regarding field site access. For example, when men in their twenties or thirties were gatekeepers of the organizations I sought to recruit participants from, they suggested they would share information about young people in exchange for my personal phone number or a one-on-one meeting with me.

These tactics proved self-serving. In 2015, a man I volunteered alongside for a summer camp for recently arrived, unaccompanied minors retrieved my personal information from an emergency contact card and began leaving small gifts at my apartment's front door. The following spring, when he was also volunteering for a university campus visit for teenaged unaccompanied teens, he made a sexual advance in a campus residence hall as we planned a group activity for the youth. On another occasion, a man who agreed to put me in touch with unaccompanied teens became angry when I refused to send him photos of myself via text message. He withheld further information about potential interviewees, and I lost contact with the organization.

These interactions reinforce the impact of researcher identity on study design, methods, and analysis beyond the questions we ask and how we interpret our data. Our identities can grant or deny access by making certain spaces safe or unsafe for us to inhabit as researchers. Women, young researchers, people of minoritized ethnoracial backgrounds, and queer scholars might be especially at risk of harassment during fieldwork.[18] I did not choose to share these experiences with others during my fieldwork, perhaps because of feelings of shame or embarrassment that I was doing ethnography wrong. In retrospect, resources like those offered by the online project The New Ethnographer would have been useful and encouraging (www.thenewethnographer.com).

Additionally, several times young men arrived at our interviews expecting that we were on a romantic date. One study participant asked me to be his girl-friend after I gave him a ride home from a youth group meeting (he was one of four young men I regularly dropped off at their apartments across Pico-Union as I made my way west from downtown Los Angeles to Koreatown, where I lived, after weekly group gatherings). Finally, young women around my age at the time expressed to the men in the groups I attended that they felt shy or insecure around me, the "American girl" who spoke English. These age, gender, citizen-ship, and language dynamics certainly informed whom I could interview and how the interviews developed. Still, the interviews I collected capture a breadth and depth of data that has yet to be considered in academic and policy conversations. I collected these data through intentional rapport building.

Admittedly, my interactions with the youth whose stories are recorded in the pages of this book served as my introduction to the existence of unaccompanied Central American and Mexican teens and young adults living in Los Angeles. I had been heavily involved in organizing with undocumented students in the years before this research, but I had yet to contemplate the possibility of undoc-umented young people growing up as workers in factories, restaurants, hotels, construction sites, and private homes across Los Angeles. The harrowing pre-migration, migration, and settlement experiences they shared with me were jarring. And it haunted me deeply that as pained as I was by the stories these youth shared, I was privileged to drive home after an interview, a group gathering, or a funeral, where I would then summarize, analyze, and theorize the events that had taken place on any given day.

Trauma and Establishing an Ethics of Care

Although conversations about researchers' health and well-being are currently more present in the social sciences, I was not privy to such discussions a decade ago. Throughout this research, I became accustomed to unsafe encounters as well as to the psychosomatic symptoms associated with the research I was doing, including migraines, constant colds, and persistent tension around my neck and shoulders. During my six years of fieldwork, I felt fatigue, anxiety, and worry. I suffered from sleeplessness at night and drowsiness during the day. I was authentic to my emotions during interviews but held back reactions during fieldwork to avoid imposing myself into a space or onto participants. I was unable to fight back tears of frustration, anger, sadness, and grief on my drives home from my field site visits or after interviews. One night I left an interview feeling sick after hearing about the sexual violence a young woman had endured and pulled over on Sixth Street in Pico-Union to vomit.

Most of the time I felt angry that this was so many people's reality. On many occasions I would leave in wonder: How could people who endured so much violence and harm embody so much resilience and hope? On other occasions I felt guilty that I was leaving, that I was *just* a researcher, a social scientist, not a social worker or even a lawyer who could give some tangible relief. I did what I could with what I knew. I began writing opinion editorials, public essays, and policy reports early in my data collection. I spoke with reporters and journalists and committed to developing partnerships with community organizations and collaboratives across Los Angeles. Engaging in work that had immediate output and impact felt like the least I could do to fulfill my "obligation to reciprocate with advocacy."[19] Scholar advocacy felt energizing.[20] But finishing the PhD requirements was challenging. Truth be told, it felt uncomfortable to launch a career as a sociologist and achieve status mobility while telling the stories of youth and young adults who had (and continue to have) few options to do the same.

It was not until I started my next project, with service providers working with unaccompanied asylum-seeking children, that I realized that I was experiencing vicarious trauma and some compassion fatigue.[21] These are psychological and emotional conditions associated with ongoing exposure to suffering and traumatized populations.[22] I had implemented strategies to minimize the retraumatization of my study participants and to honor the sensitivity of the subject matter I was discussing with them, as migration methods experts suggest, and had neglected to establish an ethic of care for myself.[23] I explain this now because people often ask me what it was like to do this research. The answer is that it was intellectually challenging, sure, but it was also physically, emotionally, and mentally challenging. It goes without saying that it was not nearly as hard for me as it is for the youth living the lives I detail in this book. Knowing that weighed on me daily. Still, this research is necessary, and equipping other researchers to engage in this type of work is essential for creating policies and programs that effectively mitigate the harms unaccompanied immigrant youth endure.

I believe researchers' health and well-being are essential components of rigorous research methods and data production. In retrospect, I wish I had equipped myself with tools for enhanced well-being. Since graduate school, I have entered therapy; found outlets for artistic expression such as painting, pottery, and creative writing; and developed a daily movement practice. These efforts are just as important for my research process as making semester plans, attending Sunday meetings, and maintaining a daily writing practice. I share these reflections to acknowledge the troubles that come alongside the triumphs of writing a dissertation and transforming that work into a book, as well as the long-term commitment to practice public sociology and scholar advocacy.[24] I offer them here, as my concluding thought, to do what my therapist reminds me to do often—"lean into being human"—and to encourage other researchers to do the same.

Notes

Introduction

1. Deferred Action for Childhood Arrivals (DACA) is an administrative executive order signed by President Barack Obama on June 15, 2012 to temporarily defer deportation from the United States for eligible undocumented youth and young adults. These young people are also granted a temporary Social Security number and a two-year work permit. To qualify, applicants must demonstrate that they (1) were under thirty-one years of age in June 2012; (2) were under the age of sixteen at the time of entry to the US and entered the US without inspection before June 2012; and (3) either are enrolled in school, have graduated from high school, have obtained a GED, or have been honorably discharged from the Coast Guard or armed forces, among other requirements. DACA was rescinded by the Trump administration in September 2017, restored by a federal judge in December 2020, and made a final rule in 2021 by the Biden administration. DACA opened access to new jobs, higher earnings, driver's licenses, health care, and banking for six hundred thousand immigrant youth.

2. Batalova and McHugh 2010.

3. Congressional Research Service 2021a.

4. US Citizenship and Immigration Services n.d.

5. Bean, Brown, and Bachmeier 2015; Gonzales 2015; Portes and Rumbaut 2001; Rumbaut and Komaie 2010; Telles and Ortiz 2009; Zhou and Bankston 1998.

6. Portes and Zhou 1993.

7. Blau and Duncan 1967; Coleman 1988; Furstenberg 1993.

8. Portes and Rumbaut 2001.

9. Portes and Zhou 1993; Golash Boza and Valdez 2018.

10. Massey, Durand, and Pren 2016. For more on differential inclusion as subordinate subjects, see Ramírez 2020. For more on racialized inclusion, see also Sáenz and Douglas 2015 and Treitler 2015.

11. Gleeson and Gonzales 2012.

12. Neckerman, Carter, and Lee 1999.

13. Portes and Fernández-Kelly 2008, 26.

14. Gonzales 2015.

15. Galli 2023.

16. Landale, Thomas, and Van Hook 2011.

17. Canizales 2023c; Diaz-Strong 2020; Martinez 2019.

18. Massey, Durand, and Malone 2003.

19. Abrego 2014.

20. Cranford 2005; Del Real 2019; Herrera 2017; Menjívar 2000; Rosales 2020.

21. Hondagneu-Sotelo 1994.

22. Feliciano 2005; Waldinger 2001.

23. Gleeson 2012.

24. Mahler 1995.

25. Canizales 2019; Rosales 2020; Hagan 1994; Hondagneu-Sotelo 2001; Menjívar 2000.

26. Bloemraad 2018; Bloemraad and Sheares 2017; Ribas 2016.

27. Ribas 2016.

28. Bronfenbrenner and Morris 1998; Suárez-Orozco et al. 2011.

29. Ribas 2016, 8.

30. Human Rights Watch 2019.

31. Van Hook, Gelatt, and Ruiz Soto 2023. Among undocumented Mexicans and Central Americans (7.4 million people total), 46 percent from originate from Mexico, 7 percent are from El Salvador, 7 percent are from Guatemala, and 5 percent are from Honduras (Van Hook, Gelatt, and Ruiz Soto 2023). Inversely, Central Americans account for three-quarters of unaccompanied minor apprehensions.

32. Congressional Research Service 2023.

33. Customs and Border Protection estimates that the total number of unaccompanied and separated Central American children apprehended at the border increased from 4,059 in FY2011 to 10,443 in FY2012, and then doubled in FY2013 to a total of 21,537 apprehensions. This rise coincided with the increase in Mexican children apprehended at the border. In FY2011, a total of 13,000 Mexican

children were apprehended by Customs and Border Protection. Another 15,709 were apprehended in FY2012, and 18,754 in FY2013.

34. About 77 percent of unaccompanied children apprehended at the US southern border originate from Central America alone, and 18 percent are of Mexican origin (Congressional Research Service 2021b).

35. Massey, Durand, and Malone 2003.

36. The states that are consistently receiving the highest rates of unaccompanied minors are Texas, California, and Florida. For information on release patterns, reference the ORR's annual "Unaccompanied Children Released to Sponsors by State" report at www.acf.hhs.gov/orr/grant-funding/unaccompanied-children-released-sponsors-state.

37. Migration Policy Institute n.d.-b.

38. Massey, Durand, and Malone 2003.

39. Hayes and Hill 2017. Undocumented immigrants make up 10 percent of the state's workforce, adding $263 billion to the state's annual gross domestic product (Hinojosa-Ojeda and Robinson 2020). Undocumented immigrants in the greater Los Angeles region contribute $87 billion to its GDP.

40. Smith 2023.

41. Loh and Richardson 2004.

42. Abrego 2011; Gomberg-Muñoz 2019; Gleeson 2016.

43. Kim 2015.

44. Estrada 2019.

45. Canizales 2021; Orellana 2009.

46. *US News and World Report* 2023.

47. RentCafe n.d.-a.

48. RentCafe n.d.-b.

49. Canizales 2023d.

50. Hagan, Hernandez-León, and Demonsant 2015.

51. Hagan, Hernandez-León, and Demonsant 2015.

52. Wellmeier 1998.

53. Canizales 2019; Gómez Cervantes 2021b; Herrera 2016; Saldaña-Portillo 2017.

54. Collins and Steinberg 2006; Muuss 1996.

55. Canizales 2022.

56. Arnett 2004.

57. Shanahan 2000.

58. Cooper 2014; Halpern-Meekin 2017; Hardie 2022.

59. Arnett 2000; 2004; Silva 2013.

60. Diaz-Strong and Gonzales 2023.

61. Martinez 2019.

62. Diaz-Strong 2021a.

63. Kwon 2022.

64. Andrews 2018; Estrada 2019; Abrego 2011.

65. Andrews 2018; Estrada 2019; Abrego 2011.

66. Bloemraad 2018; Halpern-Meekin 2017; Halpern-Meekin et al. 2015.

67. Large and Marcussen 2000; Sheeran and McCarthy 1992; Smith-Greenway and Yeatman 2020.

Chapter 1. Departures

1. Kandel and Massey 2002; Martinez 2019.

2. Ruehs 2016.

3. Hondagneu-Sotelo 1994.

4. Kandel and Massey 2002; Massey, Durand, and Malone 2003.

5. Kandel and Massey 2002.

6. Hamilton and Bylander 2020; Heidbrink 2020; Martinez 2019.

7. Escamilla García 2021.

8. Stark and Bloom 1985; Galli 2023.

9. Heidbrink 2020.

10. Heidbrink 2019, 263; 2020, 33.

11. Kennedy 2013.

12. Notably, unaccompanied immigrant youth are one segment of the total 43.3 million forcibly displaced children under the age of eighteen across the globe (UNICEF 2023). Children account for 12 percent of international migrants worldwide (UNICEF 2021).

13. Durand, Massey, and Zenteno 2001; Gómez 2020; Hamilton and Chinchilla 2001; Heidbrink 2020; Speed 2019.

14. For the purpose of this book, in which 81 percent of participants (sixty-one of seventy-five total interviewees) arrived from Central America and the remaining arrived from Mexico (fourteen total interviewees), I refrain from recounting the full history of US-Mexico entanglements that created the patterns of Mexican migration we are familiar with today. I encourage readers instead to visit works like Massey, Durand, and Malone's *Beyond Smoke and Mirrors* (2003), Hondagneu-Sotelo's *Gendered Transitions* (1994), and Fox and Rivera-Salgado's *Indigenous Mexican Migrants in the United States* (2004) for in-depth analyses of the stages of Mexican migration and their gendered and ethnoracial dynamics, respectively.

15. Padilla-Rodríguez 2022.

16. Durand, Massey, and Zenteno 2001; Rosas 2014.

17. Reichert and Massey 1980.

18. Padilla-Rodríguez 2020.

19. Massey, Durand, and Malone 2003; Massey, Goldring, and Durand 1994.

20. Fernández-Kelly and Massey 2007; Hernández-León 2008.

21. Hernández-León 2008; Massey, Durand, and Malone 2003.

22. Almeida 2008; Manz 2005; Portillo Villeda 2021.

23. Ward and Botalova 2023.

24. US Institute of Peace 1997. The heights of this "Silent Holocaust" were reached in 1978 and 1983 under the regimes of General Fernando Romeo Lucas García and General Efraín Ríos Montt. Ríos Montt implemented the scorched-earth policy that led to the eradication of over four hundred Maya villages.

25. Heidbrink 2020.

26. Heidbrink 2020.

27. Batz 2020; see also Kaenzig and Piguet 2014.

28. Portillo Villeda 2021.

29. Meyer and Seelke 2015.

30. Lopez, Connell, and Kraul 2005.

31. Coutin 2010, 2016; Golash-Boza 2014.

32. Lopez, Connell, and Kraul 2005.

33. Heidbrink 2020; Martinez 2019.

34. Heidbrink 2020.

35. Coutin 2016.

36. UN Development Programme 2021.

37. Bourgois 2003.

38. Stark and Bloom 1985.

39. Andrews 2018; Beristain, Paez, and González 2000; Erazo 2010; Schwake and Iannone 2010.

40. Menjívar 2011.

41. Kennedy 2013.

42. UN Economic Commission for Latin America 2022.

43. There is only a 6 percent margin between 29 percent reports of deprivation and 23 percent reports of violence, according to UNHCR (2016).

44. Research shows that immigrant parents migrate expecting their remittances to maximize their children's educational attainment. In this way, when older siblings migrate to support the educational attainment of their younger

siblings, they are taking on migration goals and responsibilities typically associated with adults and parents.

45. Abrego 2014; Parreñas 2015; Boehm 2008.

46. *Los Angeles Times* 2014.

47. Chavez and Menjívar 2010. In a 2011 report, UNHCR (2016) interviewed Salvadoran (104), Guatemalan (100; 48 percent Maya), Honduran (98), and Mexican (102) children about the reasons for their migration.

48. Wolseth 2008.

49. Ramos de Oliveira and Jeong 2021.

50. Hondagneu-Sotelo 1994.

51. Hondagneu-Sotelo 1994; Pessar 1999; see also Andrews 2018.

52. It is estimated that at least twelve women die of gender-based violence every day across the region, with the highest rates of femicide occurring in Honduras, the Dominican Republic, and El Salvador (UN Economic Commission for Latin America 2022).

53. The Critical Latinx Indigeneities framework (see Blackwell, Boj Lopez, and Urrieta 2017) recognizes that among the lasting legacies of colonial projects in Latin America and settler colonialism in the United States is that Indigenous and non-Indigenous Latin Americans face distinct racialization processes within and across nation-states.

54. Manz 2005.

55. Blackwell 2017, 175.

Chapter 2. Arrivals

1. Aditti 2006; Calzada, Tamis-LeMonda, and Yoshikawa 2012.

2. Menjívar 2000; Rosales 2020.

3. Bronfenbrenner and Morris 1998.

4. Keller et al. 2017.

5. Golash-Boza and Valdez 2018.

6. Hagan 1994; Hamilton and Chinchilla 2001.

7. Berger Cardoso 2018.

8. Acker 2006.

9. De Genova 2002; Enriquez 2020; Flores and Schachter 2018.

10. Migration Policy Institute n.d.-a.

11. Massey, Durand, and Malone 2003. Only individuals who arrived in the United States prior to January 1, 1982, were eligible for IRCA, making the

thousands of Central Americans who migrated during the political conflicts of the 1980s ineligible for its provisions.

12. Menjívar 2000.

13. Menjívar 2000.

14. Menjívar and Abrego 2012.

15. De Genova 2002.

16. American Immigration Council 2013.

17. The Secure Communities Program was struck down for its reliance on racial profiling and replaced with the Priority Enforcement Program between 2015 and 2017, when it was resurrected by executive order by the Trump administration. President Biden repealed the Secure Communities Program in 2021.

18. Asad 2023.

19. Gómez Cervantes and Menjívar 2020; Patler and Pirtle 2018; Suro, Suárez-Orozco, Canizales 2015.

20. Flores and Schachter 2018.

21. Asad and Clair 2018; Dreby 2015.

22. García 2014; Simmons, Menjívar, Salerno Valdez 2021.

23. Agius Vallejo 2012; Hondagneu-Sotelo and Pastor 2021.

24. Hagan 1994.

25. Obinna 2021.

26. Golash-Boza and Hondagneu-Sotelo 2013; Gómez Cervantes 2021b. On the emergence of "suddenly single mothers," see also Dreby 2015.

27. Del Real 2019; see also Cranford 2005 and Mahler 1995.

28. Menjívar and Abrego 2012.

29. State of California Department of Justice n.d.; Andrews 2018; Van Natta 2023.

30. Ward and Batalova 2023; Moslimani, Bustamante, and Shah 2023.

31. Acker 2006.

32. Da Silva et al. 2021; Hondagneu-Sotelo 1994.

33. Abrego 2014.

34. Abrego 2014.

35. Ruehs 2016.

36. González-López 2015; Valenzuela 1999.

37. Espiritu 2003.

38. The Los Angeles basin sits on Indigenous Tongva land from which its original inhabitants were displaced by Spanish (1781–1821), Mexican (1821–1847),

and US (1847–present) colonial settlers. The original pueblo was built near the Tongva village of Yaanga.

39. Nicholls 2013.

40. Gonzales 2015; Nicholls 2013.

41. Hondagneu-Sotelo 1992, 394–96. For more on patriarchal family strategies, see Hondagneu-Sotelo 1994.

42. González-López 2015.

43. Diaz-Strong 2021b.

44. A landmark Supreme Court ruling in *Plyler v. Doe* (1982) wrote into law that school districts could neither bar undocumented children from public schools nor charge them tuition. The Plyler decision affirmed the public school system as a legally permissible institution where undocumented children could receive an education. *Plyler v. Doe* included undocumented immigrant children into the country's legal and cultural framework by weaving their childhoods into the fabric of American society. The continuing inequities in access to and experiences of education after *Plyler v. Doe* are explained in Gonzales, Heredia, and Negrón-Gonzales 2015.

45. González-López 2015.

Chapter 3. (Dis)orientation

1. Boccagni and Hondagneu-Sotelo 2001.

2. Clausen 1991, 836–37.

3. Clausen 1991.

4. Small and Gose 2020.

5. Collins 1994; see also Bloch 2017.

6. For more on Central American immigrants' entrance into the low-wage labor market in the United States, and Los Angeles specifically, see Hamilton and Chinchilla 2001. For more on Mexican immigrants' entrance into the low-wage labor market in the United States, see Massey, Durand, and Malone 2003. On Central American and Mexican immigrants' position in the contemporary labor market, see Massey, Durand, and Pren 2016. For more on unaccompanied youth workers' moral obligations to left-behind family, see Canizales 2023b.

7. Hondagneu-Sotelo and Pastor 2021.

8. Galli 2023.

9. Zelizer 1985.

10. UNESCO 2016.

11. Segmented assimilation theorists posit that, along with providing material resources, parents provide immigrant children and children of immigrants with moral resources.

12. Blackwell, Boj Lopez, and Urrietta 2017.

13. Halpern-Meekin 2017, 21.

14. Hagan and Ebaugh 2003; Smith 1978.

15. Bankston and Zhou 1996.

16. Batz 2020; Herrera 2016; Loucky and Moors 2000.

17. Canizales 2019.

18. Abrego 2014; Heidbrink 2014, 2020; Hondagneu-Sotelo and Avila 1997; Levitt 2001; Schmalzbauer 2005.

19. Kasinitz et al. 2008.

20. Enriquez 2011.

Chapter 4. Adaptation

1. Portes and Rumbaut 2001.

2. The notion of institutional primacy applies to all groups. Immigrant and nonimmigrant students coming of age in a normative life-stage trajectory, for example, might experience school primacy. Students might then participate in nonschool institutions in ways that reflect and reinforce their status as students. Though the process may be the same, the institutions in which they occur, and especially in adolescence, is critical in that they determine exposure, everyday interactions that shape identity, and the point of reference from which to measure success. Furthermore, youth workers in this study navigate these processes without parents who act as buffers or guides.

3. Feliciano 2005; Gleeson 2012.

4. See Bonacich and Appelbaum (2000) for more on the Los Angeles garment industry.

5. Canizales 2019; Herrera 2016.

6. Abrego 2014; Gleeson 2016.

7. Canizales 2023e.

8. Rumbaut 2004.

9. Suárez-Orozco, Suárez-Orozco, and Todorova 2010; Waters 1999.

10. Hagan, Lowe, and Quingla 2011.

11. Hagan, Lowe, and Quingla 2011, 151–52.

12. Casanova, O'Connor, and Anthony-Stevens 2016.

13. Diaz-Strong 2021b..

14. In January 2015, California became the tenth state to permit undocumented immigrants to obtain a driver's license, through the passage of California Assembly Bill 60, the Safe and Responsible Driver's Act, which moderated the consequences of illegality by increasing immigrants' ability to participate in their local society (Enriquez, Vazquez Vera, and Ramakrishnan 2019; Stuesse and Coleman 2014). AB60 would not only facilitate undocumented immigrants' social mobility but decrease the risk of encountering immigration enforcement and therefore the risk of deportation (Armenta 2017; Romero 2006). AB60 would also buffer undocumented immigrants from the financial risks associated with confiscation of an unlicensed driver's car. Though none of the study participants had obtained a driver's license at the time of my research, they were aware of the possibility to do so and often spoke about when they would have their chance to apply. Buying a car was a first step toward learning to drive and to practicing for the eventual "behind-the-wheel" driver's test.

15. Valdivia 2019.

16. For more on how unaccompanied Maya youth develop and rely on their multilingual proficiency to navigate an array of social spaces and interactions, including interactions with non-Indigenous Latin Americans, Koreans, and White Americans, see Canizales (2021) and Canizales and O'Connor (2022).

17. California Department of Education n.d.

18. The author was nicknamed Chep by Maya youth, who said this was the K'iche' translation for Stephanie or Steph.

19. Verbatim quote of the original post.

20. Canizales and O'Connor 2022.

21. Written text reflects that of the original message.

22. Wellmeier 1998; Menjívar 2011; Canizales 2019; O'Connor and Canizales 2023.

23. For a detailed elaboration of this linguistic adaptation process, see Canizales and O'Connor (2022).

24. Gonzales, Suárez-Orozco, and Dedios-Sanguineti 2013.

25. Costa and Alinejad 2020, 1.

26. Verbatim quote of the original post.

27. Translated and paraphrased for clarity by the author.

28. Livingston and Lopez 2010. Millennials are described as "tech-savvy," while Gen Z is described as "tech native."

29. Hometown associations fulfill several important functions across transnational immigrant communities, including the transmission of financial and

social remittances (Levitt 2001; Orozco and Rouse 2007) and political influence (Andrews 2018). Hometown associations have been critical for the development of rural areas in Latin American immigrants' origin countries (Orozco and Lapointe 2004).

Chapter 5. Perdition

1. Neckerman, Carter, and Lee 1999.

2. Silva 2013.

3. Unlike in other chapters, I use the Spanish term *perdición* in the text because its most appropriate connotations appear when presented in its Spanish iteration.

4. I do not contend that gender is binary but present an analysis reflective of participants' self-identified genders. The binary expression of gender in this context may have constrained participants' naming and expression of emotions, which limits the analysis. I note this while also being aware that deconstructing gender categories is not within the scope of this book.

5. Lijtmaer 2022; Suárez-Orozco, Suárez-Orozco, and Todorova 2010.

6. Meier and Allen 2008; Morris et al. 2007.

7. Da Silva et al., 2021; Montes 2013.

8. Montes 2013.

9. Daley 2016; Menjívar 2011; Speed 2019; Tereškinas 2010.

10. Perrotte, Baumann, and Knight 2018.

11. Perrotte, Baumann, and Knight 2018.

12. Abrego 2014.

13. Da Silva et al. 2021.

14. Durkheim 1951.

15. Kidd and Carroll 2007.

16. Daley 2016; Sussman and Arnett 2014, 149.

17. Hovey 2000.

18. Meldrum and Leimberg 2018.

19. Berger Cardoso 2018.

20. Halpern-Meekin 2017.

21. Meier and Allen 2008.

22. Enriquez 2020.

23. Abrego 2014.

24. Diaz-Strong 2021b; Menjívar 2000.

25. Da Silva et al. 2021.

26. To respect participants and avoid retraumatization, I did not probe for specifics in these instances but allowed participants to provide as much or as little detail as they wanted.

27. Abrego 2014; Diaz-Strong 2021b.

28. Adams and Campbell 2012.

29. Menjívar 2000.

Chapter 6. Success

1. Canizales and Agius Vallejo 2021.

2. McCaskill 2016.

3. For more on family separation as deterrence, see Dickerson 2022. For commentary by Jeff Sessions, see Dezenski 2017.

4. Bolter, Israel, Pierce 2022.

5. Lamont 2002.

6. Agius Vallejo 2012; Clerge 2019.

7. Ramírez 2020, 82. "Moral economies of deservingness" was theorized by Chauvin and Garcés-Mascareñas 2012, 234; see also Menjívar and Lakhani 2016 for more on this.

8. Agius Vallejo and Canizales 2023; Rosales 2020.

9. "Homemaking" is "a set of practices and perspectives of migrants' way of local incorporation, with its own material, emotional, and relational underpinnings," and "while integration is a multi-dimensional and multi-scalar effort, it still rests on place-bound fields of interaction within and between groups, informed by different views and emotions about home, and by unequal possibilities to make them real" (Boccagni and Hondagneu-Sotelo 2021, 2). Focusing on "place-making and integration" allows us to move past thinking of immigrants as "subjects of exclusion, but also as agents of belonging" (Bickham Mendez and Deeb-Sossa 2020, 177).

10. Bickham Mendez and Deeb-Sossa 2020, 176–77.

11. Gomberg-Muñoz 2019.

12. Dow 2016; Espiritu 2003; Gonzalez 2022; Hondagneu-Sotelo and Pastor 2021.

13. Diaz-Strong 2021a.

Conclusion

1. US Customs and Border Protection n.d.

2. Zelizer 1985.

3. Enriquez 2020.

4. Zelizer 1985.

5. Diaz-Strong and Gonzales 2023.

6. Ribas 2016.

7. Bonilla-Silva 2005; Cooper 2014; Halpern-Meekin 2017; Silva 2013.

8. Portes and Zhou 1993.

9. Golash-Boza and Valdez 2018.

10. Enriquez 2020; Gonzales 2015.

11. Pham and Van 2021.

12. Cranford 2005; Kasinitz et al. 2008; Menjívar 2000; Gonzales 2015.

13. Borger 2018; Hamilton and Chinchilla 2001; Durand, Massey, and Zenteno 2001.

14. Canizales 2023c; Portes 2020.

15. Heidbrink 2020.

16. Nichols 2023.

17. During the Trump administration, border deaths averaged about 300 per year (Alvarez 2022). Under the Biden administration, this number rose to 850 in fiscal year 2022 alone (Rose and Peñaloza 2022).

18. Galli 2023.

19. Canizales 2023d.

20. Halpern-Meekin 2017.

21. Gleeson 2016; Gómez Cervantes and Menjívar 2020; Theodore 2013; Van Natta 2023.

22. Simmons, Menjívar, and Salerno Valdez 2021; Valdivia 2019.

23. Agius Vallejo 2012.

24. Migration Policy Institute n.d.-a.

25. Gleeson 2012.

26. US Department of Labor n.d..

27. Sherer and Mast 2023.

28. Canizales and Hondagneu-Sotelo 2022.

29. Oakland Unified School District n.d.

30. Landale, Thomas, and Van Hook 2011.

31. Patler, Gleeson, and Schonlau 2022, 356.

32. Portes and Fernández-Kelly 2008.

33. Canizales 2023c.

34. Nicholls 2013.

35. Canizales 2023a.

Appendix B. Methodological Reflections

1. McLaughlin and Alfaro-Velcamp 2015.
2. Bloemraad and Menjívar 2022.
3. Andrews 2018.
4. Livingston and Lopez 2010.
5. Estrada and Hondagneu-Sotelo 2011.
6. Gonzales 2021.
7. Small and Calarco 2022.
8. Abrego 2023.
9. Bloemraad and Menjívar 2022.
10. Deterding and Waters 2018.
11. Timmermans and Tavory 2012.
12. Small and Calarco 2022, 80–81.
13. Canizales 2022.
14. McLaughlin and Alfaro-Velcamp 2015.
15. Andrews 2018, 217.
16. Heidbrink 2020.
17. For the effectiveness of this strategy, see Lacayo 2017.
18. Congdon 2015; Kloß 2017.
19. Horton 2016, 190.
20. Hondagneu-Sotelo 1993.
21. Canizales 2023a.
22. Newell and MacNeil 2010.
23. Bloemraad and Menjívar 2022; Zapata-Barrero and Yalaz 2020.
24. Burawoy 2005.

References

Abrego, Leisy J. 2011. "Legal Consciousness of Undocumented Latinos: Fear and Stigma as Barriers to Claims-Making for First- and 1.5-Generation Immigrants." *Law & Society Review* 45(2): 337–70.

———. 2014. *Sacrificing Families: Navigating Laws, Labor and Love across Borders.* Stanford, CA: Stanford University Press

———. 2023. "Research as Accompaniment: Reflections on Objectivity, Ethics, and Emotions." In *Out of Place: Power, Person, and Difference in Socio-Legal Research*, edited by Lynnette Chua and Mark Massoud. https://escholarship .org/uc/item/34v2g837.

Acker, Joan. 2006. "Inequality Regimes: Gender, Class, and Race in Organizations." *Gender & Society* 20(4): 441–64.

Adams, Margaret E., and Jacquelyn Campbell. 2012. "Being Undocumented and Intimate Partner Violence (IPV): Multiple Vulnerabilities through the Lens of Feminist Intersectionality." *Women's Health and Urban Life* 11(1): 15–34.

Aditti, Joyce A. 2006. "Editor's Note." *Family Relations: An Interdisciplinary Journal of Applied Family Studies* 55(3): 263–65.

Agius Vallejo, Jody. 2012. *Barrios to Burbs: The Making of the Mexican American Middle Class.* Stanford, CA: Stanford University Press.

Agius Vallejo, Jody, and Stephanie L. Canizales. 2023. "Ethnoracial Capitalism and the Limits of Ethnic Solidarity." *Social Problems* 70(4): 961–80.

Almeida, Paul D. 2008. *Waves of Protest: Popular Struggle in El Salvador, 1925–2005.* Minnesota: University of Minnesota Press.

Alvarez, Priscilla. 2022. "First on CNN: A Record Number of Migrants Have Died Crossing the U.S.-Mexico Border." *CNN*, September 7. www.cnn.com /2022/09/07/politics/us-mexico-border-crossing-deaths.

American Immigration Council. 2013. "The Criminal Alien Program (CAP): Immigration Enforcement in Prisons and Jails." Washington, DC. www .americanimmigrationcouncil.org/sites/default/files/research/cap_fact _sheet_8-1_fin_0.pdf.

Andrews, Abigail L. 2018. *Undocumented Politics: Place, Gender, and Pathways of Mexican Migrants*. Oakland: University of California Press.

Armenta, Amada. 2017. *Protect, Serve, and Deport: The Rise of Policing as Immigration Enforcement*. Oakland: University of California Press.

Arnett, Jeffrey Jensen. 2000. "Emerging Adulthood: A Theory of Development from the Late Teens through the Twenties." *American Psychologist* 55(5): 469–80.

———. 2004. *Emerging Adulthood: The Winding Road from Late Teens through the Twenties*. New York: Oxford University Press.

Asad, Asad L. 2023. *Engage and Evade: How Latino Immigrant Families Manage Surveillance in Everyday Life*. Princeton, NJ: Princeton University Press.

Asad, Asad L., and Matthew Clair. 2018. "Racialized Legal Status as a Social Determinant of Health." *Social Science & Medicine* 199: 19–28.

Aufseeser, Deena, Susan Jekielek, and Brett Brown. 2006. *The Family Environmental and Adolescent Well-Being: Exposure to Positive and Negative Family Influences*. Washington, DC: Child Trends; San Francisco, CA: National Adolescent Health Information Center, University of California, San Francisco. https://nahic.ucsf.edu/wp-content/uploads/2011/02/2006-Fam EnvironBrief.pdf.

Bankston, Carl L., and Min Zhou. 1996. "The Ethnic Church, Ethnic Identification, and the Social Adjustment of Vietnamese Adolescents." *Review of Religious Research* 38(1): 18–37.

Batalova, Jeanne, and Margie McHugh. 2010. "DREAM vs. Reality: An Analysis of Potential Dream Act Beneficiaries." Washington, DC: Migration Policy Institute. www.migrationpolicy.org/pubs/DREAM-Insight-July2010.pdf.

Batz, Giovanni. 2020. "Ixil Maya Resistance against Megaprojects in Cotzal, Guatemala." *Theory & Event* 23(4): 1016–36.

Bean, Frank, Susan K. Brown, and James D. Bachmeier. 2015. *Parents without Papers: The Progress and Pitfalls of Mexican American Integration*. New York: Russell Sage Foundation.

Berger Cardoso, Jodi. 2018. "Running to Stand Still: Trauma Symptoms, Coping Strategies, and Substance Use Behaviors in Unaccompanied Migrant Children." *Children and Youth Services Review* 92: 143–52.

Beristain, Carlos Marín, Darío Paez, and José Luis González. 2000. "Rituals, Social Sharing, Silence, Emotions and Collective Memory Claims in the Case of the Guatemalan Genocide." *Psicothema* 12: 117–30.

Bickham Mendez, Jennifer, and Natalia Deeb-Sossa. 2020. "Creating Home, Claiming Place: Latina Immigrant Mothers and the Production of Belonging." *Latino Studies* 18: 174–94.

Blackwell, Maylei. 2017. "Geographies of Indigeneity: Indigenous Migrant Women's Organizing and Translocal Politics of Place." *Latino Studies* 15(2): 156–81.

Blackwell, Maylei, Floridalma Boj Lopez, and Luis Urrieta. 2017. "Special Issue: Critical Latinx Indigeneities." *Latino Studies* 15(2): 126–37.

Blau, Peter M., Otis Dudley Duncan. 1967. *The American Occupational Structure.* New York: Wiley.

Bloch, Alexia. 2017. "'Other Mothers,' Migration, and a Transnational Nurturing Nexus." *Sins: Journal of Women in Culture and Society* 43(1): 53–75.

Bloemraad, Irene. 2018. "Theorising the Power of Citizenship as Claims-making." *Journal of Ethnic and Migration Studies* 44(1): 4–26.

Bloemraad, Irene, and Cecilia Menjívar. 2022. "Precarious Times, Professional Tensions: The Ethics of Migration Research and the Drive for Scientific Accountability." *International Migration Review* 56(1): 4–32.

Bloemraad, Irene, and Alicia Sheares. 2017. "Understanding Membership in a World of Global Migration: (How) Does Citizenship Matter?" *International Migration Review* 51(4): 823–67.

Boccagni, Paolo, and Pierrette Hondagneu-Sotelo. 2021. "Integration and Struggle to Turn Space into 'Our' Place: Homemaking as a Way Beyond the Stalemate of Assimilation vs Transnationalism." *International Migration* 1: 1–14.

Boehm, Deborah A. 2008. "'For My Children': Constructing Family and Navigating the State in the U.S.-Mexico Transnation." *Anthropological Quarterly* 81(4): 777–802.

Bolter, Jessica, Emma Israel, and Sarah Pierce. 2022. "Four Years of Profound Change: Immigration Policy during the Trump Presidency." Washington, DC: Migration Policy Institute. www.migrationpolicy.org/sites/default/files/publications/mpi-trump-at-4-report-final.pdf.

Bonacich, Edna, and Richard Appelbaum. 2000. *Behind the Label: Inequality in the Los Angeles Apparel Industry.* Berkeley: University of California Press.

Bonilla-Silva, Eduardo. 2005. *Racism without Racists: Color Blind Racism and the Persistence of Racial Inequality in the United States.* New York: Rowman & Littlefield.

Borger, Julian. 2018. "Fleeing a Hell the U.S. Helped Create: Why Central Americans Journey North." *Guardian*, December 19. www.theguardian.com/us-news/2018/dec/19/central-america-migrants-us-foreign-policy.

Bourgois, Philippe. 2003. *In Search of Respect: Selling Crack in El Barrio*. 2nd ed. Cambridge: Cambridge University Press.

Bronfenbrenner, Urie, and Pamela A. Morris. 1998. "The Ecology of Developmental Processes." In *Handbook of Child Psychology*, edited by William Damon and Richard M. Lerner, 993–1028. New York: Wiley.

Burawoy, Michael. 2005. "2004 ASA Presidential Address: For Public Sociology." *American Sociological Review* 70(1): 4–28.

California Department of Education. n.d. "High School Equivalency (HSE) Test." July 31, 2023. www.cde.ca.gov/ta/tg/gd.

California Department of Justice. n.d. "California Laws Protecting Immigrants' Civil Rights." Accessed January 14, 2024. www.oag.ca.gov/immigrant/ca-law.

Calzada, Esther J., Catherine S. Tamis-LeMonda, and Hirokazu Yoshikawa. 2012. "*Familismo* in Mexican and Dominican Families from Low-Income Urban Communities." *Journal of Family Issues* 34(12): 1696–1724.

Canizales, Stephanie L. 2019. "Support and Setback: The Role of Religion in the Incorporation of Unaccompanied Indigenous Youth in Los Angeles." *Journal of Ethnic and Migration Studies* 45(9): 1613–30.

——. 2021. "Educational Meaning Making and Language Learning: Understanding the Educational Incorporation of Unaccompanied, Undocumented Latinx Youth Workers in the United States." *Sociology of Education* 94(3): 175–90.

——. 2022. "'*Si mis papas estuvieran aquí*': Unaccompanied, Undocumented Latinx Youth's Emergent Frame of Reference and Health in the U.S." *Journal of Health and Social Behavior* 64(1): 120–35.

——. 2023a. "Caught in the Dragnet: How Punitive Immigration Laws Harm Immigrant Community Helpers." *Contexts Magazine* 22(1): 38–43.

——. 2023b. "Between Obligations and Aspirations: Unaccompanied Immigrant Teen Workers' Transnational Lives and Imagined Futures." *Journal of Ethnic and Migration Studies*, November 13. https://doi.org/10.1080/1369183X.2023.2278398.

——. 2023c. "Latin American Child Migrant Labor in the U.S.: Past, Present, and Future." *Footnotes Magazine* 51(3). www.asanet.org/footnotes-article/latin-american-child-migrant-labor-in-the-u-s-past-present-and-future/.

——. 2023d. "Opinion: Our Failed Immigration Policy Is Causing a Child Labor Epidemic in the U.S." *Los Angeles Times*, October 26. www.latimes.com/opinion/story/2023-10-26/immigration-policy-child-migrants-labor.

———. 2023e. "Work Primacy and the Social Incorporation of Unaccompanied, Undocumented Latinx Youth in the United States." *Social Forces* 101(3): 1372–95.

Canizales, Stephanie L., and Jody Agius Vallejo. 2021. "Latinos and Racism in the Trump Era." *Dædalus* 150(2): 150–64.

Canizales, Stephanie L., and Pierrette Hondagneu-Sotelo. 2022. "Working-Class Latina/o Youth Navigating Stratification and Inequality: A Review of Literature." *Sociology Compass* 16(12): e13050.

Canizales, Stephanie L., and Brendan H. O'Connor. 2021. "From *Preparación* to *Adaptación*: Language and the Imagined Futures of Maya-Speaking Guatemalan Youths in Los Angeles." In *Refugee Education across the Lifespan: Mapping Experiences of Language Learning and Use*, edited by Doris S. Warriner, 103–19. New York: Springer.

———. 2022. "'Maybe Not 100%': Co-Constructing Language Proficiency in the Maya Diaspora." *International Multilingual Research Journal* 16(4): 328–44.

Casanova, Saskias, Brendan H. O'Connor, and Vanessa A. Stevens. 2016. "Ecologies of Adaptation for Mexican Indigenous Im/migrant Children and Families in the United States: Implications for Latino Studies." *Latino Studies* 14(2): 192–213.

Chauvin, Sébastien, and Blanca Garcés-Mascareñas. 2012. "Beyond Informal Citizenship: The New Moral Economy of Migrant Illegality." *International Political Sociology* 6: 241–59.

Chavez, Lilian, and Cecilia Menjívar. 2010. "Children without Borders: A Mapping of the Literature on Unaccompanied Migrant Children to the United States." *Migraciones Internacionales* 5(3): 71–11.

Clausen, John S. 1991. "Adolescent Competence and the Shaping of the Life Course." *American Journal of Sociology* 96: 805–42.

Clerge, Orly. 2019. *The New Noir: Race, Identity, and Diaspora in Black Suburbia*. Oakland: University of California Press.

Coleman, James S. 1988. "Social Capital in the Creation of Human Capital." *American Journal of Sociology* 94: S95–S120.

Collins, Patricia Hill. 1994. "Shifting the Center: Race, Class, and Feminist Theorizing about Motherhood." In *Mothering: Ideology, Experience, Agency*, edited by Evelyn Nakano Glenn, Grace Chang, and Linda Rennie Forcey, 45–65. New York: Routledge.

Collins, W. Andrew, and Laurence Steinberg. 2006. "Adolescent Development in Interpersonal Context." In *Handbook of Child Psychology*, vol. 3, *Social,*

Emotional, and Personality Development, edited by Nancy Eisenberg, William Damon, and Richard M. Lerner, 1003–67. New York: Wiley.

Congdon, Venetia. 2015. "The 'Lone Female Researcher': Isolation and Safety upon Arrival in the Field." *Journal of the Anthropological Society of Oxford* 7(1): 15–24.

Congressional Research Service. 2021a. "Child Migrants at the Border: The Flores Settlement Agreement and Other Legal Developments." https://crs reports.congress.gov/product/pdf/IF/IF11799.

———. 2021b. "Unaccompanied Alien Children: An Overview." https://sgp.fas .org/crs/homesec/R43599.pdf.

———. 2023. "Increasing Numbers of Unaccompanied Children at the Southwest Border." https://crsreports.congress.gov/product/pdf/IN/IN11638.

Cooper, Marianne. 2014. *Cut Adrift: Families in Insecure Times*. Oakland: University of California Press.

Costa, Elisabetta, and Donya Alinejad. 2020. "Experiencing Homeland: Social Media and Transnational Communication among Kurdish Migrants in Northern Italy." *Global Perspectives* 1(1): 12783.

Coutin, Susan Bibler. 2010. "Exiled by Law: Deportation and the Inviability of Life." In *The Deportation Regime: Sovereignty, Space, and the Freedom of Movement*, edited by Nathalie Peutz and Nicholas de Genova, 351–70. Durham, NC: Duke University Press.

———. 2016. *Exiled Home: Salvadoran Transnational Youth in the Aftermath of Violence*. Durham, NC: Duke University Press.

Cranford, Cynthia J. 2005. "Networks of Exploitation: Immigrant Labor and the Restructuring of the Los Angeles Janitorial Industry." *Social Problems* 52(3): 379–97.

Daley, Kathryn. 2016. "Becoming a Man: Working-Class Machismo and Substance Abuse." *Youth and Substance Abuse*, 139–68. https://doi.org/10 .1007/978-3-319-33675-6_6.

Da Silva, Nicole, Toni R. Verdejo, Frank R. Dillon, Melissa M. Ertl, and Mario De La Rosa. 2021. "Marianismo Beliefs, Intimate Partner Violence, and Psychological Distress Among Recently Immigrated Young Adult Latinas." *Journal of Interpersonal Violence* 36(7–8): 3755–77.

De Genova, Nicholas. 2002. "Migrant 'Illegality' and Deportability in Everyday Life." *Annual Review of Anthropology* 31: 419–47.

Del Real, Deisy. 2019. "Toxic Ties: The Reproduction of Legal Violence within Mixed-Status Familial and Friendship Ties." *International Migration Review* 53(2): 548–70.

Deterding, Nicole M., and Mary Waters. 2018. "Flexible Coding of In-Depth Interviews: A Twenty-First-Century Approach." *Sociological Methods and Research* 50(2): 708–39.

Dezenski, Lauren. 2017. "Sessions: Many Unaccompanied Minors Are 'Wolves in Sheep's Clothing.'" *Politico*, September 21. www.politico.com/story/2017/09/21/jeff-sessions-border-unaccompanied-minors-wolves-242991.

Diaz-Strong, Daysi X. 2020. "'*Estaba bien chiquito*' (I Was Very Young): The Transition to Adulthood and 'Illegality' of the Mexican and Central American 1.25 Generation." *Journal of Adolescent Research* 37(3): 409–38.

———. 2021a. "'When Did I Stop Being a Child?': The Subjective Feeling of Adulthood of Mexican and Central American Unaccompanied 1.25 Generation Immigrants." *Emerging Adulthood* 10(5): 1286–98.

———. 2021b. "'Why We Could Not Study': The Gendered Enrollment Barriers of the 1.25 Generation Immigrants." *Children and Youth Services Review* 122: 105889.

Diaz-Strong, Daysi X., and Roberto G. Gonzales. 2023. "The Divergent Adolescent and Adult Transitions of Latin American Undocumented Minors." *Child Development Perspectives* 17(1): 3–9.

Dickerson, Caitlin. 2022. "The Secret History of Family Separation." *Atlantic*, August 7. www.theatlantic.com/magazine/archive/2022/09/trump-administration-family-separation-policy-immigration/670604.

Dow, Dawn Marie. 2016. "The Deadly Challenge of Raising African American Boys: Navigating the Image of the 'Thug.'" *Gender & Society* 30(2): 161–88.

Dreby, Joanna. 2015. *Everyday Illegal: When Policies Undermine Immigrant Families*. Oakland: University of California Press.

Durand, Jorge, Douglas S. Massey, and Rene M. Zenteno. 2001. "Mexican Immigration to the United States: Continuities and Changes." *Latin American Research Review* 36(1): 107–27.

Durkheim, Émile. 1951. *Suicide: A Study in Sociology*. New York: Free Press.

Enriquez, Laura E. 2011. "'Because We Feel the Pressure and We Also Feel the Support': Examining the Educational Success of Undocumented Immigrant Latina/o Students." *Harvard Educational Review* 81(3): 477–500.

———. 2020. *Of Love and Papers: How Immigration Policy Affects Romance and Family*. Oakland: University of California Press.

Enriquez, Laura E., Daisy Vazquez Vera, and S. Karthick Ramakrishnan. 2019. "Driver's Licenses for All? Racialized Illegality and the Implementation of Progressive Immigration Policy in California." *Law & Policy* 41(1): 34–58.

Erazo, Juliet. 2010. "Constructing Indigenous Subjectivities: Economic Collectivism and Identity in the Ecuadorian Amazon." *Development and Change* 41(6): 1017–39.

Escamilla García, Angel Alfonso. 2021. "When Internal Migration Fails: A Cast Study of Central American Youth Who Relocate before Leaving Their Countries." *Journal of Migration and Human Security* 9(4): 297–310.

Espiritu, Yen Le. 2003. *Home Bound: Filipino American Lives across Culture, Communities, and Countries.* Berkeley: University of California Press.

Estrada, Emir. 2019. *Kids at Work: Latinx Families Selling Food on the Streets of Los Angeles.* New York: NYU Press.

Estrada, Emir, and Pierrette Hondagneu-Sotelo. 2011. "Intersectional Dignities: Latino Immigrant Street Vendor Youth in Los Angeles." *Journal of Contemporary Ethnography* 40(1): 102–31.

Feliciano, Cynthia. 2005. "Does Selective Migration Matter? Explaining Ethnic Disparities in Educational Attainment among Immigrants' Children." *International Migration Review* 39(4): 841–87.

Fernández-Kelly, Patricia, and Douglas S. Massey. 2007. "Borders for Whom? The Role of NAFTA in Mexico-US Migration." *Annals of the American Academy of Political and Social Science* 610(1): 98–118.

Flores, René D., and Ariela Schachter. 2018. "Who Are the 'Illegals'? The Social Construction of Illegality in the United States." *American Sociological Review* 83(5): 839–68.

Fox, Jonathan, and Gaspar Rivera-Salgado, eds. 2004. *Indigenous Mexican Migrants in the United States.* La Joll, CA: Center for U.S.-Mexican Studies.

Furstenberg, Frank F., Jr. 1993. "How Families Manage Risk and Opportunity in Dangerous Neighborhoods." In *Sociology and the Public Agenda,* edited by W.J. Wilson, 231–58. Newbury Park CA: Sage.

Galli, Chiara. 2023. *Precarious Protections: Unaccompanied Minors Seeking Asylum in the United States.* Oakland: University of California Press.

García, Angela S. 2014. "Hidden in Plain Sight: How Unauthorized Migrants Strategically Assimilate in Restrictive Localities in California." *Journal of Ethnic and Migration Studies* 40(12): 1895–1914.

Gleeson, Shannon. 2012. *Conflicting Commitments: The Politics of Enforcing Immigrant Worker Rights in San Jose.* Berkeley: University of California Press.

———. 2016. *Precarious Claims: The Promise and Failure of Workplace Protections in the United States.* Oakland: University of California Press.

Gleeson, Shannon, and Roberto G. Gonzales. 2012. "When Do Papers Matter? An Institutional Analysis of Undocumented Life in the United States." *International Migration* 50(4): 1–19.

Golash-Boza, Tanya. 2014. "Tattoos, Stigma, and National Identity among Guatemalan Deportees." In *The Nation and Its Peoples: Citizens, Denizens, Migrants*, edited by John Park and Shannon Gleeson, 202–22. New York: Routledge.

Golash-Boza, Tanya, and Pierrette Hondagneu-Sotelo. 2013. "Latino Immigrant Men and the Deportation Crisis: A Gendered Racial Removal Program." *Latino Studies* 11: 271–92.

Golash-Boza, Tanya, and Zulema Valdez. 2018. "Nested Contexts of Reception: Undocumented Students at the University of California, Central." *Sociological Perspectives* 61(4): 535–52.

Gomberg-Muñoz, Ruth. 2019. *Labor and Legality: An Ethnography of a Mexican Immigrant Network*. Oxford: Oxford University Press.

Gómez, Laura. 2020. *Inventing Latinos: A New Story of American Racism*. New York: The New Press.

Gómez Cervantes, Andrea. 2021a. "Language, Race, and Illegality: Indigenous Migrants Navigating the Immigration Regime in a New Destination." *Journal of Ethnic and Migration Studies* 49(7): 1610–29.

———. 2021b. "'Looking Mexican': Indigenous and Non-Indigenous Latina/o Immigrants and the Racialization of Illegality in the Midwest." *Social Problems* 68(1): 100–17.

Gómez Cervantes, Andrea, and Cecilia Menjívar. 2020. "Legal Violence, Health, and Access to Care: Latina Immigrants in Rural and Urban Kansas." *Journal of Health and Social Behavior* 61(2): 307–23.

Gonzales, Roberto G. 2015. *Lives in Limbo: Undocumented and Coming of Age in America*. Oakland: University of California Press.

Gonzales, Roberto G., Luisa L. Heredia, and Genevieve Negrón-Gonzales. 2015. "Untangling Plyler's Legacy: Undocumented Students, Schools, and Citizenship." *Harvard Educational Review* 85(3): 318–41.

Gonzales, Roberto G., Carola Suárez-Orozco, and Maria Cecilia Dedios-Sanguineti. 2013. "No Place to Belong: Contextualizing Concepts of Mental Health among Undocumented Immigrant Youth in the United States." *American Behavioral Scientist* 57(8): 1174–99.

Gonzales, Teresa I. 2021. *Building a Better Chicago: Race and Community Resistance to Urban Redevelopment*. New York: NYU Press.

Gonzalez, Shannon Malone. 2022. "Black Girls and the Talk? Policing, Parenting, and the Politics of Protection." *Social Problems* 69(1): 22–38.

González-López, Gloria. 2015. *Family Secrets: Stories of Incest and Sexual Violence in Mexico*. New York: NYU Press.

Hagan, Jacqueline M. 1994. *Deciding to Be Legal: A Mayan Community in Houston*. Philadelphia, PA: Temple University Press.

Hagan, Jacqueline M., and Helen R. Ebaugh. 2003. "Calling Upon the Sacred: Migrants' Use of Religion in the Migration Process." *International Migration Review* 37(4): 1145–62.

Hagan, Jacqueline Maria, Rubén Hernandez-León, and Jean-Luc Demonsant. 2015. *Skills of the Unskilled: Work and Mobility among Mexican Migrants*. Oakland: University of California Press.

Hagan, Jacqueline M., Nichola Lowe, and Christian Quingla. 2011. "Skills on the Move: Rethinking the Relationship between Human Capital and Immigrant Economic Mobility." *Work and Occupations* 38(2): 149–78.

Halpern-Meekin, Sarah. 2017. *Social Poverty: Low-Income Parents and the Struggle for Family and Community Ties*. New York: NYU Press.

Halpern-Meekin, Sarah, Kathryn Edin, Laura Tach, and Jennifer Sykes. 2015. *It's Not Like I'm Poor: How Working Families Make Ends Meet in a Post-Welfare World*. Oakland: University of California Press.

Hamilton, Erin R., and Maryann Bylander. 2020. "The Migration of Children from Mexico to the USA in the Early 2000s." *Population Research and Policy Review* 40: 337–61.

Hamilton, Nora, and Norma Stoltz Chinchilla. 2001. *Seeking Community in a Global City: Guatemalans and Salvadorans in Los Angeles*. Philadelphia, PA: Temple University Press.

Hardie, Jessica Halliday. 2022. *Best Laid Plans: Women Coming of Age in Uncertain Times*. Oakland: University of California Press.

Hayes, Joseph, and Laura Hill. 2017. "Undocumented Immigrants in California." Public Policy Institute of California. www.ppic.org/publication/undocumented-immigrants-in-california.

Heidbrink, Lauren. 2014. *Migrant Youth, Transnational Families, and the State: Care and Contested Interests*. Philadelphia: University of Pennsylvania Press.

———. 2019. "The Coercive Power of Debt: Migration and Deportation of Guatemalan Indigenous Youth." *Journal of Latin American and Caribbean Anthropology* 24(1): 263–81.

———. 2020. *Migranthood: Youth in a New Era of Deportation*. Stanford, CA: Stanford University Press.

Hernández-León, Rubén. 2008. *Metropolitan Migrants: The Migration of Urban Mexicans to the United States*. Berkeley: University of California Press.

Herrera, Juan. 2016. "Racialized Illegality: The Regulation of Informal Labor Space." *Latino Studies* 14(3): 320–43.

Hinojosa-Ojeda, Raul, and Sherman Robinson. 2020. "Essential but Not Disposable: Undocumented Workers and Their Mixed-Status Families." Los Angeles: UCLA Institute for Research on Labor and Employment. www.irle .ucla.edu/wp-content/uploads/2020/08/Essential-Undocumented-Workers -Final-w-Cover.pdf.

Hondagneu-Sotelo, Pierrette. 1992. "Overcoming Patriarchal Constraints: The Reconstruction of Gender Relations among Mexican Immigrant Women and Men." *Gender & Society* 6(3): 393–415.

———. 1993. "Why Advocacy Research? Reflections on Research and Activism with Immigrant Women." *American Behavioral Sociologist* 24: 56–68.

———. 1994. *Gendered Transitions: Mexican Experiences of Immigration*. Berkeley: University of California Press.

———. 2001. *Doméstica: Immigrant Workers Cleaning and Caring in the Shadows of Affluence*. Berkeley: University of California Press.

Hondagneu-Sotelo, Pierrette, and Ernestine Avila. 1997. "'I'm Here, but I'm There': The Meanings of Latina Transnational Motherhood." *Gender & Society* 11(5): 548–71.

Hondagneu-Sotelo, Pierrette, and Manuel Pastor. 2021. *South Central Dreams: Finding Home and Building Community in South LA*. New York: NYU Press.

Horton, Sarah B. 2016. *They Leave Their Kidneys in the Fields: Illness, Injury, and Illegality among U.S. Farmworkers*. Oakland: University of California Press.

Hovey, Joseph D. 2000. "Acculturative Stress, Depression, and Suicidal Ideation among Central American Immigrants." *Suicide and Life-Threatening Behavior* 30(3): 125–39.

Human Rights Watch. 2019. "US: Family Separation on Harming Children, Families." www.hrw.org/news/2019/07/11/us-family-separation-harming -children-families.

Kaenzig, Raoul, and Etienne Piguet. 2014. "Migration and Climate Change in Latin America and the Caribbean." In *People on the Move in the Changing Climate: The Regional Impact of Environmental Change on Migration*, edited by Etienne Piguet and Frank Laczko, 155–76. New York: Springer.

Kandel, William, and Douglas S. Massey. 2002. "The Culture of Mexican Migration: A Theoretical and Empirical Analysis." *Social Forces* 80(3): 981–1004.

Kasinitz, Philip, Mary C. Waters, John H. Mollenkopf, and Jennifer Holdaway. 2008. *Inheriting the City: The Children of Immigrants Come of Age.* New York: Russell Sage Foundation.

Keller, Allen, Amy Joscelyne, Megan Granski, and Barry Rosenfeld. 2017. "Pre-Migration Trauma Exposure and Mental Health Functioning among Central American Migrants Arriving at the U.S. Border." *PLoS ONE* 12(1): e0168692.

Kennedy, Elizabeth. 2013. "Unnecessary Suffering: Potential Unmet Mental Health Needs of Unaccompanied Alien Children." *JAMA Pediatrics* 167(4): 319–20.

Kidd, Sean A., and Michelle R. Carroll. 2007. "Coping and Suicidality among Homeless Youth." *Journal of Adolescence* 30(2): 283–94.

Kim, Kathleen. 2015. "Beyond Coercion." *UCLA Law Review* 62: 1158. www.uclalawreview.org/wp-content/uploads/2019/09/Kim-final_8.15.pdf.

Kloß, Sinah Theres. 2017. "Sexual(ized) Harassment and Ethnographic Fieldwork: A Silenced Aspect of Social Research." *Ethnography* 18(3): 396–414.

Kwon, Hyeyoung. 2022. "Inclusion Work: Children of Immigrants Claiming Membership in Everyday Life." *American Journal of Sociology* 127(6): 1818–59.

Lacayo, Celia. 2017. "Perpetual Inferiority: Whites' Racial Ideology toward Latinos." *Sociology of Race and Ethnicity* 3(4): 566–79.

Lamont, Michèle. 2002. *The Dignity of Working Men: Morality and the Boundaries of Race, Class, and Immigration.* Cambridge, MA: Harvard University Press.

Landale, Nancy S., Kevin J. A. Thomas, and Jennifer Van Hook. 2011. "The Living Arrangements of Children of Immigrants." *The Future of Children* 21(1): 43–70.

Large, Michael D., and Kristen Marcussen. 2000. "Extending Identity Theory to Predict Differential Forms and Degrees of Psychological Distress." *Social Psychology Quarterly* 63(1): 49–59.

Levitt, Peggy. 2001. *The Transnational Villagers.* Berkeley: University of California Press.

Lijtmaer, Ruth M. 2022. "Social Trauma, Nostalgia and Mourning in the Immigration Experience." *American Journal of Psychoanalysis* 82: 305–19.

Livingston, Gretchen, and Mario H. Lopez. 2010. *How Young Latinos Communicate with Friends in the Digital Age.* Washington, DC: Pew Research Center. www.pewresearch.org/hispanic/2010/07/28/how-young-latinos-communicate-with-friends-in-the-digital-age.

Loh, Katherine, and Scott Richardson. 2004. "Foreign-Born Workers: Trends in Fatal Occupational Injuries, 1996–2001." *Monthly Labor Review* (June): 42–53.

Lopez, Robert J., Rich Connell, and Chris Kraul. 2005. "Gang Uses Deportation to Its Advantage to Flourish in U.S." *Los Angeles Times*, October 30. www.la times.com/local/la-me-gang30oct30-story.html.

Los Angeles Times. 2014. "Obama to Central American Parents: Do Not Send Your Children to Borders." June 27. www.latimes.com/80655910-132.html.

Loucky, James, and Marilyn Moors, ed. 2000. *The Maya Diaspora: Guatemalan Roots, New American Lives*. Philadelphia, PA: Temple University Press.

Mahler, Sarah J. 1995. *American Dreaming: Immigrant Life on the Margins*. Princeton, NJ: Princeton University Press.

Manz, Beatriz. 2005. *Paradise in Ashes: A Guatemalan Journey of Courage, Terror, and Hope*. Berkeley: University of California Press.

Martinez, Isabel. 2019. *Becoming Transnational Youth Workers: Independent Mexican Teenage Migrants and Pathways of Survival and Social Mobility*. New Brunswick, NJ: Rutgers University Press.

Massey, Douglas, Jorge Durand, and Nolan J. Malone. 2003. *Beyond Smoke and Mirrors: Mexican Immigration in an Era of Economic Integration*. New York: Russell Sage Foundation.

Massey, Douglas S., Jorge Durand, and Karen A. Pren. 2016. "The Precarious Position of Latino Immigrants in the United States: A Comparative Analysis of Ethnosurvey Data." *Annals of the American Academy of Political and Social Sciences* 666(1): 91–109.

Massey, Douglas S., Luin Goldring, and Jorge Durand. 1994. "Continuities in Transnational Migration: An Analysis of Nineteen Mexican Communities." *American Journal of Sociology* 99(6): 1492–1533.

McCaskill, Nolan. 2016. "Trump Promises Wall and Massive Deportation Program." *Politico*, August 31. www.politico.com/story/2016/08/donald -trump-immigration-address-arizona-227612.

McLaughlin, Robert H., and Theresa Alfaro-Velcamp. 2015. "The Vulnerability of Immigrants in Research: Enhancing Protocol Development and Ethics Review." *Journal of Academic Ethics* 13(1): 27–43.

Meier, Anna, and Gina Allen. 2008. "Intimate Relationships Development during the Transition to Adulthood: Differences by Social Class." *New Directions in Child and Adolescent Development* 119: 25–39.

Meldrum, Ryan Charles, and Anna Leimberg. 2018. "Unstructured Socializing with Peers and Risk of Substance Use: Where Does the Risk Begin?" *Journal of Drug Issues* 48(3): 452–71.

Menjívar, Cecilia. 2000. *Fragmented Ties: Salvadoran Immigrant Networks in America*. Berkeley: University of California Press.

———. 2011. *Enduring Violence: Ladina Women's Lives in Guatemala*. Berkeley: University of California Press.

———. 2020. "Temporary Protected Status for Central American Immigrants: Advancing Immigrant Integration Despite Its Uncertainty." Los Angeles: UCLA Latino Policy and Politics Institute. https://latino.ucla.edu/wp -content/uploads/2020/08/Menjivar-LPPI_TPSBrief_8.18Final.pdf.

Menjívar, Cecilia, and Leisy J. Abrego. 2012. "Legal Violence: Immigration Law and the Lives of Central American Immigrants." *American Journal of Sociology* 117(5): 1380–421.

Menjívar, Cecilia, and Sarah M. Lakhani. 2016. "Transformative Effects of Immigration Law: Immigrants' Personal and Social Metamorphoses through Regularization." *American Journal of Sociology* 121(6): 1818–55.

Meyer, Peter J., and Clare R. Seelke. 2015. "Central American Regional Security Initiative: Background and Policy Issues for Congress." Washington, DC: Congressional Research Service. https://sgp.fas.org/crs/row/R41731.pdf.

Meyer, Sarah, H. Abigail Raikes, Elita A. Virmani, Sara Waters, and Ross A. Thompson. 2014. "Parent Emotion Representations and the Socialization of Emotional Regulation in the Family." *International Journal of Behavioral Development* 38(2): 164–73.

Migration Policy Institute. n.d.-a "Profile of the Unauthorized Population: United States." Accessed January 15, 2024. www.migrationpolicy.org/data /unauthorized-immigrant-population/state/US.

———. n.d.-b. "Unaccompanied Children Released to Sponsors by State and County, FY2014–Present." Accessed August 28, 2023. www.migrationpolicy .org/programs/data-hub/charts/unaccompanied-children-released -sponsors-state-and-county.

Montes, Veronica. 2013. "The Role of Emotions in the Construction of Masculinity: Guatemalan Migrant Men, Transnational Migration, and Family Relations." *Gender & Society* 27(4): 469–90.

Morris, Amanda Sheffield, Jennifer S. Silk, Laurence Steinberg, Sonya S. Myers, and Lara Rachel Robinson. 2007. "The Role of the Family Context in the Development of Emotion Regulation." *Social Development* 16 (2): 361–88.

Moslimani, Mohamad, Luis Noe-Bustamante, and Sono Shah. 2023. "Facts on Hispanics of Mexican Origin in the United States, 2021." Washington, DC: Pew Research Center. www.pewresearch.org/hispanic/fact-sheet/us -hispanics-facts-on-mexican-origin-latinos/.

Muuss, Rolf E. H. 1996. *Theories of Adolescence.* 6th ed. New York: McGraw-Hill.

Neckerman, Kathryn M., Prudence Carter, and Jennifer Lee. 1999. "Segmented Assimilation and Minority Cultures of Mobility." *Ethnic and Racial Studies* 22(6): 945–65.

Newell, Jason M., and Gordon A. MacNeil. 2010. "Professional Burnout, Vicarious Trauma, Secondary Traumatic Stress, and Compassion Fatigue: A Review of Theoretical Terms, Risk Factors, and Preventative Methods for Clinicians and Researchers." *Best Practices in Mental Health* 6(2): 57–68.

New Ethnographer, The. 2020. https://thenewethnographer.com.

Nichols, Briana. 2023. "Nothing Is Easy: Educational Striving and Migration Deferral in Guatemala." *Journal of Ethnic and Migration Studies* 49(7): 1919–35.

Nicholls, Walter J. 2013. *The DREAMers: How the Undocumented Youth Movement Transformed the Immigrant Rights Debate.* Stanford, CA: Stanford University Press.

Oakland Unified School District. n.d. "Newcomer Programs." Accessed July 31, 2023. www.ousd.org/newcomer.

Obinna, Denise N. 2021. "Alone in a Crowd: Indigenous Migrants and Language Barriers in American Immigration." *Race and Justice* 13(4): 488–505.

O'Connor, Brendan H., and Stephanie L. Canizales. 2023. "Thresholds of Liminality: Discourse and Embodiment from Separation to Consummation among Guatemalan Maya Youth Workers in Los Angeles." *International Journal of the Sociology of Language,* no. 279, 155–79.

Orellana, Marjorie Faulstitch. 2009. *Translating Childhoods: Immigrant Youth, Language, and Culture.* New Brunswick, NJ: Rutgers University Press.

Orozco, Manuel, and Michelle Lapointe. 2004. "Mexican Hometown Associations and Development Opportunities." *Journal of International Affairs* 57(2): 31–51.

Orozco, Manuel, and Rebecca Rouse. 2007. "Migrant Hometown Associations and Opportunities for Development: A Global Perspective." Washington, DC: Migration Policy Institute. www.migrationpolicy.org/article/migrant-hometown-associations-and-opportunities-development-global-perspective.

Padilla-Rodríguez, Ivón. 2020. "Child Migrants in 20th-Century America." *Oxford Research Encyclopedias of American History.* www.doi.org/10.1093/acrefore/9780199329175.013.855.

———. 2022. "'*Los Hijos Son la Riqueza Del Pobre*': Mexican Child Migration and the Making of Domestic (Im)migrant Exclusion, 1937–1960." *Journal of American Ethnic History* 42(1): 43–81.

Parreñas, Rhacel Salazar. 2015. *Servants of Globalization: Women, Migration and Domestic Work*. Stanford, CA: Stanford University Press.

Patler, Caitlin, Shannon Gleeson, and Matthias Schonlau. 2022. "Contesting Inequality: The Impact of Immigrant Legal Status and Education on Legal Knowledge and Claims-Making in Low-Wage Labor Markets." *Social Problems* 69(2): 356–79.

Patler, Caitlin, and Whitney L. Pirtle. 2018. "From Undocumented to Lawfully Present: Do Changes to Legal Status Impact Psychological Wellbeing from Latino Immigrant Young Adults?" *Social Science & Medicine* 119: 39–48.

Perrotte, Jessica K., Michael R. Baumann, and Cory F. Knight. 2018. "Traditional Gender Roles and the Stress–Alcohol Relationship among Latina/o College Students." *Substance Use & Misuse* 53(10): 1700–1705.

Pessar, Patricia R. 1999. "Engendering Migration Studies: The Case of New Immigrants in the United States." *American Behavioral Scientist* 32(4): 577–600.

Pham, Huyen, and Pham Hoang Van. 2021. "The Immigrant Climate Index." www.vpham415.github.io/ICI/.

Portes, Alejandro. 2020. "Bifurcated Immigration and the End of Compassion." *Ethnic and Racial Studies* 43(1): 2–17.

Portes, Alejandro, and Patricia Fernández-Kelly. 2008. "No Margin for Error: Educational and Occupational Achievement among Disadvantaged Children of Immigrants." *Annals of the American Academy of Political and Social Science* 620(1): 12–36.

Portes, Alejandro, and Rubén Rumbaut. 2001. *Legacies: The Story of the Immigrant Second Generation*. Berkeley: University of California Press.

Portes, Alejandro, and Min Zhou. 1993. "The New Second Generation: Segmented Assimilation and Its Variants." *Annals of the American Academy of Political and Social Science* 530(1): 74–96.

Portillo Villeda, Suyapa. 2021. *Roots of Resistance: A Story of Gender, Race, and Labor on the North Coast of Honduras*. Austin: University of Texas Press.

Ramírez, Catherine S. 2020. *Assimilation: An Alternative History*. Oakland: University of California Press.

Ramos de Oliveira, Clariana V., and Joshua Jeong. 2021. "Exposure to Violence, Polyvictimization, and Youth's Mental Health and Alcohol Use in El Salvador." *Child Abuse & Neglect* 118: 105–58.

Reichert, Josh, and Douglas S. Massey. 1980. "History and Trends in U.S. Bound Migration from a Mexican Town." *International Migration Review* 14(4): 475–91.

RentCafe. n.d.-a. "Cost of Living in California." Accessed January 15, 2024. www.rentcafe.com/cost-of-living-calculator/us/ca/.

———. n.d.-b. "Cost of Living in Los Angeles, CA." Accessed January 15, 2024. www.rentcafe.com/cost-of-living-calculator/us/ca/los-angeles/.

Ribas, Vanesa. 2016. *On the Line: Slaughterhouse Lives and the Making of the New South*. Oakland: University of California Press.

Rohde, Nicholas, K. K. Tang, Lars Osberg, and Prasada Rao. 2016. "The Effect of Economic Insecurity on Mental Health: Recent Evidence from Australian Panel Data." *Social Science & Medicine* 151: 250–58.

Romero, Mary. 2006. "Racial Profiling and Immigration Law Enforcement: Rounding up of Usual Suspects in the Latino Community." *Critical Sociology* 32(2–3): 447–73.

Rosales, Roció. 2020. *Fruteros: Street Vending, Illegality, and Ethnic Community in Los Angeles*. Oakland: University of California Press.

Rosas, Ana Elizabeth. 2014. *Abrazando el Espiritu: Bracero Families Confront the U.S.-Mexico Border*. Oakland: University of California Press.

Rose, Joel, and Marisa Peñaloza. 2022. "Migrant Deaths at the U.S.-Mexico Border Hit a Record High, in Part Due to Drownings." *NPR*, September 29. www.npr.org/2022/09/29/1125638107/migrant-deaths-us-mexico-border-record-drownings.

Ruehs, Emily M. 2016. "Adventures in *El Norte*: The Identities and Immigration of Unaccompanied Youth." *Men and Masculinities* 20(3): 364–84.

Rumbaut, Rubén. 2004. "Age, Life Stages, and Generational Cohorts: Decomposing the Immigrant First and Second Generations in the United States." *International Migration Review* 38(3): 1160–1205.

Rumbaut, Rubén G., and Golnaz Komaie. 2010. "Immigration and Adult Transitions." *The Future of Children* 20: 39–63.

Sáenz, Rogelio, and Karen Manges Douglas. 2015. "A Call for the Racialization of Immigration Studies: On the Transition of Ethnic Immigrants to Racialized Immigrants." *Sociology of Race and Ethnicity* 1(1): 166–80.

Saldaña-Portillo, María Josefina. 2017. "Critical Latinx Indigeneities: A Paradigm Shift." *Latino Studies* 15: 138–55.

Schmalzbauer, Leah. 2005. *Striving and Surviving: A Daily Life Analysis of Honduran Transnational Families*. New York: Routledge.

Schwake, Sonja A., and Gyles Iannone. 2010. "Ritual Remains and Collective Memory: Maya Examples from West Central Belize." *Ancient Mesoamerica* 21(2): 331–39.

Shanahan, Michael J. 2000. "Pathways to Adulthood in Changing Societies: Variability and Mechanisms in the Life Course Perspective." *Annual Review of Sociology* 26: 667–92.

Sheeran, Paschal, and Eunice McCarthy. 1992. "Social Structure, Self-Conception and Well Being: An Examination of Four Models with Unemployed People." *Journal of Applied Social Psychology* 22(2): 117–33.

Sherer, Jennifer, and Nina Mast. 2023. *Child Labor Laws Are under Attack across the Country*. Washington, DC: Economic Policy Institute. www.epi.org/publication/child-labor-laws-under-attack.

Silva, Jennifer M. 2013. *Coming Up Short: Working-Class Adulthood in an Age of Uncertainty*. New York: Oxford University Press.

Simmons, William Paul, Cecilia Menjívar, and Elizabeth Salerno Valdez. 2021. "The Gendered Effects of Local Immigration Enforcement: Latinas' Social Isolation in Chicago, Houston, Los Angeles, and Phoenix." *International Migration Review* 55(1): 108–34.

Small, Mario L., and Leah E. Gose. 2020. "How Do Low-Income People Form Survival Networks? Routine Organizations as Brokers." *Annals of the American Academy of Political and Social Science* 689(1): 89–109.

Small, Mario Luis, and Jessica McCrory Calarco. 2022. *Qualitative Literacy: A Guide to Evaluating Ethnographic and Interview Research*. Oakland: University of California Press.

Smith, Dakota. 2023. "L.A. City Council Moves 'Sanctuary City' Ordinance Forward." *Los Angeles Times*, June 9. www.latimes.com/california/story/2023-06-09/l-a-city-council-moves-sanctuary-city-ordinance-forward.

Smith, Timothy. 1978. "Religion and Ethnicity in America." *American Historical Review* 83(5): 1115–85.

Smith-Greenway, Emily, and Sara Yeatman. 2020. "Unrealized Educational Expectations and Mental Health: Evidence from a Low-Income Country." *Social Forces* 98(3): 1112–42.

Speed, Shannon. 2019. *Incarcerated Stories: Indigenous Women Migrants and Violence in the Settler-Capitalist State*. Chapel Hill: University of North Carolina Press.

Stark, Oded, and David E. Bloom. 1985. "The New Economics of Labor Migration." *Economic Development and Cultural Change* 31: 191–96.

State of California Department of Justice. n.d. "California Laws Protecting Immigrants' Civil Rights." Accessed August 31, 2023. https://oag.ca.gov/immigrant/ca-law

Stuesse, Angela, and Mathew Coleman. 2014. "Automobility, Immobility, Altermobility: Surviving and Resisting the Intensification of Immigrant Policing," *City & Society* 26 (1): 51–72.

Suárez-Orozco, Carola, Hee Jin Bang, and Ha Yeon Kim. 2010. "I Felt Like My Heart Was Staying Behind: Psychological Implications of Family Separations & Reunifications for Immigrant Youth." *Journal of Adolescent Research* 26(2): 222–57.

Suárez-Orozco, Carola, Marcelo M. Suárez-Orozco, and Irina Todorova. 2010. *Learning a New Land: Immigrant Students in American Society.* Cambridge, MA: Harvard University Press.

Suárez-Orozco, Carola, Hirokazu Yoshikawa, Robert T. Teranishi, and Marcelo M. Suárez-Orozco. 2011. "Growing Up in the Shadows: The Developmental Implications of Unauthorized Status." *Harvard Educational Review* 81(3): 438–72.

Suro, Roberto, Marcelo M. Suárez-Orozco, and Stephanie L. Canizales. 2015. "Removing Insecurity: How American Children Will Benefit from President Obama's Executive Action on Immigration." Los Angeles: USC Price Tomas Rivera Policy Institute and the Institute for Immigration, Globalization, and Education at UCLA. https://socialinnovation.usc.edu/wp-content/uploads /2017/09/research_report.pdf.

Sussman, Steve, and Jeffrey Jensen Arnett. 2014. "Emerging Adulthood: Developmental Period Facilitative of Addictions." *Evaluation and the Health Professions* 37(2): 147–55.

Telles, Edward E., and Vilma Ortiz. 2009. *Generations of Exclusion: Mexican Americans, Assimilation, and Race.* New York: Russell Sage Foundation.

Tereškinas, Artūras. 2010 "Men and Social Suffering in Contemporary Lithuania." *Anthropology of East Europe Review* 28(1): 23–39.

Theodore, Nik. 2013. *Insecure Communities: Latino Perceptions of Police Involvement in Immigration Enforcement.* Oakland, CA: PolicyLink. www.policylink .org/sites/default/files/INSECURE_COMMUNITIES_REPORT_FINAL.PDF.

Timmermans, Stefan, and Idoo Tavory. 2012. "Theory Construction in Qualitative Research: From Grounded Theory to Abductive Analysis." *Sociological Theory* 30(3): 167–86.

Treitler, Vilna Bashi. 2015. "Social Agency and White Supremacy in Immigration Studies." *Sociology of Race and Ethnicity* 1(1): 153–65.

UN Development Programme. 2021. "Trapped: High Inequality and Low Growth in Latin America and the Caribbean." www.undp.org/latin-america

/press-releases/trapped-high-inequality-and-low-growth-latin-america-and
-caribbean.

UN Economic Commission for Latin America. 2022. "Poverty Rates in Latin
America Remain above Pre-Pandemic Levels in 2022, ELAC Warns." Press
release. www.cepal.org/en/pressreleases/poverty-rates-latin-america
-remain-above-pre-pandemic-levels-2022-eclac-warns.

United Nations Education, Science, and Culture Organization (UNESCO).
2016. "Education Policies: Recommendations in Latin America Based on
TERCE." https://unesdoc.unesco.org/ark:/48223/pf0000244976_eng.

United Nations High Commissioner for Refugees (UNHCR). 2016. "Children on
the Run." www.unhcr.org/us/media/children-run-full-report.

——. 2023. "Child Displacement." https://data.unicef.org/topic/child
-migration-and-displacement/displacement/

——. n.d. "Refugee Data Finder." Accessed July 31, 2023. www.unhcr.org
/refugee-statistics.

United Nations International Children's Emergency Fund (UNICEF). 2021.
"Child Migration." https://data.unicef.org/topic/child-migration-and
-displacement/migration.

——. 2023. "Number of Displaced Children Reaches New High of 43.3
Million." www.unicef.org/press-releases/number-displaced-children
-reaches-new-high-433-million.

US Citizenship and Immigration Services. n.d. "Special Immigrant Juveniles."
Accessed July 31, 2023. www.uscis.gov/working-in-US/eb4/SIJ.

US Customs and Border Protection. n.d. "Southwest Land Border Encounters."
Accessed January 15, 2024. https://www.cbp.gov/newsroom/stats/southwest
-land-border-encounters.

US Department of Labor. n.d. "Child Labor." Accessed August 1, 2023.
https://www.dol.gov/agencies/whd/data/charts/child-labor.

US Institute of Peace. 1997. "Truth Commission: Guatemala." www.usip.org
/publications/1997/02/truth-commission-guatemala

US News and World Report. 2023. "Most Expensive Places to Live in the U.S. in
2023–2024." Accessed January 15, 2024. www.realestate.usnews.com/places
/rankings/most-expensive-places-to-live.

Valdivia, Carolina. 2019. "Expanding Geographies of Deportability: How
Immigration Enforcement at the Local Level Affects Undocumented and
Mixed-Status Families." *Law & Policy* 41: 103–19.

Valenzuela, Abel. 1999. "Gender Roles and Settlement Activities among Children and Their Immigrant Families." *American Behavioral Scientist* 42(4): 720–42.

Van Hook, Jennifer, Julia Gelatt, and Ariel G. Ruiz Soto. 2023. "A Turning Point for the Unauthorized Immigrant Population in the United States." Washington, DC: Migration Policy Institute. www.migrationpolicy.org/news/turning -point-us-unauthorized-immigrant-population?eType=EmailBlastContent& eId=28e358e3-27cd-4194-8326-cbc896cda2c4.

Van Natta, Meredith. 2023. *Medical Legal Violence: Health Care and Immigration Enforcement against Latinx Noncitizens.* New York: NYU Press.

Waldinger, Roger. 2001. *Strangers at the Gates: New Immigrants in Urban America.* Berkeley: University of California Press.

Ward, Nicole, and Jeanne Botalova. 2023. "Central American Immigrants in the United States." Washington, DC: Migration Policy Institute. www .migrationpolicy.org/article/central-american-immigrants-united-states.

Waters, Mary C. 1999. *Black Identities: West Indian Immigrant Dreams and American Realities.* Cambridge, MA: Harvard University Press, 1999.

Wellmeier, Nancy. 1998. *Ritual, Identity, and the Mayan Diaspora.* New York: Garland Publishing.

Wolseth, Jon. 2008. "Everyday Violence and the Persistence of Grief: Wandering and Loss Among Honduran Youths." *Journal of Latin American and Caribbean Anthropology* 13(2): 311–35.

Zapata-Barrero, Ricard, and Evren Yalaz. 2020. "Qualitative Migration Research Ethics: A Roadmap for Migration Scholars." *Qualitative Research Journal* 20(3): 269–79.

Zelizer, Viviana. 1985. *Pricing the Priceless Child: Changing Social Values of Children.* Princeton, NJ: Princeton University Press.

Zhou, Min, and Carl Bankston. 1998. *Growing Up American: How Vietnamese Children Adapt to Life in the United States.* New York: Russell Sage Foundation.

Index

Aarón, 111, 115–17, 158, 215

abandonment, 2, 40, 52, 54, 59–60, 85, 136, 213

Abrego, Leisy J., 267

Adán, 109, 118, 174–79, 183–87, 193, 202, 218

adaptation *(adaptación)*, 7, 19, 22, 28, 131, 134–36, 175, 213, 268; definition, 13–14; and family, 165–72; and incorporation, 97; and orientation, 14, 137–38, 148, 150–57, 162–67, 172–73, 179, 204, 206–10, 215, 218–19, 224, 228, 230, 233–34, 239–42, 247, 249, 254–55; and perdition, 28, 178–79, 186–87, 193, 197–203, 206, 240; and spatial/social landscape, 148–51; and work, 138–48, 151–65, 218–19, 238–39, 250

addiction, 46, 98, 110, 128, 167, 182–84, 186, 198, 215–16, 218, 225. *See also* substance abuse

Affordable Care Act (2010), 66

agency, 6, 33, 206, 241, 263, 268; and adaptation, 137, 143, 153, 155, 165, 172–73, 239; activating, 120–33; and

orientation, 27, 96, 113–34; and risk, 58; and social structure, 12, 21, 62, 232

aguantando, 68, 81

Akateko (language), 26

Alcoholics Anonymous (AA), 202

Alejandro, 94

Alliance for Prosperity Program (2015), 39

Álvaro, 52–53

American Baptist Churches (ABC) v. Thornburgh (1991), 64–65

American Dream, 27, 95, 125, 222, 232

Ander, 80, 82, 114–15, 150–51, 220

Andrés, 42–45, 50, 108, 112, 168–69, 201

Andrews, Abigail, 269

Annalisa, 113

Anti-Drug Abuse Act (1988), 65

anti-immigrant sentiment, 111

anti-Indigenous racism, 19, 42, 56–57, 95, 111–13, 115, 140–41, 162

Antiterrorism and Effective Death Penalty Act (1996), 65

anxiety, 112, 120, 126, 194, 203, 272

Ariel, 83–84

arrival contexts, 5, 16, 25, 58–59, 64–66, 68, 92–93, 136, 241, 246–47, 249, 252; and departure contexts, 34, 235–36; and disorientation, 13, 100–101, 106, 206; gendered, 27, 60–63, 67, 69–70, 77–91; and incorporation, 95; and intersectional expectations, 69–70; and orientation, 13, 100–101, 104, 106, 133, 175, 198, 206, 237; welcoming, 70–77, 98–99, 204

assimilation. *See* segmented assimilation theory

asylum, 2, 64, 205, 245–46, 254, 272. *See also* refugees

asylum transit ban (2023), 246

Avila, Rodrigo, 39

belonging, 7, 10, 19, 41, 46, 49, 51, 175, 204, 241, 268, 286n9; and adaptation, 173; and family, 62, 84, 95, 176; gendered, 55, 84; and giving back, 217, 229; and language learning, 155, 159; and *metas*, 27, 30, 33; and orientation, 28; and place-making, 214, 286n9; and role modeling, 215; and romantic relationships, 187; and work, 151, 211

Benicio, 94, 104–6

Bianca, 149, 169, 200

Bickham Mendez, Jennifer, 214

Biden, Joe, 246, 275n1, 281n17, 287n17

bisexuality, 128–29

Bracero Program/Mexican Farm Labor Program (1942–64), 35

Bush, George W., 39

Caleb, 131–32, 135–37, 144, 198, 200–202; and family, 30–32, 34, 95; and methodology of book, 23–24;

and orientation, 99–101, 114; and unburdening, 122–23

Camelia, 44–46, 147–49, 226–28

Caribbean, 35

Carlos, 103, 139

Catholicism, 115, 117, 186, 225. *See also* churches

Central American Free Trade Agreement (CAFTA, 2004), 39

Central American Minors Program, 245

Central American Regional Security Initiative (CARSI, 2008), 38–39

Central Valley, CA, 71

Chicago, IL, 21

Child Protective Services, 60

choice, 6, 33, 41, 49

churches, 24, 109, 115, 149, 185–86, 193, 197, 225, 239, 264; community support at, 115–16, 123, 166, 167, 213, 216–17; limits of support at, 117–20, 166, 190. *See also* Catholicism; Protestantism

citizenship, 3, 140, 250, 269

Clinton, Bill, 39

Cold War, 36

collective memory, 255

collectivism, 22, 33, 51, 58, 130, 195, 217, 255; collective mobility, 27; collective responsibility, 32, 256; collective success, 219–28; and migration *metas,* 27, 34, 40–49, 157, 171

colonialism, 32, 56, 243; settler, 57, 280n52, 281n38; Spanish, 35, 281n38. *See also* imperialism

communism, 37–38

compassion fatigue, 273

"competent adult/teen" discourse, 21, 229

Compton, CA, 71

compulsion, 33, 41, 60, 108

Contras, 38

coping strategies, 14, 28, 53, 171, 177–83, 187, 197, 203, 239–40

COVID-19 pandemic, 40

coyotes, 31–32

Criminal Alien Program (2006), 65

criminalization, 66, 206, 232, 245

Cristhian, 4–7

Critical Latinx Indigeneities, 280n53

critical youth studies, 19

Danilo, 101–2, 146, 221–22

Deeb-Sossa, Natalia, 214

Deferred Action for Childhood Arrivals (DACA), 1–3, 25, 73–74, 76–77, 124, 205, 255, 275n1. *See also* Dreamers

Delia, 113, 119–20, 188–90, 194

Del Real, Deisy, 67

Department of Health and Human Services: Office of Refugee Resettlement (ORR), 2, 16, 22, 253

Department of Homeland Security (DHS), 2

Department of Labor, 249–50

departure contexts, 26–27, 30–41, 67, 232, 241, 244–45, 252; and arrival contexts, 34, 66, 235–36; and escape, 50–57; and family, 49–50; and migration *metas*, 41–49, 58, 219

deportability, 65, 68, 248

deportation, 35, 39, 68, 232, 275n1; gendered, 67; protection from, 1, 64, 248; risk of, 60, 65–66, 236

depression, 98, 100, 123, 145, 175, 177, 184, 194, 196

deservingness, 7, 92, 208, 214, 229, 286n7

Diego, 167–68

differential inclusion, 9

discrimination, 38, 96, 110, 176, 245; anti-Indigenous, 19, 42, 56–57, 95, 111–13, 115, 140–41, 162; buffers from, 9; ethnoracial, 8, 40, 51, 117, 127, 140; gender, 11, 40, 51, 55–56, 67, 95, 140–41, 237

disorientation *(desorientación)*, 7, 19, 27, 82, 93–96, 123, 167, 204, 214, 229, 233, 238, 252; and agency, 113–33; and an emergent frame of reference, 107–10; definition, 13; and independence, 101–7; and inequality, 110–13; and orientation pathways, 97–101; and perdition, 14, 28, 177, 182, 190, 193, 200, 206, 218, 230, 239, 247

displacement, 5, 26, 32, 34–35, 41, 47, 111, 175, 180, 244–46, 252, 265, 278n12; and incorporation, 12; by US immigration policy, 204, 232; by violence, 36–37, 40, 58, 255

dispossession, 36–37, 58

domestic violence, 40, 51, 53–54, 59, 74–75, 88, 98, 119, 188–94, 198. *See also* femicide; intimate partner violence

downward mobility, 9, 136, 233

Dreamers, 25, 76, 255. *See also* Deferred Action for Childhood Arrivals (DACA)

driver's licenses, 67, 275n1, 284n14

drug trade, 38, 40, 51

drug use, 31, 101, 110, 167, 181–85, 196, 215–16. *See also* addiction; substance abuse

dual labor market, 11–12. *See also* secondary labor market

Durkheim, Émile, 182

18th Street gang, 39

Elías, 48–49, 103–4, 114, 117, 158–59, 199

El Salvador, 15, 25, 53–54, 74, 81, 174, 259–60, 276n31; civil war, 37–38, 121; earthquakes in, 40; violence in, 36–39, 51–52, 221, 280n52. *See also* Salvadorans

emergent frame of reference, 20, 95–96, 107–10, 175, 192, 223, 237

English-language development (ELD) courses, 152–57, 169

Entry Without Inspection (EWI), 3

Esmeralda, 46–47, 88–90

Esteban, 195–97

Facebook, 149, 157, 169–71, 176, 196, 265, 268

familismo, 61, 69, 90, 236

family separation, 14, 65, 122, 192, 205, 236, 248

femicide, 56, 280n52. *See also* domestic violence; gender-based violence; intimate partner violence; sexual violence

femininity, 69, 180–81

financial independence, 21, 47, 60, 79, 80–81, 101, 109, 219

Flaco, 199–201

Flores Settlement Agreement (1997), 2

food insecurity, 39, 62

futurity, 16–17, 53, 57, 176–77, 186, 209–10, 215, 220, 223, 236, 240, 244, 266, 268; and adaptation, 136–38, 154, 156–57, 165; and anti-Indigeneity, 56; collective, 41–49, 217, 219; gendered, 55; and giving back, 218–19; and migration *metas*, 5, 26, 30–34, 41–49, 58, 171, 206; and orientation, 96, 98, 104, 117, 122, 126, 130–31, 179, 192; perdition curtailing, 180, 182; right to, 253–56; and success, 223–28; violence

curtailing, 40–41, 51, 245; and work, 9

Gabriel, 170–71, 194–95

Gael, 106–7, 222–27

gangs, 31, 40, 58, 71, 106, 148, 174, 205, 221–22; 18th Street, 39; MS-13, 39, 148

GED (general education development) certificates, 152–53, 275n1

gender, 19–20, 33, 99, 148, 161, 236, 250, 278n14; and arrival contexts, 27, 60–63, 67, 69–70, 77–91; and belonging, 55, 84; and deportation, 67; gender discrimination, 11, 40, 51, 55–56, 67, 95, 140–41, 237; and incorporation, 82, 87; and left-behind families, 88, 226–27; and methodology of book, 162, 259–60, 265, 268, 270–72, 285n4; and orientation, 111–12; and perdition, 28, 178–82, 186–95, 239–40; and trauma, 119–20, 181; and unburdening, 69, 190–91. *See also* femicide; gender-based violence; *machismo*; *marianismo*; masculinity; patriarchy

gender-based violence, 56, 85, 87–90, 113, 119, 148, 178–79, 181, 186–94, 270–72, 280n52. *See also* domestic violence; femicide; intimate partner violence; patriarchy; sexual violence

genocide, 37, 41, 57, 279n24

Gen Z, 171, 284n28

Gilberto, 81–82

giving back, 29, 207–29, 242, 254

González-López, Gloria, 85, 89

"good immigrant" discourse, 21–22, 68, 229

Guatemala, 5, 15, 51, 105, 127, 164, 259–60, 270, 276n31; Ander leaving, 220; anti-Indigeneity in, 56–57; Caleb's family in, 30–31, 136; Camelia's family in, 44; civil war, 37; Delia leaving, 188–89; education in, 224, 226; Elías's family in, 48, 104; Esteban's family in, 196; Gabriel's family in, 194; Gael leaving, 106; Huehuetenango, 156; hurricanes in, 40; Jayson leaving, 109; Joaquín leaving, 79; Marcos leaving, 71; Quetzaltenango, 198; resources in, 103, 139; Tacajalbé, 56; Tomás leaving, 54–55, 59; Totonicapán, 171; Usher's family in, 49; violence in, 36–38, 54, 59–60; work in, 108

Guatemalans, 52, 144, 163, 190, 276n31, 280n47; and *ABC* settlement, 65; Maya, 4, 26, 42, 46, 56–57, 111, 113, 128; and methodology of book, 25–26; and Voces de Esperanza, 22, 265; and work, 42

Gustavo, 78–79

Halpern-Meekin, Sarah, 112

Héctor, 199–201

Homeland Security Act (2002), 15

homemaking, 214, 260, 286n9

hometown associations, 171, 284n29

homosexuality, 128–29

Hondagneu-Sotelo, Pierrette, 85, 214

Honduras, 15, 25, 36–37, 40, 51, 211, 259–60, 276n31, 280n47; civil war, 38; femicide violence in, 280n52

housing insecurity, 246–47. *See also* unhoused youth

humanitarian crisis (2014), 36, 206

Hurricane Eta, 40

Hurricane Iota, 40

Hurricane Mitch, 40

Hurricane Stan, 40

hybrid hegemonies, 111, 140

hypercommodification, 102–3, 107, 153, 176, 219, 239

Ignacio, 185–86

Illegal Immigration Reform and Immigrant Responsibility Act (IIRIRA, 1996), 65

illegality, 10, 91, 284n14; construction of, 17, 64–66, 68

Immigration and Nationality Act (1965): 287(g) provision, 65

Immigration Reform and Control Act (IRCA, 1986), 64–65, 280n11

imperialism, 36, 243; US, 32, 35. *See also* colonialism

incorporation, 3, 17, 19, 20–21, 24, 27–28, 175, 203, 227–29, 232–37, 240–43, 246–47, 250, 263, 268; and adaptation, 22, 173, 206–7; and arrival contexts, 63, 70, 73, 76–77, 91–92; and community, 251–53; definition, 6; and departure contexts, 34; downward, 6–7; gendered, 82, 87; and giving back, 208, 215, 218–19; and homemaking, 286n9; as ongoing process, 7, 26, 29; and orientation, 22, 94–95, 97, 120–21, 124–25, 206–7; and perdition, 22, 177, 179, 192; theories of, 8–14; and work primacy, 18

Indigenous peoples, 11, 126, 130, 197, 252, 259–60, 280n52; and adaptation, 162–65, 237–38; anti-Indigenous racism, 19, 42, 56–57, 95, 111–13, 115, 140–41, 162; and collectivism, 40; and colonialism,

mentors, 73, 121, 132, 176, 209–10, 218, 225, 255

Mérida Initiative (2008), 38–39

methodology of book, 22–26, 263–73

Mexicans, 1, 4, 15, 23, 66–67, 190, 247, 252, 259–60, 265, 268, 269, 271, 276n31, 276n33, 277n34; in California, 16; and departure contexts, 55, 57; and displacement, 34–36; and humanitarian crisis, 2; and incorporation, 233; and legalization, 64; and migration *metas,* 33; and poverty, 68; racism against, 205; relation to Central American migrants, 38; research on, 10–11, 21, 63; working conditions for, 154

Mexico, 25, 87, 191–92, 276n31, 278n14; displacement in, 34–36, 232, 243–46; Guatemala-Mexico border, 31; left-behind families in, 155, 171; migration through, 101; resources in, 103; US-Mexico border, 2–3, 15–16, 36, 68, 205, 231, 245–46, 254, 277n34, 287n17; violence in, 40, 51. *See also* Mérida Initiative (2008)

migration debt, 17, 78, 80–81, 83, 100, 106, 188, 201, 238, 246

migration deterrence, 205, 245–46

migration *metas* (goals), 136, 184, 192, 221, 233, 236, 255; and adaptation, 138, 155, 157, 167–68, 173; and belonging, 27, 30, 33; and collectivism, 27, 34, 40–49, 157, 171; and (dis)orientation, 109, 117, 126, 134, 173, 239; and futurity, 5, 26, 30–34, 41–49, 58, 171, 206; and gender, 226–27; and giving back, 29, 208–9, 219–20, 229; and poverty, 27, 32–33, 44, 46–48, 222; and work primacy, 28, 137

militarization, 38, 52, 205, 246

millennials, 171, 284n28

Moisés, 198–202

MS-13 gang, 39, 148

multigenerational punishment, 232

National Labor Relations Act (1935), 249

National Science Foundation (NSF), 267

neoliberalism, 39, 68, 102, 207, 229, 235

nested context of reception framework, 27, 62

The New Ethnographer, 271

New York City, 21

Nicaragua, 37, 40, 64; civil war, 38

Nicaraguan Adjustment and Central American Relief Act (1997), 64–65

Nicolás, 165–66, 215–18

North American Free Trade Agreement (NAFTA), 36, 39

Oakland Unified School District: Newcomer Program, 251

Obama, Barack, 1, 39, 275n1

Office of Refugee Resettlement (ORR), 16, 22, 253

1.5-generation immigrants, 9, 23

orientation *(orientación),* 94, 174, 176, 178, 180, 183, 203, 236, 268; and adaptation, 14, 137–38, 148, 150–57, 162–67, 172–73, 179, 204, 206–10, 215, 218–19, 224, 228, 230, 233–34, 239–42, 247, 249, 254–55; and agency, 27, 96, 113–34; and arrival contexts, 13, 100–101, 104, 106, 133, 175, 198, 206, 237; to childhood, 107–10; definition, 13; and futurity, 96, 98, 104, 117, 122, 126, 130–31, 179, 192; and incorporation, 22,

right to stay, 243–46

Ríos Montt, Efraín, 279n24

Rolando, 102

role modeling, 215–19, 254

Romero Lucas García, Fernando, 279n24

sacrifice, 69, 127, 129, 195, 208–9, 216, 222–28, 268

Safe and Responsible Driver's Act (AB 60, 2015, CA), 284n14

Salvadorans, 15, 23, 53–54, 64–65, 74–75, 81, 101, 123, 149, 200, 221, 259–60, 276n31, 280n47. *See also* El Salvador

Samuel, 185, 211–15

sanctuary status, 16–17, 67, 237

Sandinistas, 38

San Fernando Valley, CA, 135, 149

secondary labor market, 11, 17, 67, 138–39, 172, 244

second-generation immigrants, 9

Secure Communities Program (2008), 65, 281n17

segmented assimilation theory, 9, 283n11

self-esteem, 21, 56–57, 110, 119, 158

self-harm, 28, 179, 182, 194, 203, 240

Serafina, 55–56, 154–55, 215

Sessions, Jeff, 205

settler colonialism, 57, 280n52, 281n38

sexualization, 63, 88–90

sexual violence, 88–90, 113, 148, 188, 270–72. *See also* femicide; gender-based violence

Silent Holocaust, 279n24

social death, 51

social exclusion, 6, 64, 92, 256

social inclusion, 6, 92, 207

socialization, 9–10, 69, 97, 197, 233–34, 237–38, 246

social media, 170

social mobility, 1, 36, 146, 284n14

social responsibility, 208

socioecological theory, 12

soledad y agonía, 175, 177–78, 180, 182, 187, 202, 204, 240

solitos, 4, 63, 114

Southern Border Program (2014), 39

Soviet Union, 36–37

Special Immigrant Juvenile (SIJ) status, 2–3, 253

sponsors, 2, 16, 68, 75, 253–54

structural violence, 5, 40, 55, 57, 247. *See also* colonialism; criminalization; housing insecurity

substance abuse, 14, 28, 181–84, 213. *See also* addiction

success, 6–8, 10, 12, 44, 58, 136, 204, 205–9, 241, 243, 252, 254, 257; and adaptation, 154, 157; collective, 219–28; and departure contexts, 34; and futurity, 223–28; and giving back, 210–30, 242; and incorporation, 20–21, 26, 28, 92, 233–35; and perdition, 179, 182, 187; and work primacy, 19

suicide/suicidal ideation, 171, 178–80, 182, 193–97, 240

superando, 68

Susana, 54, 59–60

Temporary Protected Status, 64

Thalia, 87–88, 190

Theo, 84

Tía Marta, 74–77, 90, 97–98, 105

Tío Hugo, 74–75

Title 42 (2020), 246

Tomás, 54–55, 59–61, 85, 110, 140–42, 153

Tongva people, 281n38

toxic ties, 67

Founded in 1893,
UNIVERSITY OF CALIFORNIA PRESS
publishes bold, progressive books and journals
on topics in the arts, humanities, social sciences,
and natural sciences—with a focus on social
justice issues—that inspire thought and action
among readers worldwide.

The UC PRESS FOUNDATION
raises funds to uphold the press's vital role
as an independent, nonprofit publisher, and
receives philanthropic support from a wide
range of individuals and institutions—and from
committed readers like you. To learn more, visit
ucpress.edu/supportus.